Copyright, Data and Creativity in the Digital Age

The Supreme Court of the United States in *Feist v. Rural* (1991) required that databases must have a minimal degree of creativity for copyright. The judgment was highly significant and the subsequent period is understood as the post-Feist era. It has been globally influential. However, the decision is extremely complex and remains unsatisfactorily interpreted. In particular, it has been impossible to illuminate the creativity requirement.

The book gives an account of the decision's conceptual structure, focusing on its full delineation of the opposite to creativity. In a radical and unprecedented innovation, it is correlated with an automatic computational process. Creativity itself is understood as non-computational or directly human activity concerned with meaning. Determining the presence of creativity is reduced to a four-stage test. This work then has acute practical current relevance to property in data in the digital age; it will also be of theoretical interest to, and is aimed at, researchers in, practitioners, and students of intellectual property worldwide.

Julian Warner is a faculty member at Queen's Management School, Queen's University Belfast.

Routledge Research in Intellectual Property

Available:

Biodiversity, Genetic Resources and Intellectual Property
Developments in Access and Benefit Sharing
Edited by Kamalesh Adhikari and Charles Lawson

Pharmaceutical Patent Protection and World Trade Law
The Unresolved Problem of Access to Medicines
Jae Sundaram

Patent Pools, Competition Law and Biotechnology
Devdatta Malshe

Copyright Law and Derivative Works
Regulating Creativity
Omri Rachum-Twaig

The Patentability of Software
Software as Mathematics
Anton Hughes

Annotated Leading Trademark Cases in Major Asian Jurisdictions
Edited by Kung-Chung Liu

SEPs, SSOs and FRAND
Asian and Global Perspectives on Fostering Innovation in Interconnectivity
Edited by Kung-Chung Liu and Reto M. Hilty

Towards an Ecological Intellectual Property
Reconfiguring Relationships Between People and Plants in Ecuador
David J Jefferson

For more information about this series, please visit https://www.routledge.com/Routledge-Research-in-Intellectual-Property/book-series/INTELLPROP

Copyright, Data and Creativity in the Digital Age

A Journey through *Feist*

Julian Warner

Routledge
Taylor & Francis Group
LONDON AND NEW YORK

First published 2021
by Routledge
2 Park Square, Milton Park, Abingdon, Oxon OX14 4RN

and by Routledge
52 Vanderbilt Avenue, New York, NY 10017

Routledge is an imprint of the Taylor & Francis Group, an informa business

British Library Cataloguing-in-Publication Data
A catalogue record for this book is available from the British Library

Library of Congress Cataloging-in-Publication Data
Names: Warner, Julian, 1955- author.
Title: Copyright, data and creativity in the digital age : a journey through Feist / Julian Warner.
Description: Abingdon, Oxon ; New York, NY : Routledge, [2021] |
Series: Routledge research in intellectual property |
Includes bibliographical references and index. |
Identifiers: LCCN 2020015105 | ISBN 9780367902858 (hardback) |
ISBN 9781003083009 (ebook)
Subjects: LCSH: Copyright--Databases | Copyright infringement. |
Creation (Literary, artistic, etc.) | Copyright infringement--United States. |
Copyright--Databases--United States.
Classification: LCC K1443.D37 W37 2021 | DDC 346.048/2--dc23
LC record available at https://lccn.loc.gov/2020015105

ISBN: 978-0-367-90285-8 (hbk)
ISBN: 978-0-367-53714-2 (pbk)
ISBN: 978-1-003-08300-9 (ebk)

Typeset in Galliard
by Taylor & Francis Books

For Sue

Contents

Illustrations

Figures

Tables

Boxes

Acknowledgments

I would like to record my appreciation of the encouragement and assistance offered by Kenneth Crews, Michael Buckland, Graham Brownlow, and Jonathan Bardon.

Some material has been adapted from the following previously published articles.

Warner, Julian (2013). Creativity for Feist. *Journal of the American Society for Information Science and Technology*. 64(6), 1173–1192.
Warner, Julian (2010). So mechanical or routine: the not original in Feist. *Journal of the American Society for Information Science and Technology*. 61(4) 820–834.
Warner, Julian (2010). The absence of creativity in Feist and the computational process. *Journal of the American Society for Information Science and Technology*. 61(11) 2324–2336.

1 Introduction

The convergence of the twain

Introduction

The Supreme Court of the United States denied copyright protection to telephone white pages, and thereby to similar compilations or collections of data, for their lack of creativity in 1991 in *Feist Publications, Inc. v. Rural Tel. Service Co.* (Feist Publications, Inc. v. Rural Tel. Service Co., Inc., 1991). The judgment specified that compilations or databases, and other works, must have a minimal degree of creativity to be copyrightable. The decision has been widely regarded as the most significant of modern intellectual property decisions for the information or digital age (Goldstein, 1991). Creativity is not directly elucidated and remains poorly understood. Creativity was described, as recently as 2012, as 'the *sine qua non* and the *je ne sais quoi* of copyright' (Bridy, 2012, p. 9) [the without which nothing and the I know not what of copyright]. No satisfactory reading of the decision has been made, in the nearly 30 years since it was issued. Establishing an understanding of creativity remains a live issue and is a compelling task.

In the introduction here we progressively address the decision, including its relation to the digital age, the reading of the decision to be developed, the approach on which that reading rests, and the structure of the subsequent work, including the use of narrative motifs. Finally, we conclude on the harmony the work enables for the convergence of copyright with the digital age.

The decision

For the decision, we distinguish its significance, diffusion, continuing status as law and the implications of this, the circumstances and progress of the case, and the decision's relation to the digital age.

Significance

The decision dismissed 'sweat of the brow' or 'industrious collection' (Feist Publications, Inc. v. Rural Tel. Service Co., Inc., p. 352) as the criterion for intellectual property, insisting on creativity and originality as the constitutional requirement for copyright. The dismissal of industrious collection places it in tension with the often dominant labor theory of copyright, which had demonstrated its utility by its long endurance and wide diffusion for over 200 years in the United States and in other jurisdictions (Ager v. Peninsula, 1884; Breyer, 1970, pp. 284–285), whatever its imperfections (Breyer, 1970).

Elevating creativity to a constitutional requirement for copyright (Narayanan, 1993–1994, pp. 341, 350; Raskind, 1991–1992, pp. 331–334; VerSteeg, 1995, p. 586) and the dismissal of industrious collection was received as both highly significant and extremely disruptive. The Supreme Court was characterized as having 'dropped a bomb' on United States copyright law by the then Register of Copyrights, in testimony before the House of Representatives (Copyright Act Hearing, 1991; also quoted in Samuelson, 1992, p. 27; Polivy, 1997–1998, p. 782). In an analogous contemporaneous image – '[l]ike the proverbial handful of pebbles dropped in a pond' – the *Feist* decision was described as having 'the potential over time to generate a series of widening, if not necessarily concentric, consequences for the basic doctrines of copyright law' (Raskind, 1991–1992, p. 331).

The disruption and discontinuity – 'dropp[ing] a bomb', the potential for multiple interpretations – 'not necessarily concentric [,] consequences', and the extensive diffusion – 'widening ... consequences', vividly anticipated by commentators immediately subsequent to the decision have since been amply fulfilled. The discontinuity implied by the term 'post' is matched by the significance of the discontinuity and of *Feist* itself, understood as the 'now-governing case' (Nimmer and Nimmer, 1978/2020, 13.01n.5.1). Disruption and discontinuity for subsequent copyright practice is confirmed by current references to the 'post-Feist era' in the major treatise by Nimmer and Nimmer (1978/2020, 1.01[B][2][b]n.48).

The absence of concentricity from the consequences of the decision for copyright law is revealed in the contrasting interpretations developed by different circuits (Polivy, 1997–1998). Commentaries also attribute an intention to the Supreme Court of encouraging a unified interpretation of property in data by the lower courts, although any such intention has been frustrated rather than fulfilled by the diversity of subsequent interpretations.

Diffusion

The diffusion of the decision includes its extension to comprehend material not prepared as data for compilations. For instance, a decision, concerned with the use of players' statistics by newspapers for fantasy baseball, took *Feist* as controlling for considerations of copyright preemption. Baseball players' names and playing records were considered to be analogous to the 'names, towns, and telephone numbers in a phone book' (C.B.C. Distribution, 2006, p. 73). Crucially, the decision, in a direct citation to *Feist*, held that statistics of players' performance lacked the '*sine qua non* of copyright – originality', and refused to allow intellectual property to inhere such data (pp. 70, 73).

Other jurisdictions have also encountered similar issues and may have been indirectly influenced by the *Feist* judgment. The *European Community Database Directive* (Narayan, 1993–1994, pp. 469–472), *sui generis* in the sense that it is not directly part of copyright legislation, was introduced (Gupta, 2017). Such developments can also be understood as part of the process of technological diffusion. At the same time, the reaction in the sphere of legal consciousness is different and indicates possibilities for difference within a dynamic with extensive commonalities. A commonality in outcome has been observed.

> Congress' record in meeting the challenge of the new dissemination technologies invites comparison with the high protectionist model of the continental author's rights traditions.... the practical results on both continents have been roughly the same.
>
> (Goldstein, 1991, p. 115)

In this instance, protection for compilations can be integrated within copyright or as *sui generis* provision, on the European Union model. The standard for the lack of copyrightability in the decision has begun to diffuse globally (Gervais, 2002; Judge and Gervais, 2010).

The increasing number of citations to the case, and its global impact, imply that its significance has increased, rather than diminished, over time. In the period from 1991 to 2020, paralleling the diffusion of the judgment, the internet has grown, databases have expanded greatly in size and number, and search engines have become increasingly prominent. The definitive removal of restrictions on the development of large collections of data by the decision may have partly enabled this development. The global diffusion of the judgment further implies an international need for an authoritative reading of the decision.

Status as law

The decision remains law – 'Like it or not, Feist is the law in the U.S.' (Resnik, 2003, p. 309) – without the prospect of change. The Court itself has not revisited the decision, despite opportunities to do so. The most that can be read from the absence of revisiting is that the Court is not sufficiently dissatisfied with the decision or with its effects, to expend its time in reviewing it. Constitutionally, Congress, as the legislature, cannot immediately override the Supreme Court (Fallon, 2004; Nimmer and Nimmer, 1978/ 2020, §1.01[B][2][a]). Although there have been a number of proposals for *sui generis* legislation to protect property for data in databases, these have not been passed into law. *Sui generis* proposals for legislation have not insignificant deliberation costs and, if enacted, can reduce the consistency and increase the complexity of the law (Trosow, 2004–2005). The status of the decision as current law, and the recognition of the costs of change, must then be accepted, as the founding basis for our considerations.

Circumstances and progress of the case

Rural Telephone Service Company were 'a certified public utility providing telephone service to several communities in Kansas' and were required to publish a directory of their subscribers, '[p]ursuant to state regulation'. A 'typical telephone directory, consisting of white pages and yellow pages' was published. Feist Publications, Inc., by contrast, was 'a publishing company that specialize[d] in area-wide telephone directories covering a much larger geographic range than directories such as Rural's' (Feist, 1991a, Syllabus).

The copying activities which gave rise to the Supreme Court case of 1991 can be traced to 1978. When Rural refused to license its white pages listings to Feist for a directory covering 11 different telephone service areas, Feist extracted the listings it needed from Rural's directory without Rural's consent. Although Feist altered many of Rural's listings, several were identical to listings in Rural's white pages (Feist, 1991a, Syllabus).

Only Rural, of the 11 telephone service providers covered by the Feist directory, had refused to license their listings to Feist. Rural's refusal stemmed from an unlawful purpose 'to extend its monopoly in telephone service to a monopoly in yellow pages advertising' (Feist, 1991a, p. 343). However, Rural's refusal to license and possibly unlawful purpose, to create a monopoly, are deliberately excluded from consideration in the oral proceedings of the Supreme Court – 'Mr. Caplinger, before you sit down, just as a matter of curiosity, what is the status of the antitrust aspect of this case?' (Feist, 1991b, p. 48). They can then be acknowledged but continue to be placed out of scope, for our subsequent considerations. Feist's use of license agreements may imply that they had initially held the common understanding that publishers of directories had property in their listings. Feist also conducted some independent research to add street addresses to entries.

The dispute was partly prompted by a transition in the production methods used by Feist for selecting and arranging data for their collective directories. For the alphabetization of data, Feist had further supplemented human labor by automated computer-based processes by 1983 (Feist, 1990a, pp. 45, 46; Feist, 1991b, pp. 25, 53; Rural, 1990, pp. 29–33, 36–38, 45–57), reflecting concurrent transitions in information technologies. Feist used human labor to keyboard data copied from Rural's white pages directory, and sent files to a vendor for production of the collective printed directory, which would have included the integration of previously separate alphabetical arrangements. Interrogation of computer-held data, and the imposition of different orderings on coordinated units as part of the search process, was not yet fully part of the commercial practice for such directories.

The progress of the case can be traced. The District Court 'granted summary judgment to Rural, explaining that "[c]ourts have consistently held that telephone directories are copyrightable" and citing a string of lower court decisions'. The Court of Appeals for the Tenth Circuit affirmed 'for substantially the reasons given by the district court', in an unpublished opinion (Feist, 1991a, Syllabus). The Supreme Court selects cases offered for appeal on the basis of their wide potential significance.

> We granted certiorari, 498 U.S. 808 (1990), to determine whether the copyright in Rural's directory protects the names, towns, and telephone numbers copied by Feist.
>
> (Feist Publications, Inc. v. Rural Tel. Service Co., Inc., 1991, p. 344)

The Supreme Court reversed the judgment of the Court of Appeals, breaking with an apparently settled and not fully questioned consensus.

Cultural and legal aspects distinctive of the United States can be discerned. Provision of telephone services is by region, with no national provider. Feist's directory aggregated together listings from different telephone service providers, in order to facilitate communication between and to their subscribers. There is also a strong commitment to public information embodied in the judgment.

The role of information technology in prompting the dispute implies some relation to the digital age.

Feist *and the digital age*

The decision has been widely regarded as the most significant of modern intellectual property cases for the digital or information age, for the current epoch.

> Just as the Supreme Court's 1879 decision in *Baker v. Selden*, describing the respective spheres of copyright and patent law, was a defining event for copyright in the industrial age, so *Feist* is a defining event for copyright in the information age.
>
> (Goldstein, 1991, p. 118)

The view of *Feist* as 'a defining event for copyright … in the information age' (Goldstein, 1991, p. 118), then, intimates a significant relation of the case to contemporaneous information developments, but does not fully explore the nature of that relation. The comment cites *Baker v. Selden* for its significance to the distinction of copyright from patent but does not attend to the late-nineteenth-century information technologies – books for entering accounts and economizing on the direct human labor involved – in the case. A limited historical awareness with regard to information technology is, then, discernible. The subsequent critical understanding of the judgment then shows a strong consensus that it is the crucial judgment for copyright in the digital age. The precise significance of the judgment for the digital age remains unarticulated, although there has been some further specificity.

In particular, developments in information technology, including computational technologies, were early recognized as a highly relevant context (Samuelson, 1992). Recognizing the presence, and also the influence, of technology is valuable for locating the judgment in real historical practice, particularly with regard to changes in the methods of production and distribution of data. The time and geopolitical place of the *Feist* decision does offer further clues which enable us to sharpen our focus in the search for a specific relation to the digital age. The case itself emerges in the 1980s, in connection with a transition to more intensively computer-based methods of directory production. The congruence in time and geopolitical space – 1991 and the United States – between the judgment and the diffusion of the internet as the World Wide Web is striking. The specific relation can then be sought in the diffusion of the computer and of the signal transmission technologies of the internet. The decision emerged earlier in the United States than similar movements in other jurisdictions, supporting its relation to the digital age as residing in the in the global diffusion of technologies, a movement proceeding slightly earlier in the United States than in other jurisdictions. A relevant context for explanation can, then, be found in the concurrent diffusion of information and communication technologies.

A technologically deterministic explanation which arises in connection with the recognition of an influence from technology – that, by 1991, technological developments had made public policy control over the movement of data impossible to exert – is initially attractive. It can be considered from a technologically and historically informed perspective. The implications for copyright of the increased ease of duplication or copying of material conferred by modern computational technologies were discussed (Resnik, 2003, p. 304n). For instance, by 1993, the economic significance of electronic databases was recognized, while noting that, 'personal computers are widely available and their use to "move" information cannot feasibly be regulated by legislative means or contractually controlled by producers or other private interests', and concluding that, '[t]echnological barriers to the piracy of these valuable resources … remain practically nonexistent' (Narayan, 1993–1994, pp. 459, 481). Similarly, in 2003, it was noted that the ease of copying, transformation, and transmission of digital information made it very convenient to use but also difficult to control (Resnik, 2003, p. 304). The influence from technology has emerged fully as a central theme and often in connection with a critique of the judgment as abandoning public policy control over an increasingly economically significant activity. Technically, however, constraints on copying have been developed and proved effective. In subsequent history, the contractual measures taken by database producers have also proved generally sufficient to protect their interests. A technologically deterministic account of the decision's relation to the digital age, then, emerges as insufficient technically and historically.

The consensus, then, of commentaries is that *Feist* is somehow intimately related to the current epoch, to the digital age. However, this consensus does not extend to specifying the precise or particular relation that exists. On the basis of the consensus of commentaries, we can accept a deep relation to the digital age and adopt as our task, the exposure of that specific, and still deep, relation.

Conclusion

In conclusion, then, a reading of the decision must substantiate creativity, acknowledge its significance, explain its diffusion, accept its status as law, fully contextualize its circumstances, and specify its relation to the digital age. Economy and conviction in explanation would be achieved if the central component of the reading fulfilled all these functions.

Reading of the decision

A satisfactory and comprehensive reading of the decision can be developed. The work accepts the judgment as in force, rather than querying its correctness as an interpretation of copyright, in contrast to other critiques. The *Feist* (Feist Publications, Inc. v. Rural Tel. Service Co., Inc. 1991) decision has been recognized as unresolved but generally regarded as a wrong turn by the Supreme Court, rather than critiqued and explicated. Crucially, the work accepts the judgment as law and explicates and elucidates it. The argument of the work is close to the advice issued by the Copyright Office (2017, 308.2), which quotes 'so mechanical or routine' and its associated clauses from *Feist* to characterize what is not copyrightable. It differs from, and builds on, that advice by, by developing a positive interpretation of creativity. The survival of the judgment over time is taken to imply that it is self-consistent and in accord with real world determining forces.

The creativity required for copyright is left undefined by *Feist* (Feist Publications, Inc. v. Rural Tel. Service Co., Inc., 1991) and has resisted subsequent elucidation. The opposite or antithesis to creativity is extensively characterized by the judgment and has the potential to clarify the decision. Specifically, the antithesis to creativity can be very strongly correlated with conceptions of computability and, specifically, with a routine automatic computational process. Accordingly, creativity is understood as non-computational human activity, above a certain level of routinicity. The non-computable itself is understood as direct human interaction with meaning. The reading comprehends all aspects of the decision, has strong analytic and future proofing possibilities, and reduces the dissonance of the decision with previous understandings of copyright.

New meanings, related to modern digital technologies, are imported from specialized discourses remote from the ordinary discourse and precedents available to the Supreme Court. Models of the computational process and characterizations of computability, have been developed in logic, mathematics, and theoretical computer science, but were in 1991, and still in 2020, not widely present in ordinary discourse, lagging behind the diffusion of computational processes and of the computer as a material technological product. They are also remote from the humanist tradition of the law and legal scholarship, although formal or symbolic logic might be one mediating intellectual influence. Reference has been made to the undeveloped nature of information concepts in law (Bygrave, 2015). The potentially unfamiliar, such as the theory of computability, is here explained in ordinary discourse terms.

The fully argued position established, that copyright should continue to reside in the products of intellectual labor, is largely in accord with independently developing practice. It also explicitly restores the incentive function of copyright, by recognizing and protecting the costs of human intellectual and creative activity. A continuity is revealed with the understanding of copyright as the natural right of an author to benefit from their intellectual labor, an understanding which has dominated since Jefferson and which was thought to be threatened by the requirement for creativity.

Comparisons are also made between the understanding of the absence of copyrightability and copyrightability established for *Feist* (1991) and standards in the European Union and in jurisdictions globally. The creativity required for *Feist* is mapped to the labor generally more directly required in other jurisdictions. A high degree of congruence is similarly found between the interpretation established of *Feist* (Feist Publications, Inc. v. Rural Tel. Service Co., Inc., 1991) and European Union and global standards, adding to the integrative effect of the work.

The reading of the decision given is original, compelling, concise, and practically implementable, absorbing and resolving disputes which have persisted since 1991. The correlation of the antithesis to creativity with a routine automatic computational process as the central component of the reading gives the economy and conviction desired.

Approach

Complementary techniques are used for the reading of the decision.

- A close textual exegesis establishes the senses of critical term in the judgment and the relation between the senses established.
- A classic legal technique of correlation of the senses and their relations with a real world and more objective correlative is then introduced. 'So mechanical' (Feist Publications, Inc. v. Rural Tel. Service Co., Inc., 1991, p. 362) in the judgment is correlated with an automatic computational process (both as theoretically understood in discussions of computability and as widely realized in contemporary everyday practice).
- The argument is also expressed as a sequence of formally logical propositions. It is developed discursively and uses graphic support, with diagrams and tables. The logical propositions are not conceived as autonomous from the primary discourse and long inferential sequences within them, which would be characteristic of mathematics, are not employed.

These techniques are employed, in a cumulative manner, moving from exegesis to correlation and from discursive to formally logical presentation.

Two of the techniques adopted, of close textual exegesis and correlation, are well established in law. In relation to exegesis, advice to students of the law is that, 'You have to read *much* more carefully' (Kerr, 2005, p. 5). Correlation is also a classic legal mode of development (Holmes, 1881/1991), although the specific correlation made is entirely unprecedented.

In contrast, the deliberate translation into logical propositions, used here, is apparently antithetical to a significant view of the nature of the law. Oliver Wendell Holmes famously and influentially (Leiter, 2005; Stone, 2002) remarked,

> The life of the law has not been logic: it has been experience.
>
> (Holmes, 1881/1991, p. 1)

Logic, in this instance, is understood as involving 'the syllogism' and as treating the 'law [which] embodies the story of a nation's development through many centuries ... as if it contained only the axioms and corollaries of a book of mathematics' (Holmes, 1881/1991, p. 1). The 'official theory', which is exposed as a partial fiction, is 'that each new decision follows syllogistically from existing precedents' (Holmes, 1881/1991, p. 35). A contrasting, and more positive understanding of logic as associated with rationality, opposed to more primitive 'personifying metaphors' (Holmes, 1881/1991, p. 383), coexists with the primary understanding of logic. However, logical method itself is endorsed for certain purposes and with certain limitations:

> The business of the jurist is to make known the content of the law; that is, to work upon it from within, or logically, arranging and distributing it, in order, from is *summum genus* to its *infima species*, so far as practicable.
>
> (Holmes, 1881/1991, p. 219)

Logic can, then, be used to give coherence and organization to experience.

Here, formal logic is used consistently with the reservations on its applicability to the law and with its contrasting endorsement. In accord with the priority given to experience, ordinary discourse and discursive expression is treated as primary; consistently with the endorsement of logic as a method for making known the content of the law from within, logical propositions are used to give clearer and more intelligible form to discursively expressed arguments.

The dependence of the reading only on deeply grounded and complementary techniques are indicative of the depth, simplicity, and potential wide acceptance of the argument.

Structure

The work is structured to enable directed economy in attention, for different purposes – for a full and deep reading of the case and the work here, for a more summary recall or rereading of the major conclusions of each chapter, and for overview or recollection of the complete argument.

Each chapter of the book directly concerned with the case is structured to allow reading in depth and for summary recall.

- For depth in reading, the full presentation of the exegesis of the judgment enables highly specific and fully critical reading. The relation to the European Union and potentially to other jurisdictions is also indicated in a separate section following the reading established in that chapter. Text boxes are used for summary and ordinary language exposition of concepts, such as computability, which might be unfamiliar to some readers.
- For more summary recall or rereading of specific chapters, each chapter directly concerned with the reading includes a chapter summary, towards the end of the chapter, which includes an indication of the argument in formal logic.

- For an overview and recollection of the argument, individual chapters are synthesized into an overall summary and formally logical development, which includes a full sequence of the logical propositions, in Chapter 9 – 'Qualities of Reading'.

Directed economy of attention, for complementary purposes, is thereby enabled.

Individual chapters are organized into a simple and strongly symmetrical overall structure. The introduction and the next chapter on critiques of the decision are paralleled by a conclusion and the chapter on the qualities of the reading, which revisits the themes derived from critiques to consider how far they have been resolved. Within this symmetrical envelope, a progressive reading of the decision is given.

The argument is graphically mapped as well as verbally developed. The written discursive exposition of the reading is supported by an overall map of the journey through the judgment, in figures linked to the text. Progress along the journey is marked on the map, allowing the reader to locate the position of discussions of specific concepts within the overall argument. The diagram or map is progressively developed and reveals the structure and cohesion of the argument. We finally arrive back where we started, but with deeper understanding of the judgment.

Departure and returning with deeper understanding, is reminiscent of quest literature. Accordingly, the work is further structured around a metaphorical journey.

Narrative motifs

Narrative motifs derived from familiar stories are adopted to give unity, progression, and clarity to the reading. For instance, comparing originality to Odysseus clarifies that originality simultaneously contains all subordinate concepts, including creativity, but is nothing in itself, analogous to Odysseus adopting the name of Nobody to be restored as every man on his return to Ithaca. The overall significance of the journey narratives incorporated – Brer Rabbit's escape to the briar patch, Bunyan's pilgrim's progress along a narrow path to salvation, and Odysseus's journey to Ithaca – can be understood as the overcoming of obstacles, negotiating the labyrinth of creativity, and as absorbing the technical and computational within the human.

For each particular motif, the connection from the reading to the motif will be explained within the chapter in which the motif is embedded.

Conclusion

The introduction's own narrative motif derives from Thomas Hardy's poem, *The Convergence of the Twain*, concerned with the *Titanic* and its convergence with an iceberg.

Well: while was fashioning
This creature of cleaving wing,
The Immanent Will that stirs and urges everything

Prepared a sinister mate
For her – so gaily great –
A Shape of Ice, for the time far and dissociate.
(Hardy, 1912/1923)

The work brings together, or converges, the decision with the digital age. In contrast to the *Titanic*, the knowledge offered by the work enables the convergence of a decision of the Supreme Court with the digital age to become a harmonious basis for future practice and theory.

We begin our journey in the next chapter, by establishing further specific criteria for a satisfactory reading of the decision.

References

Ager v. Peninsula (1884). Ager v. Peninsula and Oriental Steam Company. *The Law Reports: Chancery Division*. 26, 637–643.

Breyer, S. (1970). The uneasy case for copyright: A study of copyright in books, photocopies, and computer programs. *Harvard Law Review*. 84(2), 281–351.

Bridy, A. (2012). Coding creativity: Copyright and the artificially intelligent author. *Stanford Technology Law Review*, 5, 1–28. At http://stlr.stanford.edu/pdf/bridy-coding-creativity.pdf (January 8, 2014).

Bygrave, L.A. (2015). Information concepts in law: Generic dreams and definitional daylight. *Oxford Journal of Legal Studies*. 35, 91–120.

C.B.C. Distribution (2006). C.B.C. Distrib. and Mktg., Inc. v. Major League Baseball Advanced Media, L.P., 443 F. Supp. 2d 1077 (E.D. Mo. 2006).

Copyright Act Hearing (1991). Copyright Act: Hearing before the House Subcommittee on Intellectual Property and Judicial Administration, 102d Cong., 8 (1991) (Testimony of Ralph Oman, Register of Copyrights).

Copyright Office (2017). *U.S. Copyright Office: Compendium of U.S.Copyright Office practices* (3rd edn), § 101.

Fallon, R.H. (2004). *The dynamic constitution: An introduction to American constitutional law*. Cambridge and New York: Cambridge University Press.

Feist (1990a). Feist Publications, Inc., Petitioner v. Rural Telephone Service Company, Inc. Respondent. Certiorari granted October 1, 1990. On writ of certiorari to the United States Court of Appeals for the Tenth Circuit. Joint Appendix.

Feist Publications, Inc. v. Rural Tel. Service Co., Inc. (1991a). Feist Publications, Inc. v. Rural Tel. Service Co., Inc. 499 U.S. 340 (1991).

Feist (1991b). Feist Publications, Inc. Petitioner v. Rural Telephone Service Company, Inc. No. 89-1909. Supreme Court of the United States. 1991 U.S. Trans Lexis 165. January 9, 1991, Washington, D.C. [Transcript of the Oral Argument].

Gervais, D.J. (2002). Feist goes global: A comparative analysis of the notion of originality in copyright law. *Journal of the Copyright Society of the U.S.A.* 49, 949–981.

Goldstein, P. (1991). Copyright. *Journal of the Copyright Society of the U.S.A.* 38, 109–122.

Gupta, I. (2017). *Footprints of Feist in European Database Directive: A legal analysis of IP law-making in Europe*. Singapore: Springer.

Hardy, T. (1912/1923). The convergence of the twain. In T. Hardy. *Collected poems of Thomas Hardy*. London: Macmillan.

Holmes, O.W. (1881/1991). *The common law* (pp. 288–289). With a new introduction by Sheldon M. Novick. New York: Dover.

Judge, E.F. and Gervais, D. (2010). Of silos and constellations: Comparing notions of originality in copyright law. *Cardozo Arts and Entertainment*. 27, 373–407.

Kerr, O.S. (2005). How to read a judicial opinion: A guide for new law students. At http://euro.ecom.cmu.edu/program/law/08-732/Courts/howtoreadv2.pdf (August 9, 2018).

Leiter, B. (2005). American legal realism. In M.P. Golding and W.A. Edmundson (eds). *The Blackwell guide to the philosophy of law and legal theory* (pp. 50–67). Malden, MA: Blackwell Publishing.

Narayanan, A.S. (1993–1994). Standards of protection for databases in the European Community and the United States: Feist and the myth of creative originality. *George Washington Journal of International Law and Economics*. 27, 457–500.

Nimmer, M.B. and Nimmer, D. (1978–2020). *Nimmer on copyright: A treatise on the law of literary, musical and artistic property, and the protection of ideas*. New York: Matthew Bender. Continually updated resource.

Polivy, D.R. (1997–1998). Feist applied: Imagination protects, but perspiration persists – the basis for copyright protection for factual compilations. *Fordham Intellectual Property Media and Entertainments Law Journal*. 8, 773–835.

Raskind, L.J. (1991–1992). Assessing the impact of Feist. *University of Dayton Law Review*. 12, 331–344.

Resnik, D.B. (2003). Strengthening the United States' database protection laws: Balancing public access and private control. *Science and Engineering Ethics*. 9, 301–318.

Rural (1990). Feist Publications, Inc., Petitioner, v. Rural Telephone Service Company, Inc., Respondent. No. 89–1909. Supreme Court of the United States. On Writ of Certiorari to the United States Court of Appeals for the Tenth Circuit. Brief for the respondent.

Samuelson, P. (1992). Copyright law and electronic compilations of data. *Communications of the ACM*. 35, 27–32.

Stone, M. (2002). Formalism. In J. Coleman, S. Shapiro, and K.E. Himma (eds), *The Oxford handbook of jurisprudence and philosophy of law* (pp. 166–205). Oxford: Oxford University Press.

Trosow, S.E. (2004–2005). Sui generis database legislation: A critical analysis. *Yale Journal of Law and Technology*. 7, 1–109.

VerSteeg, R. (1995). Sparks in the tinderbox: Feist, 'creativity', and the legislative history of the 1976 Copyright Act. *University of Pittsburgh Law Review*. 56, 549–588.

2 Critiques of the decision

Introduction

The *Feist* (Feist Publications, Inc. v. Rural Tel. Service Co., Inc., 1991) decision required that databases must have a minimal degree of creativity to be copyrightable and that, in contrast to some previous understandings, sweat of the brow or industrious collection would not confer copyrightability. The judgment remains law but presents great difficulties of interpretation. As current law, the decision requires understanding and elucidation.

Commentaries on the judgment, by contrast, have focused on critiquing, rather than explicating, the decision. They were published predominantly, but not exclusively, in the period immediately following the decision. The issues they raise remain largely unresolved. They remain valuable for their exposure of crucial issues to be addressed.

We can consider the themes of critiques, in broadly descending order of significance and conceptual dependence. Conditions for a satisfactory reading of the decision can be simultaneously generated.

Themes of critiques

We can begin with the apparent complexity of the decision.

Complexity

Commentaries characterized the decision as complex and difficult to interpret, 'inordinately Delphic even by Supreme Court standards' (Strong, 1994, p. 39).[1]

1 The judgment may be 'inordinately Delphic', in the sense of being particularly difficult to interpret, but all Supreme Court judgments can be considered Delphic in a radical etymological sense, when it is recalled that the term *Delphic* is derived from the oracle at Delphi.

The limited dialogue between questioner and responder at the oracle at Delphi normally allowed no direct sensory or visual contact between the questioner and responder. Questioning of the oracular utterance delivered was forbidden at Delphi and of other oracles. The priestess' voice was changed for response to enquiries (Aune, 1987; Bremmer, 1987; Parke & Wormell, 1956; Price, 1985). Commentators were

There is effectively universal agreement on the complexity of the decision. Commentaries also indirectly testify to the complexity of the decision and its resistance to interpretation, as a conceptual structure has not yet been fully revealed. On the basis of the explicit recognition of complexity, and indirect testimony to this, we can confirm the apparent complexity of the decision.

The explicit concerns of critiques, and their indirect testimony, can yield a significant, and, at first sight, curious, further implication. Despite the number and diversity of commentaries, and the long period since the decision, no self-contradiction within the decision has been detected. We can therefore assume, or, more technically, presume, that the decision is self-consistent, even though the particular form of self-consistency has not yet been fully revealed.

A counter critique should, then, reveal the coherence which we may legitimately assume is discoverable behind, or within, the complexity.

Creativity

The absence of an elucidation of creativity emerges as the principal aspect of the complexity and resistance to interpretation of the decision.

The poor definition of creativity in the decision is the most persistent and significant specific concern, common to a number of commentaries (Clifford, 2004; Ginsburg, 1992; Greetham, 1996; Narayanan, 1993–1994; Raskind, 1991–1992; Resnik, 2003; Strong, 1994; VerSteeg, 1995). The discussion of creativity in the decision is considered to be diffuse. 'Here, the Court's opinion [where it moves to a discussion of creativity (Feist Publications, Inc. v. Rural Tel. Service Co., Inc., 1991, pp. 348–349)] loses its almost Wagnerian sense of mastery and descends to platitudes' (Strong, 1994, p. 45). The decision does not say what sort of manner of selection and arrangement of facts will reach the standard for protection.

> *Feist* demands that we seek creativity in the selecting and arranging of data. This is no small metaphysical task. It requires that we understand the nature of the creative act that goes into making a compilation.
>
> (Strong, 1994, p. 45)

Further, the need for an understanding of creativity that satisfies ordinary discourse understandings and everyday practice as well as copyright is noted. 'Whatever definition we arrive at must satisfy not only the ordinary human meaning of creativity but also the strictures of copyright law' (Strong, 1994, p. 45). *Feist* (Feist Publications, Inc. v. Rural Tel. Service Co., Inc., 1991) fails to answer the basic question of how intellectual creativity is to be recognized: 'Without a test

debarred from questioning the producer of the significant utterance about its underlying meanings or intentions.

Analogously, commentators on Supreme Court judgments are debarred from questioning the producer of the significant utterance about its underlying meanings or intention, and have to turn to exegesis or close reading.

that concentrates attention on the essence of *Feist* and the nature of human inventiveness – choice making by a human author – too many works that are incomprehensible or unappreciated by the court will be denied copyright protection' (Clifford, 2004, p. 299). Commentaries have noted that the arrangement must not only be original, or not copied from another source, but also creative and that no court, including the Supreme Court, has been able to explicate this standard (Strong, 1994, p. 40). The poor definition of creativity is considered to have had significant effects, particularly making it difficult to fulfill the decision's assurance that property will continue to subsist in the 'vast majority of compilations' (Feist Publications, Inc. v. Rural Tel. Service Co., Inc., 1991, p. 359). Commentaries continue to accept that creativity is poorly defined but they have not developed a more satisfactory and robust concept.

A counter critique needs to resolve the lack of development of creativity identified by commentaries. It can similarly acknowledge the centrality of creativity, but must substantiate it, isolate creativity in relation to compilations and other works, ensure consistency with ordinary discourse, and render the presence of creativity testable.

Dissonance with existing understandings

The requirement for a minimal degree of creativity, as part of originality, and the denial of protection to works solely the product of industrious collection, has been thought to place the judgment at odds with the classic understanding that copyright protected and rewarded the intellectual labor of authors. A dissonance with the labor theory of copyright, by which an author has a right to benefit from their intellectual labor, is detected. The tension was noted at an early date.

> Locke's argument that the labors of the mind, as they produce identifiable 'works', should be analogous with real estate and the ownership of land ... has been rendered moot by the *Feist* decision in which labor in and of itself does not produce proprietorship.
>
> (Greetham, 1996, p. 59)

The term 'moot' (Greetham, 1996, p. 59) implies some uncertainty as to the degree of dissonance, which remains unresolved. The uncertainty does leave scope for reconciliation and reintegration.

A counter critique can accept the appearance of difference from or dissonance with preceding understandings of copyright and then clearly and specifically identify and substantiate difference, and, if possible, also reveal any underlying continuity.

Incentive role

Critiques of the decision have considered that, by not rewarding the labor of authors, it grossly neglects the incentive function of copyright (Ginsburg, 1992, pp. 341, 350), particularly its incentive role in rewarding the production of works, including databases (Branscomb, 1994, pp. 38–40).

A counter critique would restore the incentive role of copyright, for databases and other works.

Appeal to nineteenth-century precedents

The citation by the Supreme Court of some nineteenth-century cases as significant precedents is thought to revive and give unexpected importance to precedents which had been out of fashion – '[f]ew intellectual property lawyers expected the Supreme Court in *Feist* to reinvigorate these musty old cases'. The result of the case, which exempted Feist from liability, had been expected by informed observers, but reasoning, which incorporated these citations, was not widely, if at all, anticipated (Goldstein, 1991, p. 118).

A counter critique should explain the appeal to the nineteenth-century precedents.

Consonance with natural justice

It has been noted that provisions enforced by the courts need to be in accord with conceptions of natural justice, if they are to survive, specifically in relation to *Feist* (1991). 'Courts and commentators will doubtless continue to be moved by an equitable sense of "fair" commercial conduct and by an abhorrence of "piracy"' (Raskind, 1991–1992, p. 332). More broadly, a deep relation to the extra-legal context is consistent with classic, and deeply historically embedded, perspectives, which recognize that the law must embody collective sentiment or consciousness. The *I Ching* noted that legal provisions must accord with wider public consciousness, if they are to be accepted and effectively instantiated. 'It is the same with human society: only such laws as are rooted in popular sentiment can be enforced, while laws violating this sentiment merely arouse resentment' (*I Ching* 32/2003, p. 68). Law should then be in accord with collective feeling.

A counter critique should either specifically identify the dissonance with natural justice, or, preferably, expose an underlying congruence with concepts of natural justice.

Feist *and the digital age*

Feist (Feist Publications, Inc. v. Rural Tel. Service Co., Inc., 1991) has been regarded as the crucial copyright judgment for the digital age (Goldstein, 1991). However, its precise relation to the digital age has not been established. Survival within the United States and its increasing global diffusion indicates that the judgment must have a basis in real world determining forces, in the digital age.

A critique should specify the precise relation to the digital age and its basis in real world determining forces.

European Union

The decision has been regarded as influential in the formulation of the European Database Directive, as a reaction to the lack of protection for databases apparently offered by *Feist* (Feist Publications, Inc. v. Rural Tel. Service Co., Inc., 1991). The standard for the lack of copyrightability in the decision has also begun to diffuse globally (Gervais, 2002; Judge and Gervais, 2010; Gupta, 2017).

A counter critique must identify precisely differences and similarities with the European Union, and, more generally, with the labor oriented standards for copyrightability which may be held by other jurisdictions. A preference again would be for revealing an underlying continuity, as this would make for integration and economy in effort.

Review and synthesis

We have identified the major issues raised by critiques of the judgment:

- the complexity of the judgment is universally agreed;
- the lack of substantiation of creativity is widely considered a crucial aspect of its complexity;
- a tension with previous understandings of copyright has been detected;
- the incentive role of copyright is considered to have been neglected;
- the appeal to nineteenth-century precedents by the Supreme Court has been regarded as idiosyncratic;
- at the same time, it is still conceded that any implementation of copyright must be consonant with natural justice.
- the relation of the decision to the digital age is not fully specified.
- the judgment has an uncertain and complex relation to developments in other jurisdictions (particularly the European Union).

Commentaries were published predominantly in the period immediately following the decision, with some diminution in their number in recent years, but the issues they raise remain largely unresolved.

Conclusion

In concluding summary, then, the continuing status of the decision as law and the need for elucidation are recognized. We also reviewed critiques of the decision and registered their concerns, which were primarily with the complexity and difficulty of interpretation of the decision and with its poor delineation of creativity. Further specific issues to be addressed by a counter study were also isolated. An indication of the absence of self-contradiction was derived from the collectivity of critiques and transformed into a presumption of self-consistency, whose particular form awaits revelation.

The task for the work is understood as resolving the criticisms made, through a reading of the decision. A counter critique must accept the complexity of the decision. It should also reduce the appearance of complexity, while remaining comprehensive with regard to the decision, revealing its structure and preserving distinctions in that revealed structure. The analysis can be conducted on the presumption of an underlying internal conceptual coherence.

On the basis of the need for elucidation and of presumption of self-consistency, we can construct a reading of the decision which can then be reviewed in relation to the criteria we have established for our counter study.

We begin, in the next chapter, with an account of what could usefully be called, the conceptual structure of the decision. The structure hidden behind or disguised by the apparent complexity will be revealed.

References

Aune, D.E. (1987). Oracles. In M. Eliade (ed.). *The encyclopaedia of religion* (vol. 2, pp. 80–87). New York: Macmillan.

Branscomb, A.W. (1994). *Who owns information? From privacy to public access.* New York: Basic Books.

Bremmer, J. (1987). Delphi. In M. Eliade (ed.). *The encyclopedia of religion* (vol. 4, pp. 277–279). New York: Macmillan.

Clifford, R.D. (2004). Random numbers, chaos theory, and cogitation. A search for the minimal creativity standard in copyright law. *Denver University Law Review.* 82, 259–299.

Feist Publications, Inc. v. Rural Tel. Service Co., Inc. (1991). Feist Publications, Inc. v. Rural Tel. Service Co., Inc. 499 U.S. 340 (1991).

Gervais, D.J. (2002). Feist goes global: A comparative analysis of the notion of originality in copyright law. *Journal of the Copyright Society of the U.S.A.* 49, 949–981.

Ginsburg, J.C. (1992). No 'sweat'? Copyright and other protection of works of information after Feist v. Rural Telephone. *Columbia Law Review.* 92, 338–388.

Goldstein, P. (1991). Copyright. *Journal of the Copyright Society of the U.S.A.* 38, 109–122.

Greetham, D. (1996). The telephone directory and Dr. Seuss: Scholarly editing after Feist versus Rural Telephone. *Studies in the Literary Imagination.* 29, 53–74.

Gupta, I. (2017). *Footprints of Feist in European Database Directive: A legal analysis of IP law-making in Europe.* Singapore: Springer.

I Ching (32/2003). *I Ching or Book of changes.* The Richard Wilhelm translation, rendered into English by Cary F. Baynes. Foreword by C.G. Jung. Preface to the Third Edition by H. Wilhelm. London: Penguin.

Judge, E.F. and Gervais, D. (2010). Of silos and constellations: Comparing notions of originality in copyright law. *Cardozo Arts and Entertainment.* 27, 373–407.

Narayanan, A.S. (1993–1994). Standards of protection for databases in the European Community and the United States: Feist and the myth of creative originality. *George Washington Journal of International Law and Economics.* 27, 457–500.

Parke, H.W. and Wormell, D.E.W. (1956). *The Delphic Oracle. Volume I: The history. Volume II: The oracular responses.* Oxford: Basil Blackwell.

Price, S. (1985). Delphi and divination. In P.E. Easterling and J.V. Muir (eds). *Greek religion and society* (pp. 128–154). Cambridge: Cambridge University Press.

Raskind, L.J. (1991–1992). Assessing the impact of Feist. *University of Dayton Law Review.* 12, 331–344.

Resnik, D.B. (2003). Strengthening the United States' database protection laws: Balancing public access and private control. *Science and Engineering Ethics*. 9, 301–318.

Strong, W.G. (1994). Database protection after Feist v. Rural Telephone Co. *Journal of the Copyright Society of the U.S.A.* 42, 39–67.

VerSteeg, R. (1995). Sparks in the tinderbox: Feist, 'creativity', and the legislative history of the 1976 Copyright Act. *University of Pittsburgh Law Review*. 56, 549–588.

3 Creativity in the decision

Into the briar patch

Introduction

Critics have recognized that creativity is highly significant and fundamental to the decision (Clifford, 2004; Ginsburg, 1992; Greetham, 1996; Narayanan, 1993–1994; Nimmer, 2001; Nimmer & Nimmer, 1978–2020; Polivy, 1997–1998; Raskind, 1991–1992; Resnik, 2003; Strong, 1994; Trosow, 2004–2005, p. 109; VerSteeg, 1995; 2007). However, they have not articulated the precise sense in which creativity is both significant and fundamental. Critical scrutiny had not revealed self-contradiction within the decision and this implied that the decision was internally consistent. The internal consistency of the decision further implies that creativity must have a definite place within it. The apparent complexity of the decision can be reduced and the precise position of creativity revealed, by a careful and comprehensive analysis. The purpose of this chapter is to reveal that place, as a preliminary to elucidating creativity.

Brer Rabbit's briar patch is adopted as an image of something which appears strange and threatening, but which can be made familiar and navigated, like the *Feist* decision itself. The Supreme Court could be said to have thrown copyright into the briar patch, through the *Feist* decision (Feist Publications, Inc. v. Rural Tel. Service Co., Inc., 1991), in two, related, senses – first, a location which is initially strange and threatening, but can be made familiar, and, second, in creativity being embedded in a maze, which can, finally, be navigated. Brer Rabbit, it will be recalled, pleaded not to be thrown into the briar patch.

> 'Drown me! Roast me! Hang me! Do whatever you please,' said Brer Rabbit. 'Only please, Brer Fox, please don't throw me into the briar patch.'
>
> (American Folklore, 2020)

Yet once in the briar patch, where had lived all his life, Brer Rabbit can calmly comb tar from his fur. The briar patch can then be read as an image for an apparently complex and confused, possibly maze-like, place, which might appear to scratch and to harm, but which can be navigated, and protects, given local knowledge and discernment. An apparently negative situation can be transformed, by intelligence and wit, into something positive.

Establishing the place of creativity in the decision can reveal the precise sense in which creativity is significant and fundamental. The relation of creativity to originality and to a minimal degree of creativity, the immediate requirements for copyrightability, must first be established. Conditions for creativity and a minimal degree of creativity will be simultaneously derived from the decision. All readings of both the semantics and grammar of the decision are ordinary language, unless otherwise indicated.

We determine the place of creativity in the decision. Originality is the immediate requirement for copyright and includes a minimal degree of creativity. Creativity is included in a minimal degree of creativity, on an ordinary language reading. Creativity is, then, foundational to the decision, in the sense that it is a constituent of a minimal degree of creativity and thereby of originality.

Creativity itself is not disaggregated into further concepts and nor is it linked to semantically related terms. Creativity can then be regarded as primitive, classically open to elucidation but not to further decomposition. Creativity is also antithetically implied by the creativity utterly lacking distinguished by the judgment and this is the only resource for the elucidation of creativity, from within the decision. In the absence of any further, including technical, development, creativity must be understood as consistent with its ordinary discourse sense. From its application to all works, it must range from very low to the highest possible levels of creativity.

Creativity in the decision

Originality

Originality is required for all works: 'a compilation, *like any other work*, is copyrightable only if it satisfies the originality requirement. ... the originality requirement *applies to all works*' (Feist Publications, Inc. v. Rural Tel. Service Co., Inc., 1991, p. 357 [emphases added]).

A statement specifying what original means is given once, and only once, within the opinion. As a unique occurrence, the statement must be received as exhaustive of the meaning of original. 'Original, as the term is used in copyright, means only that the work was independently created by the author (as opposed to copied from other works), and that it possesses at least some minimal degree of creativity' (Feist Publications, Inc. v. Rural Tel. Service Co., Inc., 1991, p. 345).

The qualification immediately following '[o]riginal', 'as the term is used in copyright', indicates a meaning specific to copyright. '[O]nly' in 'means only' (p. 345) must be read rigorously as, entirely restricted to. The 'and' (p. 345) connecting 'independently created' (p. 345) and 'at least some minimal degree of creativity' (p. 345) indicates that both independent creation and at least some minimal degree of creativity are essential to originality. The meaning of original is, then, specific to copyright, but not technical, and can then be understood as a more precise instantiation of an ordinary discourse sense, consistently with the need to be applicable to all works. '[A]t least' in 'at least some minimal degree of creativity' (p. 345) indicates a lower threshold for a minimal degree of creativity.

Crucially, originality is solely constituted by independent creation and at least some minimal degree of creativity (Figure 3.1).

Independent creation is parenthetically explicated, at its introduction.

> the work was independently created by the author (as opposed to copied from other works).
>
> (Feist Publications, Inc. v. Rural Tel. Service Co., Inc., 1991, p. 345)

Creativity is not directly included in any of the formulations for independent creation (Box 3.1).

Box 3.1 References to independent creation

Original, as the term is used in copyright, means only that the work was **independently** created **by the author (as opposed to copied from other works)** (p. 345).

Originality requires **independent creation** (p. 346).

These choices as to selection and arrangement, so long as they are **made independently by the compiler** and entail a minimal degree of creativity, are *sufficiently original that Congress may protect such compilations through the copyright laws* (p. 348).

Under the doctrine [of sweat of the brow], the only defense to infringement was **independent creation** (p. 353).

Originality requires only that the author make the selection or arrangement **independently (i.e., without copying that selection or arrangement from another work)** (p. 358).

Note: The references to independent creation are given in **bold** and the primary evidence for their assimilation in *italics*.

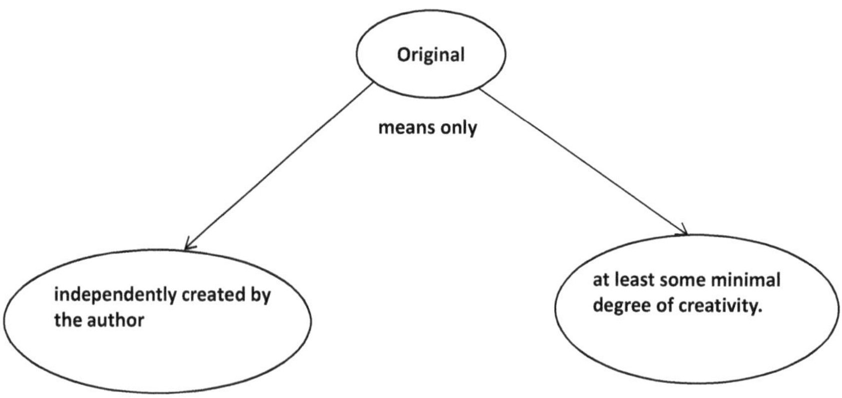

Figure 3.1 The meaning of originality

A minimal degree of creativity

'[A]t least some minimal degree of creativity' (Feist Publications, Inc. v. Rural Tel. Service Co., Inc., 1991, p. 345) would include a minimal degree of creativity. A minimal degree of creativity disaggregates into a required level and sufficient amount 'some minimal degree of creativity. To be sure, the requisite level of creativity is extremely low; even a slight amount will suffice'. (Feist Publications, Inc. v. Rural Tel. Service Co., Inc., 1991, p. 345) [citations omitted].

A minimal degree of creativity is then, first, constituted by a required level of creativity, and, second, by an amount of creativity at that level. The level of creativity required must be knowable, from its explicit specification as one of the requirements of a test for originality. 'Originality requires ... that the author makes the selection or arrangement independently ... and that it display some minimal level of creativity. Presumably, the vast majority of compilations will pass this test' (Feist Publications, Inc. v. Rural Tel. Service Co., Inc., 1991, pp. 358–359).

The combination of level and amount for a minimal degree of creativity should also be discernible, to fulfill the requirements of the test.

The further references which can be assimilated to a minimal degree of creativity and which include the words *creativity* and *creative* link them only to terms which can be understood as corresponding to 'minimal degree', such as 'modicum', 'component', or 'minimal spark' (Feist Publications, Inc. v. Rural Tel. Service Co., Inc., 1991, pp. 345, 346, 362, 363) (Box 3.2). Creativity and creative are not then further explicated or linked to semantically similar terms, within the references to a minimal degree of creativity. The different terms, *creativity* and *creative*, are revealed, on inspection, to be equivalent in their inclusion of creativity[1] but the predominance of creativity (five as contrasted with three mentions) implies a concern with the substantive phenomenon of creativity. Creativity would then be included in a minimal degree of creativity and would also be a mediated constituent of originality, from the inclusion of a minimal degree of creativity within originality (Figure 3.2).

1 The difference between the noun, *creativity*, and the adjective, *creative*, contains the possibility of a significant difference, in their meaning or in the inclusion of creativity. However, a closely subsequent reference to the first reference to a 'minimal degree of creativity', 'some creative spark' (p. 345), uses 'creative' as a term, implying an equivalence between creativity and creative, within a minimal degree of creativity. The variation between 'creativity' (pp. 345, 346, 348, 362, 363) and 'creative' (pp. 345, 346, 363) can, in this and every subsequent reference which can be assimilated to a minimal degree of creativity, be connected with the grammatical requirements of the surrounding phrase. The possibility of a significant distinction is not, then, realized.

Box 3.2 References which can be assimilated to a minimal degree of creativity

Original, as the term is used in copyright, means only ... that it [the work] *possesses* at least **some minimal degree of creativity**. ... The vast majority of works *make* **the grade** quite easily, as they *possess* **some creative spark**. (p. 345).

The Court explained that originality requires ... **a modicum of creativity** (p. 346).

the Court emphasized **the creative component** *of originality* (p. 346).

so long as they ... entail **a minimal degree of creativity**, *are sufficiently original* (p. 348).

Originality requires ... **some minimal level of creativity** (p. 358).

the Constitution mandates **some minimal degree of creativity** (p. 362).

the modicum of creativity *necessary to transform mere selection into copyrightable expression* (p. 362).

the minimal creative spark *required by the Copyright Act and the Constitution*. (p. 363).

As a constitutional matter, copyright protects ... **more than a *de minimis* quantum of creativity** (p. 363).

Note: The initial reference to the at least some minimal degree of creativity required for copyrightability is followed by further references which can be assimilated to it. They can be identified from their connection to the initial reference (Feist Publications, Inc. v. Rural Tel. Service Co., Inc., 1991, p. 345), and from their linking to originality (pp. 345, 346, 348), to the Constitution (pp. 362–363), and to copyrightable expression (p. 362).

The references which can be assimilated to a minimal degree of creativity are given in **bold** and the primary evidence for their assimilation in *italics*.

The creative spark utterly lacking or so trivial as to be virtually nonexistent.

A creative spark below the level of creativity required for originality is also distinguished (see Box 3.3).

> There remains a narrow category of works in which the creative spark is utterly lacking or so trivial as to be virtually nonexistent. ... Such works are incapable of sustaining a valid copyright.
>
> (Feist Publications, Inc. v. Rural Tel. Service Co., Inc., 1991, p. 359)

'There remains' (p. 359) indicates that the creative spark 'so trivial as to be virtually nonexistent' begins immediately after a minimal degree of creativity, without a significant interval.

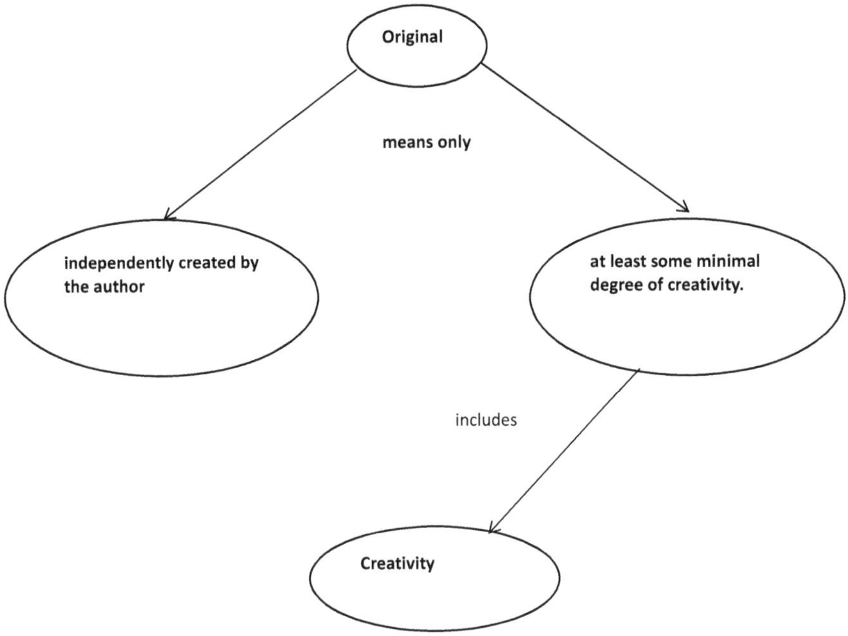

Figure 3.2 Originality, at least some minimal degree of creativity, independent creation, and creativity

Note: **Bold** is used for terms and phrases directly derived from the decision.

Box 3.3 References to the creative spark utterly lacking or so trivial as to be virtually nonexistent

Originality requires that ... it [the work] display some minimal level of creativity. ... the vast majority of compilations will pass this test, but not all will. There remains a narrow category of works in which **the creative spark is utterly lacking or so trivial as to be virtually nonexistent**. ... *Such works are incapable of sustaining a valid copyright* (pp. 358–359).

The question that remains is whether *Rural selected, coordinated, or arranged these uncopyrightable facts in an original way. The selection and arrangement of facts cannot be* so mechanical or routine as to require **no creativity whatsoever** (p. 362).

Rural's white pages are entirely typical ... [t]he end product is a garden-variety white pages directory, **devoid of even the slightest trace of creativity** (p. 363).

Rural expended ... **insufficient creativity** (pp. 362–363).

The *white pages do nothing more than list Rural's subscribers in alphabetical order ... there is* **nothing remotely creative** *about arranging names alphabetically in a white pages directory* (p. 363).

a *de minimis* quantum of creativity. *Rurals' white pages ... fall short of the mark* (p. 363).

Note: Further references to the creative spark without the level required for originality, after its initial introduction (Feist Publications, Inc. v. Rural Tel. Service Co., Inc., 1991, pp. 358–359) are identifiable from their direct connection with Rural's activities in construction of the directory or the directory itself (pp. 362–363), given that Rural's white pages fall below the level of creativity required for originality (p. 363).

The references to the creative spark without the level required for originality are given in **bold** and the primary evidence for their reference in *italics*.

The 'creative spark' (Feist Publications, Inc. v. Rural Tel. Service Co., Inc., 1991, p. 359) below the level of creativity required for originality contains a further distinction. The creative spark 'so trivial as to be virtually nonexistent' (p. 359) is differentiated from the creative spark 'utterly lacking' (p. 359) (neither gives rise to copyright) (Figure 3.3). The clauses corresponding to 'utterly lacking' (Feist Publications, Inc. v. Rural Tel. Service Co., Inc., 1991, p. 359) form the thematically and quantitatively, understood as the number of references, dominant part of the creative spark below the level of creativity required for originality (Figure 3.3).

The creative spark 'so trivial as to be virtually nonexistent' (p. 359) can be understood as a real level and amount of creativity and would include creativity. The creative spark 'utterly lacking' (p. 359), by contrast, would exclude creativity in a positive sense (Figure 3.4). Creativity as included in, and as excluded from, the creative spark can be understood as identical to each other. The concern with the substantive phenomenon of creativity established for a minimal degree of creativity is sustained.[2]

The clauses corresponding to 'utterly lacking' (Feist Publications, Inc. v. Rural Tel. Service Co., Inc., 1991, p. 359) can be read to imply, as well as to exclude, creativity. '[U]tterly lacking' (Feist Publications, Inc. v. Rural Tel. Service Co., Inc., 1991, p. 359) can be read to imply, *creativity fully present*, as its antithesis or complement. '[N]o creativity whatsoever' (p. 362) implies *some creativity at all*, as its own antithesis. It then indicates an immediate transition from the absence of creativity to creativity. The clause also explicitly includes the absence of creativity – 'no creativity' (p. 362) – which had been strongly implied by, 'utterly lacking' (p. 359). '[D]evoid of even the slightest trace of creativity' (p. 362) implies, *with the slightest trace of creativity*. It can then be similarly understood to 'no creativity whatsoever'

2 The pattern of occurrence of creativity and creative within the creative spark 'utterly lacking or so trivial as to be virtually nonexistent' (Feist Publications, Inc. v. Rural Tel. Service Co., Inc., 1991, p. 359) is similar to that within a minimal degree of creativity. The variation between 'creativity' (pp. 358, 362, 363) and 'creative' (pp. 359, 363) can be connected with grammatical requirements of the surrounding phrase, the difference is not semantically significant, and 'creativity' (pp. 358, 362, 363) occurs more frequently.

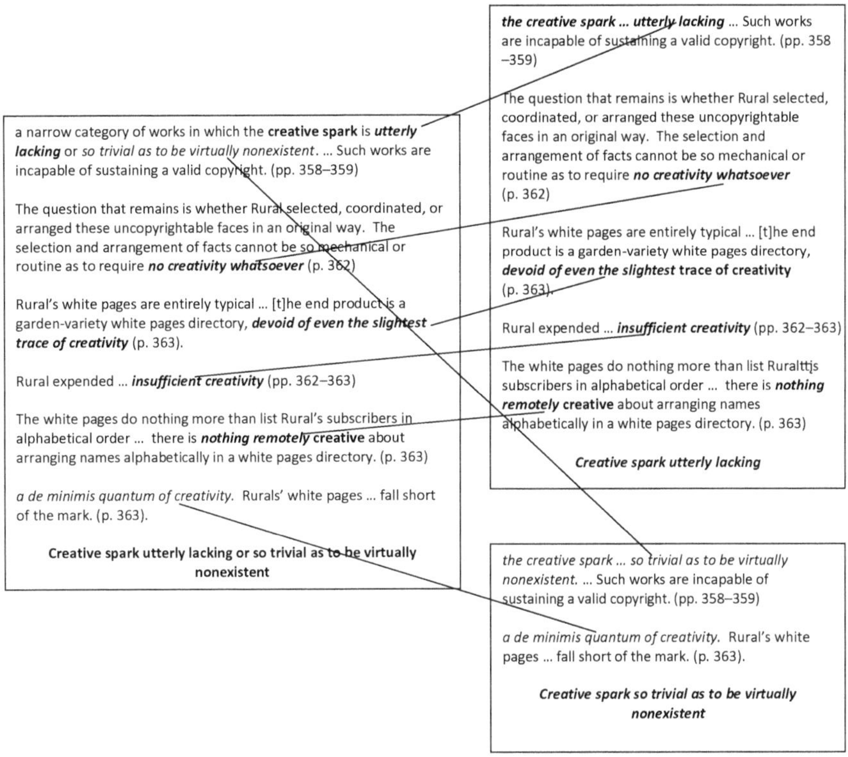

Figure 3.3 The creative spark utterly lacking and so trivial as to be virtually nonexistent
Note: The reference to the creative spark utterly lacking or so trivial as to be nonexistent is given in **bold**, references to the creative spark utterly lacking in ***bold italics*** and to the creative spark so trivial as to be virtually nonexistent in *italics.*

(p. 362) as indicating an immediate transition from the absence of creativity to creativity. The reference to a product in 'end product ... devoid of even the slightest trace of creativity' (p. 362) adds the significant possibility of reading the absence of creativity from the product, from the 'trace' (p. 362) left by processes of selection, coordination, and arrangement. The two consecutive clauses are then mutually complementary. 'Insufficient creativity' (p. 362) implies *sufficient creativity* as its opposite. The final clause, 'nothing remotely creative' (p. 363) implies creativity as remote from its own antithesis, as *something fully creative.* The initial clause and its implication, of creativity fully present, then comprehends all the subsequent clauses and their implications of, some creativity at all, with the slightest trace of creativity, sufficient creativity, and something fully creative.

An extended characterization of 'no creativity whatsoever' (Feist Publications, Inc. v. Rural Tel. Service Co., Inc., 1991, pp. 362–363), forms the basis for the conclusion that, 'the names, towns, and telephone numbers copied by Feist were not original to Rural' (p. 362). The characterization constitutes the strongly

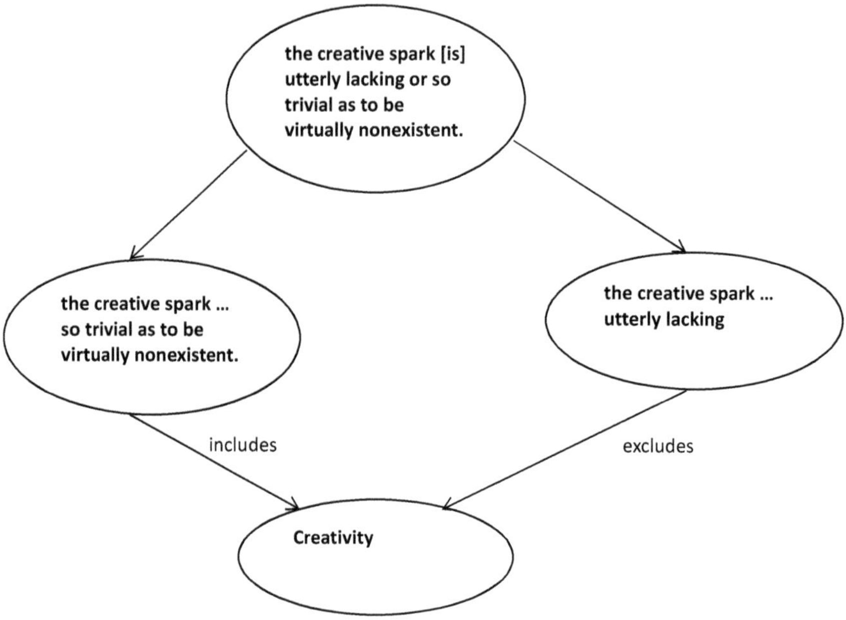

Figure 3.4 Creativity, the creative spark so trivial as to be virtually nonexistent, and creativity utterly lacking
Note: **Bold** is used for terms and phrases directly derived from the decision.

predominant part of a passage immediately preceding the conclusion to the opinion, from '[t]he question remains' (p. 362) to '[w]e conclude that' (p. 363) It can then be understood as highly significant, technically as the *ratio decidendi*, or rationale for the decision, as its crux or crucial turning point.

Overview

Combining the references to the minimal degree of creativity required for originality and to the creative spark below the requisite level of creativity is informative (Figure 3.5). The clause, 'more than a *de minimis* quantum of creativity' (Feist Publications, Inc. v. Rural Tel. Service Co., Inc., 1991, p. 363) can be read as a whole to refer to a minimal degree of creativity, and a part of it, 'a *de minimis* quantum' (p. 363), to correspond to the creative spark 'so trivial as to be virtually nonexistent' (p. 359), with 'creativity' (p. 359) as a common term. The strongly implied equivalence between creativity in a minimal degree of creativity and in the 'creative spark ... so trivial as to be virtually nonexistent' (p. 359) is, then, confirmed. The totality of the combined references includes all instances of the terms creativity and creative, in the direct text of the decision (Figure 3.5). The references are thereby exhaustive of creativity, for the purposes of the decision.

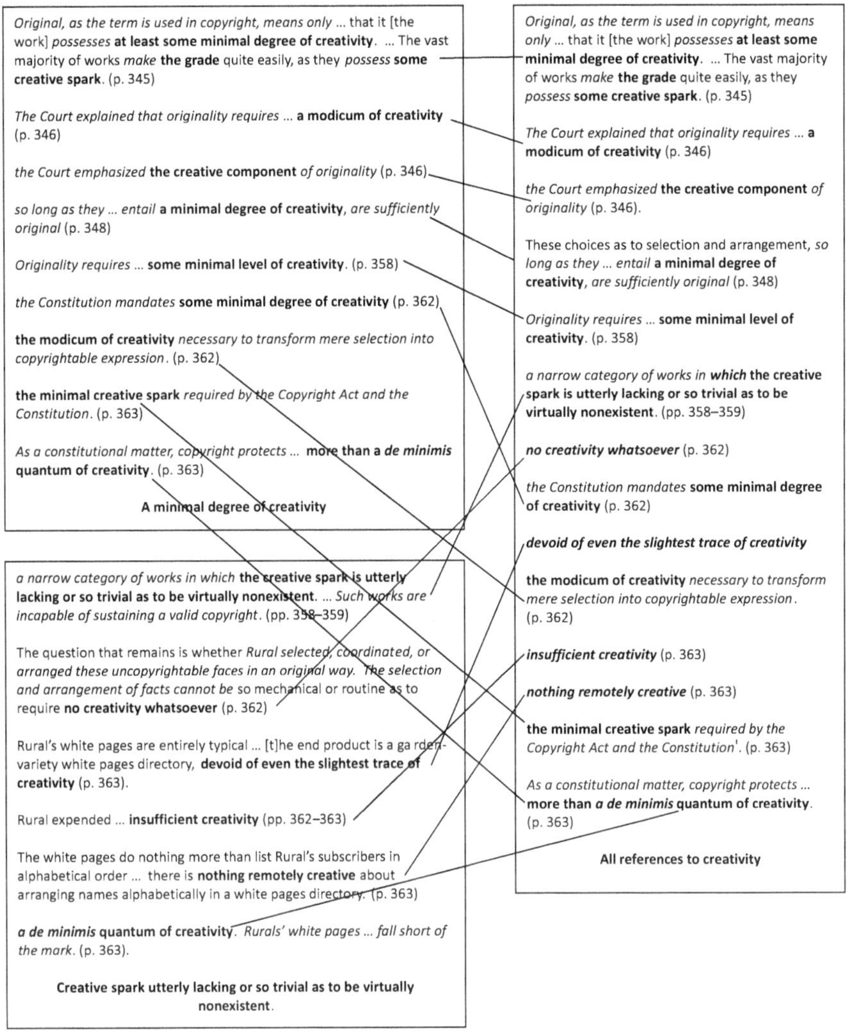

Figure 3.5 All references to at least some minimal degree of creativity, the creative spark utterly lacking or so trivial as to be virtually nonexistent, and to creativity in the direct text of the decision

Note: References are given in **bold** and the primary evidence for the reference in *italics*.

The treatment of creativity in the decision within the exhaustive set of references contrasts significantly with the treatment of other crucial terms in the decision. Creativity is nowhere assigned a meaning specific to copyright, unlike originality, nor is it explicated, unlike independent creation. It must then be understood to default to consistency with ordinary discourse. Creativity is not disaggregated, in contrast to a minimal degree of creativity. It is not connected to semantically similar or overlapping terms, contrasting with other parts of the judgment, such as the characterization of the absence of creativity, as 'an age old practice, firmly rooted in tradition and so commonplace that it has come to be expected as a matter of course' (Feist Publications, Inc. v. Rural Tel. Service Co., Inc., 1991, p. 359). An understanding of creativity cannot then be obtained by referral to subordinate or related terms.

The place of creativity in the decision can be fully revealed, by combining all previous considerations, including the implication of creativity from the creative spark utterly lacking (see Figure 3.6). The implication of creativity from the 'creative spark … utterly lacking' (p. 359) is, then, the only means for generating an understanding of creativity, from within the decision.

Conditions for the understanding of creativity generated can be derived from its inclusion in originality, in a minimal degree of creativity, and in the creative spark 'so trivial as to be virtually nonexistent' (Feist Publications, Inc. v. Rural Tel. Service Co., Inc., 1991, p. 359). From its inclusion within originality, it must be applicable to all works. Such works would exhibit very high and historically rare levels of creativity and creativity must then also comprehend a range from the minimal to the very highest level. From its inclusion in a minimal degree of creativity, creativity must give rise to level and to level and amount in combination. It must also occupy the 'extremely low' level required for a minimal degree of creativity. It must be sufficiently knowable to be incorporated into the possibility of obtaining knowledge of the level of creativity required for a minimal degree of creativity. Creativity must also occupy the level 'so trivial as to be virtually nonexistent' (p. 359). From the absence of the assignment of a meeting specific to copyright, it

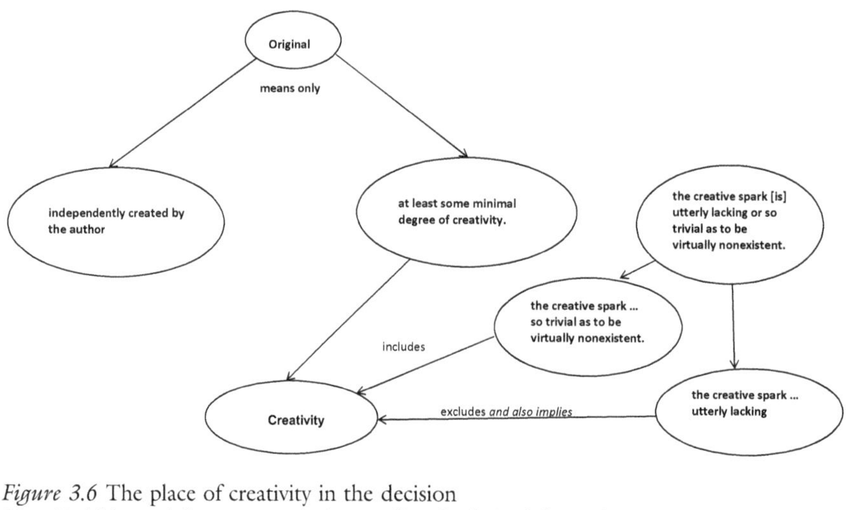

Figure 3.6 The place of creativity in the decision
Note: **Bold** is used for terms and phrases directly derived from the decision.

must be consistent with ordinary discourse. In summary, then, creativity should be applicable to all works, range from the highest possible level, through an 'extremely low' (p. 345) level, to a 'virtually nonexistent' (p. 369) level. It should give rise to level and amount in combination, be knowable, and consistent with ordinary discourse.

Narrative motif

Brer Rabbit has recognized the briar patch as home, begun to recognize his locale, and has found a progressive structure within an apparent maze. Like Brer Rabbit, we have used emotional intelligence, close observation, and intuition, to adapt to more powerful forces, emblematic of the *Feist* decision and of the work's approach.

Conclusion

Establishing the conceptual structure of the decision has then revealed the precise sense in which creativity is significant and fundamental. Its significance derives from its incorporation into the originality and the minimal degree of creativity, directly required for copyright. It is fundamental in the sense of being a primitive term, not further disaggregated. It would then be open to elucidation, but not to further decomposition, in Wittgenstein's sense of elucidation. 'The meaning of primitive signs can be explained by elucidations. Elucidations are propositions which contain the primitive signs. They can, therefore, only be understood when the meaning of these signs are already known' (Wittgenstein, 1922/1981, § 3.263). We have then addressed the preliminaries to our journey, by constructing a map for it.

Creativity in the decision: chapter summary

Originality is required for copyright and the originality requirements apply to all works, including, but not limited to, compilations. As a logical formulation, the requirement for originality could be represented as

$$\vdash \text{copyright} \leftrightarrow \text{originality}$$

The meaning of originality for copyright is given once only in the decision. It must be received as exhaustive and authoritative.

> Original, as the term is used in copyright, means only that the work was independently created by the author (as opposed to copied from other works), and that it possesses at least some minimal degree of creativity.
>
> (Feist Publications, Inc. v. Rural Tel. Service Co., Inc., 1991, p. 345)

A work is original, then, if and only if, it has at least some minimal degree of creativity and is independently created. In formal logic, this would read.

> **Original ↔ ((at least some minimal degree of creativity) ^ (independently created))**

We then have an authoritative understanding of originality and can turn to its components, a minimal degree of creativity and independent creation.

A minimal degree of creativity would include creativity. From inclusion we can understand that if there is a minimal degree of creativity then there is creativity, or

> A minimal degree of creativity → creativity.

Independent creation is parenthetically explicated at its introduction, as 'opposed to copied from other works' (p. 345). A minimal degree of creativity immediately disaggregates into a level of creativity and an amount of creativity at that level but is not further explicated.

A minimal degree of creativity is differentiated from 'the creative spark … utterly lacking or so trivial as to be virtually nonexistent' (p. 358).

> There remains a narrow category of works in which the creative spark is utterly lacking or so trivial as to be virtually nonexistent. … Such works are incapable of sustaining a valid copyright.
>
> (Feist Publications, Inc. v. Rural Tel. Service Co., Inc., 1991, p. 359)

The 'creative spark utterly lacking or so trivial as to be virtually nonexistent' (p. 358) can be understood as contiguous with a minimal degree of creativity, which also includes creativity, or,

> A minimal degree of creativity ↔ ~ (creative spark utterly lacking or so trivial as to be virtually nonexistent)

A minimal degree of creativity is then differentiated from its neighbor.

The 'creative spark … utterly lacking or so trivial as to be virtually nonexistent' (p. 358) contains a further distinction, between 'utterly lacking' and 'so trivial as to be virtually nonexistent' (p. 358). The 'creative spark … trivial as to be virtually nonexistent' (p. 358) can be understood as corresponding to a real level and amount of creativity. As such, it would include creativity, or

> creative spark so trivial as to be virtually nonexistent creativity → creativity

The 'creative spark … utterly lacking' (p. 358), by contrast, excludes creativity. The 'creative spark … utterly lacking' (p. 358) can also be understood to imply creativity as its own antithesis.

Creativity itself is not assigned a meaning specific to copyright, decomposed into further terms, nor connected to semantically similar or overlapping terms. The implication of creativity from 'the creative spark ... utterly lacking' (p. 358) then emerges as the only way of generating an understanding of creativity, from within the decision. At this stage, we can concentrate on the negative aspect of this implication, that a work is not creative, if and only if, the creative spark is utterly lacking, or

~ creativity ↔ (creative spark utterly lacking)

Conditions for an understanding of creativity can be generated from the inclusion of creativity within originality, in a minimal degree of creativity, and in the 'creative spark ... so trivial as to be virtually nonexistent' (p. 358). It must apply to all works, extend from the lowest to the highest possible level, give rise to level and amount in combination, be knowable, and be consistent with ordinary discourse.

Our task is to generate an understanding of creativity, from the creative spark utterly lacking, which meets these conditions.

We can use the map to navigate carefully through the decision. The intended journey is graphically represented as a map and progress along our journey will be marked throughout the work (see Figure 3.6).

We must now follow the initial stages of the path discerned, beginning with a fuller understanding of the 'creative spark ... utterly lacking' (Feist Publications, Inc. v. Rural Tel. Service Co., Inc., 1991, p. 362), of the antithesis to creativity, which is extensively characterized in the judgment and which is located at the bottom right of the figure showing the place of creativity in the decision (see Figure 3.6).

References

American Folklore (2020). Brer Rabbit and the Tar Baby. A Georgia folktale, retold by S. E. Schlosser. At http://americanfolklore.net/folklore/2010/07/brer_rabbit_meets_a_tar_baby.html (6 January 2020).

Clifford, R.D. (2004). Random numbers, chaos theory, and cogitation. A search for the minimal creativity standard in copyright law. *Denver University Law Review*. 82, 259–299.

Feist Publications, Inc. v. Rural Tel. Service Co., Inc. (1991). Feist Publications, Inc. v. Rural Tel. Service Co., Inc. 499 U.S. 340 (1991).

Ginsburg, J.C. (1992). No 'sweat'? Copyright and other protection of works of information after Feist v. Rural Telephone. *Columbia Law Review*. 92, 338–388.

Greetham, D. (1996). The telephone directory and Dr. Seuss: Scholarly editing after Feist versus Rural Telephone. *Studies in the Literary Imagination*. 29, 53–74.

Narayanan, A.S. (1993–1994). Standards of protection for databases in the European Community and the United States: Feist and the myth of creative originality. *George Washington Journal of International Law and Economics*. 27, 457–500.

Nimmer, D. (2001). Copyright in the Dead Sea Scrolls: Authorship and originality. *Houston Law Review*. 38, 1–222.

Nimmer, M.B. and Nimmer, D. (1978–2020). *Nimmer on copyright: A treatise on the law of literary, musical and artistic property, and the protection of ideas.* New York: Matthew Bender. Continually updated resource.

Polivy, D.R. (1997–1998). Feist applied: Imagination protects, but perspiration persists – the basis for copyright protection for factual compilations. *Fordham Intellectual Property Media and Entertainments Law Journal.* 8, 773–835.

Raskind, L.J. (1991–1992). Assessing the impact of Feist. *University of Dayton Law Review.* 12, 331–344.

Resnik, D.B. (2003). Strengthening the United States' database protection laws: Balancing public access and private control. *Science and Engineering Ethics.* 9, 301–318.

Strong, W.G. (1994). Database protection after Feist v. Rural Telephone Co. *Journal of the Copyright Society of the U.S.A.* 42, 39–67.

Trosow, S.E. (2004–2005). Sui generis database legislation: A critical analysis. *Yale Journal of Law and Technology.* 7, 1–109.

VerSteeg, R. (1995). Sparks in the tinderbox: Feist, 'creativity', and the legislative history of the 1976 Copyright Act. *University of Pittsburgh Law Review.* 56, 549–588.

VerSteeg, R. (2007). Originality and creativity in copyright law. In P.K. Yu (ed.), *Intellectual property and information wealth: Issues and practices in the digital age. Volume 1: Copyright and related rights* (pp. 1–31). Westport CT and London: Praeger.

Wittgenstein, L. (1922/1981). *Tractatus Logico-Philosophicus.* Translated by C.K. Ogden. London and New York: Routledge and Kegan Paul.

4 Creativity utterly lacking

Through the Wicket Gate

Introduction

We must begin with the 'creative spark … utterly lacking' (Feist Publications, Inc. v. Rural Tel. Service Co., Inc., 1991, p. 359), located at the bottom right hand corner of the figure showing the place of creativity in the decision (see Figure 4.1). The 'creative spark utterly lacking' (p. 359) is extensively delineated within the *ratio decidendi* of the decision, or the statement of the principles that determine the outcome of the case (Greenberg, 1997, p. 47).

One analogy for our journey through *Feist* was *The Pilgrim's Progress.* On this model, we have passed through the Slough of Despond, or despair at the apparent complexity of the decision, and elucidated the position of creativity within the decision and have begun to discern the path we must follow. We can now make a new beginning, on the basis on the understanding of the place of creativity in the decision. We must pass through the Wicket Gate (Bunyan, 1678/1985, pp. 12–25) and travel along the narrow and strait path given by the decision and which can be used to obtain a full understanding of the decision.

The judgment gives a full account of the negative of creativity, as 'so mechanical or routine as to require no creativity whatsoever' (Feist Publications, Inc. v. Rural Tel. Service Co., Inc., 1991, p. 362). The decision does imply an understanding for creativity by clauses with an antithetical character, most significantly by 'so mechanical or routine as to require no creativity whatsoever' (p. 362), which would imply creativity as neither so mechanical nor so … routine.

The delineation of the negative of, or antithesis to, a complex and difficult concept is consistent with a classic strategy used by the Supreme Court. Confronted with complex or elusive, but inescapable, concepts – 'the task of trying to define what may be indefinable' (Jacobellis v. Ohio, p. 197) – the Court has resorted to indirect methods of delineation (Fallon, 2004, p. 46). In one significant instance, concerned with obscenity, further definition of 'hard-core pornography' was deliberately avoided and a sufficient test for recognition of it – 'I know it when I see it' – substituted (p. 197). In the case of *Feist*, there is not a comparably clearly articulated avoidance of definition of the complex

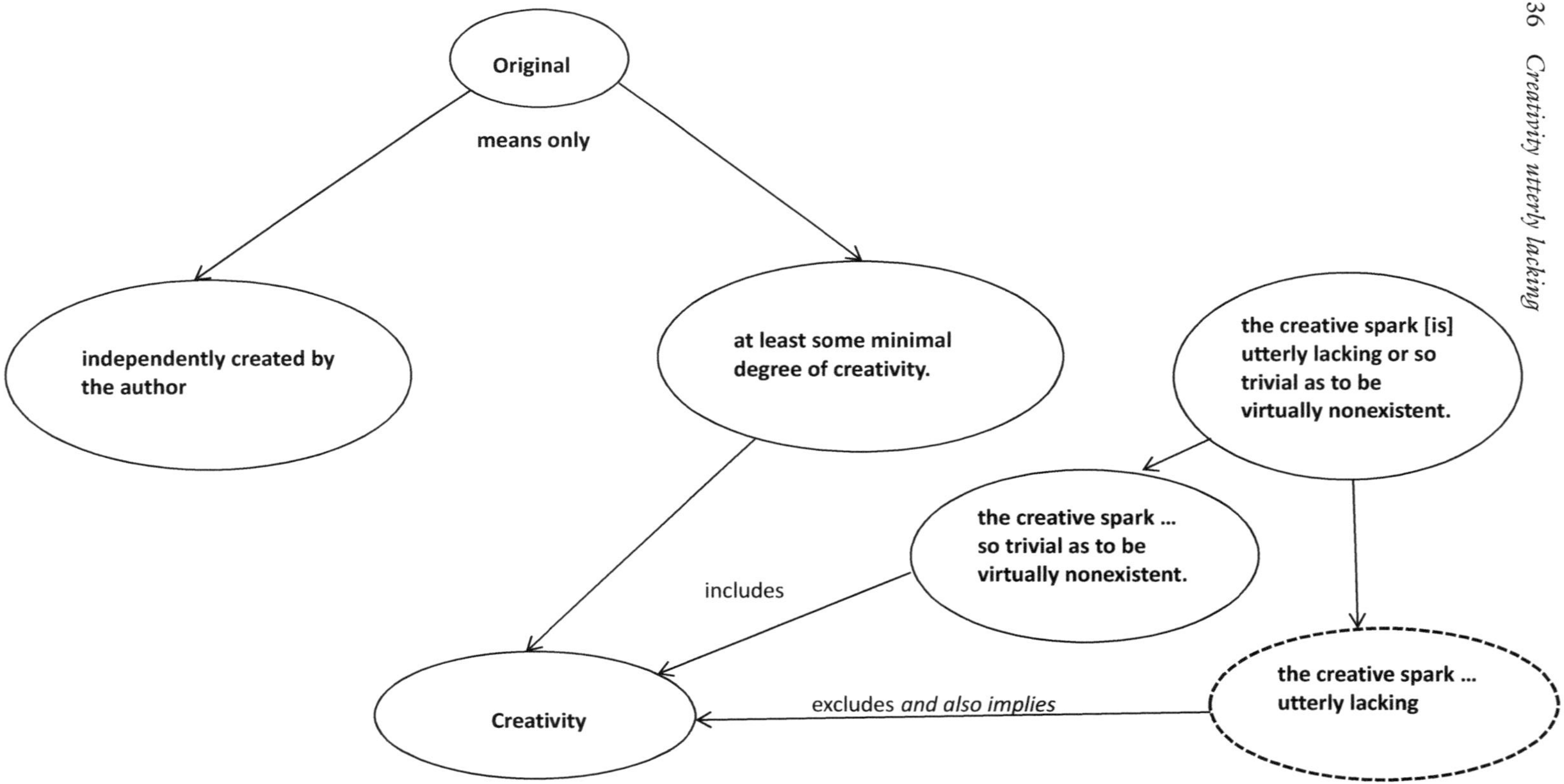

Figure 4.1 Map for the journey
Note: **Bold** is used for terms and phrases directly derived from the decision. The broken line indicates the current focus for the journey.

concept, of creativity, or a recourse to recognition. Rather, there is a focus on, and characterization of, the more definite, and possibly, simpler, antithesis to creativity, the absence of creativity, as the final rationale for the denial of property. The problematic history of creativity as a concept in copyright would definitely have been known to the Supreme Court, who cite a seminal case, Bleistein v. Donaldson Lithographing Co. (Feist Publications, Inc. v. Rural Tel. Service Co., Inc., 1991, p. 359), which allowed copyright to inhere in circus posters. The Supreme Court can then be understood as deliberately concentrating on delineating the antithesis to creativity rather than creativity itself, in the knowledge that it was more likely to be open to significant elucidation.

The characterization of the absence of or antithesis to creativity has not been subject to a close exegesis, beyond the recognition of the relative explicitness with which the not original as a whole has been delineated. One commentary at least has contrasted the explicitness with which the not original is characterized compared to the original – '[t]he Feist opinion is more explicit in describing what is not original than in delineating what is' (Ginsburg, 1992, p. 343). Commentaries have not seized upon the characterization for exegesis, or, as a further possibility, recognized it as a resource for the clarification of the decision (Nimmer and Nimmer, 1978/2020). The crucial characterization, 'so mechanical or routine', is increasingly frequently cited in widely scattered sources as a central criterion for the absence of property. The combination of recognition of clarity of delineation and the implication of the significance of the clause with an absence of further development promises the potential for a powerful analysis. The analysis can transform the implicit, emerge into the explicit, and integrate and unify scattered, but potentially congruent sources.

Critiques have recognized the existence, but not the potential significance, of the delineation of the absence of a modicum of creativity to the decision. Authors who recognized the focus on what was excluded from copyright in the opinion it simultaneously qualified its value – 'Where earlier Supreme Court decisions in this century – *Bleistein v. Donaldson Lithographing, Mazer v. Stein* – told us what subject matter falls within copyright's embrace, *Feist* took the hard road of telling what us what subject matter falls outside of copyright' (Goldstein, 1991, p. 118). Alternatively, recognition is followed by dismissal of the significance of the delineation: 'The *Feist* opinion is more explicit in describing what is not original than in delineating what is. ... The Court's word choice might best be viewed as rhetorical excess' (Ginsburg, 1992, p. 344). Even the recognition of the extended treatment of the absence of a modicum of creativity has not been consistently sustained by critiques, which have been more concerned with the poor positive definition of creativity as a positive concept (Clifford, 2004; Greetham, 1996; Narayanan, 1993–1994; Raskind, 1991–1992; Resnik, 2003; Strong, 1994; VerSteeg, 1995).

The beginning of the *ratio decidendi* is clearly marked.

> The question that remains is whether Rural selected, coordinated, or arranged these uncopyrightable facts in an original way.
>
> (Feist Publications, Inc. v. Rural Tel. Service Co., Inc., 1991, p. 362)

Similarly, its conclusion is also clearly signaled.

> We conclude that the names, towns, and telephone numbers copied by Feist were not original to Rural.
>
> (p. 363)

The crux of the decision is, then, captured in 'not original to' (Feist Publications, Inc. v. Rural Tel. Service Co., Inc., 1991, p. 363).

'[N]ot original to' (Feist Publications, Inc. v. Rural Tel. Service Co., Inc., 1991, p. 363) can be understood as the negation of originality. Originality is constituted by 'independent creation' and 'a minimal degree of creativity' (p. 346). '[N]ot original to' (p. 363) would be conversely constituted by the absence of independent creation and of a minimal degree of creativity. The absence of a minimal degree of creativity is populated by the 'creative spark … utterly lacking or so trivial as to be virtually nonexistent' (p. 359). '[N]ot original to' (p. 363) is, then, potentially constituted by the absence of independent creativity, the creative spark utterly lacking, and the creative spark so trivial as to be virtually nonexistent.

'[N]ot original to' (Feist Publications, Inc. v. Rural Tel. Service Co., Inc., 1991, p. 363) is extensively characterized in a series of consecutive paragraphs between the opening and the conclusion of the *ratio decidendi*, with crucial clauses proceeding from 'so mechanical or routine' to 'practically inevitable … time-honored tradition' (Feist Publications, Inc. v. Rural Tel. Service Co., Inc., 1991, pp. 362–363). The focus of this chapter is, then, on the delineation of 'not original to' (p. 363), with the aim of isolating the delineation of the 'creative spark … utterly lacking' (p. 359) and developing an understanding of it.

Creativity utterly lacking

The delineation of 'not original to' (Feist Publications, Inc. v. Rural Tel. Service Co., Inc., 1991, p. 363) can be scrupulously studied, with close attention given to all significant clauses.

So mechanical or routine

The not original is introduced at the beginning of the *ratio decidendi.*

> The question that remains is whether Rural selected, coordinated, or arranged these uncopyrightable facts in an original way. As mentioned, originality is not a stringent standard; it does not require that facts be presented in an

> innovative or surprising way. It is equally true, however, that the selection and arrangement of facts cannot be so mechanical or routine as to require no creativity whatsoever.
>
> (Feist Publications, Inc. v. Rural Tel. Service Co., Inc., 1991, p. 362)

The clause immediately characterizing the not original is, 'so mechanical or routine as to require no creativity whatsoever' (p. 362). The reference of the clause is directly to the absence of creativity, 'no creativity whatsoever (p. 362)'. As such, it constitutes a characterization of the absence of creativity in its strongest or most central sense, corresponding to the 'creative spark … utterly lacking' (p. 359). The meaning of the content-bearing terms, 'mechanical' and 'routine' and the relation between them needs to be considered.

Neither *mechanical* nor *routine* occur elsewhere in the decision, and in their unique occurrences, are not accompanied by citations or other indications of intended specialized or technical senses. They can then be understood in their ordinary discourse senses. These can be illuminated by definitions taken from a monolingual dictionary, understood as a register of acceptable usages. A culturally and chronologically proximate source is, *Webster's Third New International Dictionary of the English Language*, in its immediately preceding edition.

Mechanical is there defined as, 'done as if by a machine: seeming uninfluenced by will or emotion: automatic, involuntary' (Webster, 1981). The clause, 'done as if by a machine', is given first in the definition, with the other and subsequent clauses acting as elaborations or illuminating qualifications on it. The sense, 'done as if by machine' can then be regarded as the primary meaning of mechanical in ordinary discourse and adopted to interpret its occurrence in the decision. The qualification within the definition, '*as if* by machine', implies the inclusion of processes conducted by direct human work, but by a human acting mechanically, and of direct machine work. The definition of routine, as an adjective corresponding to its use in the decision is, 'of a commonplace or repetitious character: ordinary, usual' Webster, 1981), and this sense can also be adopted.

The qualifier 'so' in 'so mechanical or routine' applies directly to 'mechanical' and indicates that the term is to be understood in its most intense sense. It could also legitimately be understood as qualifying 'routine'. '[S]o mechanical' and 'routine', then, are distinct, but not contradictory, in meaning, and have a common referent in 'no creativity whatsoever' (Feist Publications, Inc. v. Rural Tel. Service Co., Inc., 1991, p. 362).

The linking of semantically distinct terms by 'or' does not strike a native reader of written English as dissonant, but emerges as unusual when compared with other occurrences of or within the decision and with its customary use in written English. The expression *or* is used within the decision with semantically overlapping or contiguous adjectives or adjectival clauses for instance, 'humble or obvious', 'utterly lacking or so trivial' (Feist Publications, Inc. v. Rural Tel. Service Co., Inc., 1991, pp. 345, 359). *Or* in ordinary modern English language written discourse is most commonly used to link semantically strongly overlapping terms (Metaphysics Research Lab, Stanford University, 2020). The unusual linking of semantically distinct terms is significant as it affects the relation and the preferred logical translation for the 'so mechanical or routine'.

The expression *or* has been translated from discursive prose into formal logic in two contrasting ways. In early modern logic, with Boole (1854), it was translated as an exclusive disjunction [either (p AND NOT- q) or else (NOT- p AND q)], but this was subsequently transformed into an inclusive reading (p OR q).[1] The inclusive reading includes the exclusive disjunction, but also includes the conjunction or AND, which was excluded from the exclusive disjunction. The crucial point of difference is then the inclusion or exclusion of the conjunction. Studies suggest that uses of *or* corresponding to exclusive disjunction in ordinary language are not common and that it is normally inclusive (Metaphysics Research Lab, Stanford University, 2020). With formulations with semantically overlapping terms, the expectation would be that the overlap or conjunction of the terms would normally describe most of the referents to be included, with some few only having one characteristic of belonging to the exclusive disjunction of the terms. '[S]o mechanical or routine' contrasts with such uses, as the content bearing terms are semantically relatively distinct rather than immediate alternatives. The expression 'or' (p. 362) in the decision would, then, normally predispose a logical translation towards an inclusive reading, but this predisposition must be qualified by the unusual semantic distinctness of the conjoined terms.

The particular logical translation for the ordinary language clause 'so mechanical or routine' is crucial as it leads to highly significant contrasts in the scope of the absence of creativity. The most extensive semantic scope would be given by logical OR, with negation, conjunction, and exclusive disjunction more restricted. Alternatives can be progressively considered and eliminated.

- *Negation.* Negation of both terms can be definitively eliminated from a reading of the ordinary language expression 'or' (p. 362) either as an exclusive disjunction or as inclusive.
- *Conjunction.* Conjunction, *so mechanical* AND *so … routine*, can be rejected as an exclusive reading, on the received understanding of *or* as corresponding to either an exclusive or inclusive disjunction.
- *Exclusive disjunction.* A reading that was intended to be restricted to exclusive disjunction could have been easily marked, without departing from ordinary language. An exclusive disjunction could have been phrased as, *either so mechanical or else so routine*, without loss of clarity or a departure from ordinary discourse. The commonality of reference, to 'no creativity whatsoever' (Feist Publications, Inc. v. Rural Tel. Service Co., Inc., 1991, p. 362), also does not favor reading as an exclusive disjunction, which would normally

1 Consider the parody of the use of *or* as an exclusive disjunction by Lewis Carroll (1871/1998, p. 213).

'It's long,' said the Knight, 'but very, *very* beautiful. Everybody that hears me sing it – either it brings the *tears* into their eyes, or else –'

'Or else what?' said Alice, for the Knight had made a sudden pause.

'Or else it doesn't, you know.'

require two separate referents, or a single referent with a dual aspect, to remain true when one term does not apply. Semantically, OR as an exclusive disjunction can be used for exclusive or contradictory terms. The terms *mechanical* and *routine* were not semantically contradictory or exclusive, on the reading established here. A reading of 'or' in 'so mechanical or routine' as restricted to exclusive disjunction is then not favored, by a reading of the expression, reference, or semantics of the decision.

- *Inclusive disjunction.*The expression *or* is used elsewhere within the decision in a clearly inclusive sense, although for semantically overlapping or contiguous adjectives or adjectival rather than distinct terms. The absence of a semantic contradiction between mechanical and routine, on the meanings established, still allows for the inclusion of a reading as a conjunction (a contradiction would normally debar a conjunct reading). An inclusive reading, which would include conjunction and exclusive disjunction, can then be accepted, in accord with modern practice.

'[N]o creativity whatsoever' (Feist Publications, Inc. v. Rural Tel. Service Co., Inc., 1991, p. 362) is then best understood as something which is *so mechanical OR routine*, with the qualifier 'so' applying directly and strongly to 'mechanical' and indirectly to 'routine' (p. 362) (see Figure 4.2).

Within *so mechanical OR routine*, the conjunction, *so mechanical AND routine*, can be understood as the strongest or most intense sense, as both substantive terms are realized. *So mechanical AND NOT routine* can be understood as the next most intense sense, as the primary term is realized. *So … routine AND NOT so mechanical* can be understood as the least intense sense, as only the secondary term is realized. The relative semantic distinctness of 'mechanical' (Feist Publications, Inc. v. Rural Tel. Service Co., Inc., 1991, p. 362) and 'routine' has, then, been incorporated and transformed into a recognition of difference intensities of senses within the inclusive OR reading. The different intensities of senses distinguished are also in accord with the normal distribution of combinations in a truth table.

The terms directly qualified by 'so mechanical or routine' (Feist Publications, Inc. v. Rural Tel. Service Co., Inc., 1991, p. 362) are the nouns, 'selection and

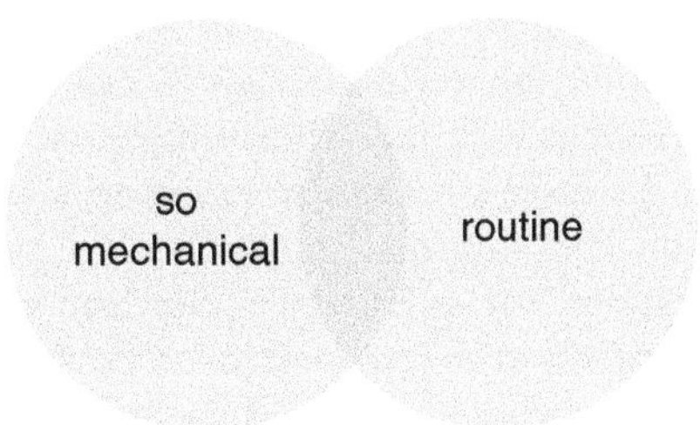

Figure 4.2 Logical representation of *so mechanical or routine*

arrangement' (p. 362), which could be understood as both processes and as a product. In turn, these noun forms refer back to the verbs 'selected, coordinated … arranged' (p. 362), directly referring to processes. '[S]o mechanical or routine' (p. 362) and 'no creativity whatsoever' (p. 362) must then be understood as having a strong underlying reference to the processes of selection, coordination, and arrangement, but also as qualifying the products of those processes.

In summary, both 'mechanical' and 'routine' could be understood in central ordinary discourse senses. Intensity was conferred directly on the mechanical by *so* and indirectly on the routine. An inclusive OR was the preferred logical translation for 'so mechanical or routine' (Feist Publications, Inc. v. Rural Tel. Service Co., Inc., 1991, p. 362), with different intensities of combination distinguished within the inclusive OR. The primary concern was with processes lacking creativity.

Entirely typical … end product … garden-variety

The decision then continues to characterize the selection, coordination, and arrangement of Rural's white pages.

> As mentioned at the outset, Rural's white pages are entirely typical. Persons desiring telephone service in Rural's service area fill out an application, and Rural issues them a telephone number. In preparing its white pages, Rural simply takes the data provided by its subscribers and lists it alphabetically by surname. The end product is a garden-variety white pages directory, devoid of even the slightest trace of creativity.
>
> (Feist Publications, Inc. v. Rural Tel. Service Co., Inc., 1991, p. 362)

The level of creativity at concern is, 'devoid of even the slightest trace of creativity' (p. 362). As such, it characterizes the absence of creativity, which would be contained within the scope of the 'creative spark … utterly lacking' (p. 359) and could extend to the extreme antithesis to creativity, which was also contained within the immediately previous reference to, 'no creativity whatsoever' (p. 362). The reference is also to Rural's white pages rather than a general characterization of creativity utterly lacking. Rural's white pages are characterized as 'entirely typical … end-product … garden-variety' (p. 362).

The senses of 'entirely typical' and 'garden-variety' need to be considered. The meaning of *typical*, although not of *garden-variety*, can be elucidated from its other occurrences within the decision. Typical can be understood as representative of a type, consistent with its ordinary discourse usage (also present in more technical usage, for instance when referring to a token of a type). The opening of the decision characterizes Rural's product as a 'typical telephone directory' (Feist Publications, Inc. v. Rural Tel. Service Co., Inc., 1991, p. 342), where *typical* can be understood as representative of a type. Feist's directory, by contrast, is not typical as in this way – '[u]nlike a typical directory, which covers only a particular calling area' (pp. 342–343). It is still characterized as, 'a typical Feist listing' (p. 344), where *typical* can be understood as representative of its own type. In the current passage, the decision refers back to the initial characterization of Rural's directory – 'as mentioned at the outset' (p. 362) – and then characterizes Rural's white pages as 'entirely typical' (p. 362). '[E]ntirely' (p. 362) confers intensity, and 'entirely typical' (p. 362) must then be understood as representative of the more normal and widely distributed type. '[G]arden-variety' (p. 362) is a unique occurrence and can be understood in its ordinary discourse senses, with a similar meaning to 'entirely typical' (p. 362). A semantic parallelism is also implied by the proximity and common structure of the sentence in which they occur.

The similarity in meaning between 'entirely typical' and 'garden-variety' implies that the terms would cover contiguous and overlapping domains in a semantic or intellectual space. The commonality of immediate reference to Rural's white pages directory, and of deeper conceptual reference, to the extreme absence of creativity, strengthens the case for their contiguity and overlap. An inclusive reading of the relation between 'entirely typical' and 'garden-variety' is then strongly preferred, with the further expectation of significant overlap or commonality between them.

The relation of 'entirely typical' and 'garden-variety' to the previous, and possibly encompassing, characterization of the absence of creativity as 'so mechanical or routine' can also be considered. The clauses are close in meaning to the routine but not in contradiction or tension with the mechanical. 'Entirely typical' (p. 362), as representative of a normal type, fully belongs to the routine.

The clauses can be regarded as explicating, although not exhausting or fully occupying the routine. In an approach to a stricter logical formulation, they could be conceived as a list of species – although without clear differentiation between the species – for the genus, routine. Classically, from Aristotle, it is 'more informative and apt to give the species than the genus', and further, 'the genera can be predicated of the species but the species are not predicated reciprocally of the genera' (Aristotle, 323BC/1989, p. 7). The OR reading of the relation between the clauses is strengthened by the consideration of the clauses as species of a genus. The conjunction of the 'so mechanical' with the routine is not disturbed. On the level of expression, 'routine' is closer to the clauses than 'so mechanical'. They further explicate the routine, without disturbing the conjunction of the routine with the mechanical.

'[E]ntirely typical' and 'garden variety' qualify Rural's white pages, characterized as an 'end product … devoid of even the slightest trace of creativity' (Feist Publications, Inc. v. Rural Tel. Service Co., Inc., 1991, p. 362). A product is specially designated in 'end *product*' (p. 362) [emphasis added] and 'end product' can be understood as the final outcome of a set of processes. '[T]race' (p. 362) can be understood as the evidence for those processes left in the product. *Product* can then be understood as analogous to, although not fully identical with, the marked term as recognized from a linguistic perspective, where the marked term is the variant of the unmarked term (actress/actor), and process as the unmarked, and here implicit, term. The sequence as a whole can then be represented as a logical formulation as *((entirely typical OR garden variety) AND end product)* (see Figure 4.3).

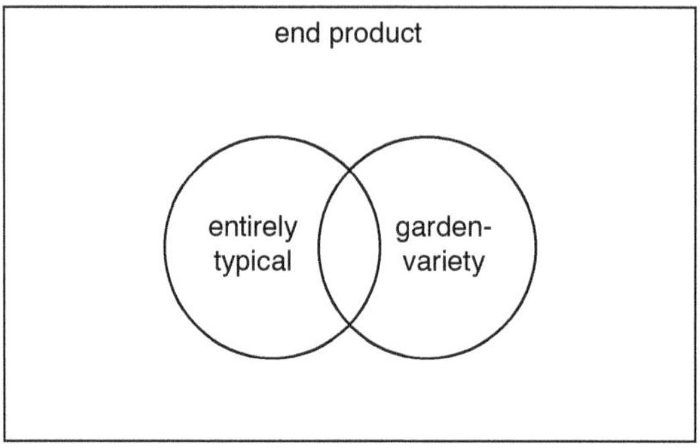

Figure 4.3 Logical representation of *entirely typical ... end product ... garden-variety*

In summary, 'entirely typical', 'garden-variety', and 'end product ... devoid of even the slightest trace of creativity' (Feist Publications, Inc. v. Rural Tel. Service Co., Inc., 1991, p. 362) could be understood in central ordinary discourse senses. A product rather than a process is at issue and 'entirely typical' (p. 362) and 'garden-variety' existed in an OR relation to each other and could be understood as contained within the routine.

Could not be more obvious ... the most basic information

The decision is next concerned with Rural's selection of listings.

> Rural's selection of listings could not be more obvious: It publishes the most basic information – name, town, and telephone number – about each person who applies to it for telephone service. This is 'selection' of a sort, but it lacks the modicum of creativity necessary to transform mere selection into copyrightable expression. Rural expended sufficient effort to make the white pages directory useful, but insufficient creativity to make it original.
>
> (Feist Publications, Inc. v. Rural Tel. Service Co., Inc., 1991, pp. 362–363)

The concern with Rural's white pages directory identifies the level of creativity as continuous with 'devoid of even the slightest trace of creativity' (p. 362). '[I]nsufficient creativity' (p. 362) must be read, from the connection to Rural's directory, as referring to the absence of creativity. '[I]nsufficient' (p. 362), as a term, also implies a level contiguous to the boundary with creativity. The nature of selection involved in 'insufficient creativity' (p. 362) is characterized as 'could not be more obvious ... the most basic information ... "selection" of a sort' (pp. 362–363).

Obvious occurs elsewhere in the decision, in quotations, as self-evident and can be similarly interpreted here (Feist Publications, Inc. v. Rural Tel. Service Co., Inc., 1991, pp. 345, 359). *Basic* is used both as fundamental – 'basic copyright principles' (p. 354) – and as simple or the lowest possible level – 'basic subscriber information' (p. 363) – and simple and lowest possible level can be understood here. Information in compilations is consistently differentiated from data, intensely from 'raw data' (p. 361), as data organized into a more coherent form. '[M]ost basic' in conjunction with 'information' then implies data that has been subject to a simple transformation into information.

Information, in the decision, functions as the final term in a hierarchy, *raw data, data, information*, in which each term is differentiated from the preceding term by processing conducted.

'[S]election' in 'Rural's selection of listings' (Feist Publications, Inc. v. Rural Tel. Service Co., Inc., 1991, p. 362) is linked to verbs, immediately to 'publishes', and, later in the paragraph, to 'expended' (p. 362), revealing a concern with selection as a process.

The similarity in meaning between the significant clauses coupled with their syntactic parallelism – 'could not be more obvious: it publishes the most basic information' (Feist Publications, Inc. v. Rural Tel. Service Co., Inc., 1991, p. 362) – and the commonality of their reference, to 'Rural's selection of listings' (p. 362), implies that they are closely related alternatives to each other, corresponding to an inclusive OR (see Figure 4.4). '[O]bvious' and 'most basic' are cognate with the routine, but not in contradiction with the mechanical, particularly when we are concerned with mechanical reasoning (Babbage, 1989, pp. 246–247). The clauses can then be understood as belonging to the routine and as consistent with the proximity of the routine to the mechanical.

In summary, then, 'insufficient creativity' refers to a level of creativity continuous with 'devoid of even the slightest trace of creativity' (Feist Publications, Inc. v. Rural Tel. Service Co., Inc., 1991, p. 362). All the terms characterizing 'insufficient creativity' (p. 362), 'could not be more obvious', 'the most basic information' (p. 362), could be understood in their ordinary discourse senses. The clauses primarily qualified processes, stood in an OR relation to each other, and primarily belonged to the routine.

Dictated by state law

The treatment of selection is then further developed, directly in connection with not meeting the originality requirement:

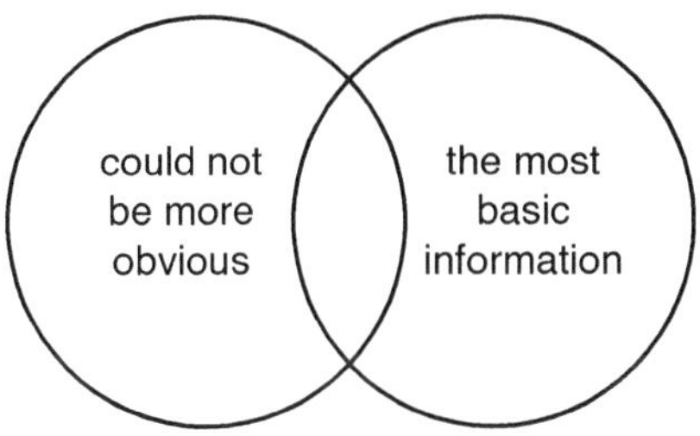

Figure 4.4 Logical representation of *could not be more obvious ... the most basic information*

> We note in passing that the selection featured in Rural's white pages may also fail the originality requirement for another reason. Feist points out that Rural did not truly 'select' to publish the names and telephone numbers of its subscribers; rather, it was required to do so by the Kansas Corporation Commission as part of its monopoly franchise. ... Accordingly, one could plausibly conclude that this selection was dictated by state law, not by Rural.
>
> (Feist Publications, Inc. v. Rural Tel. Service Co., Inc., 1991, p. 363)[2]

The reference of the passage is directly to the 'originality requirement' (p. 363) rather than to a level of creativity. The qualification, 'note in passing' (p. 363) also implies a departure from the direct concern with levels of creativity and 'for another reason' (p. 363) a concern with another constituent of originality. The only other constituent of the not original is the absence of independent creation, and this must be understood as indicated, rather indirectly. The determination of the process of selection by an outside body precludes the presence of independent creation, also indicated by the 'to' in 'not original to' (p. 363), in the conclusion of the *ratio decidendi*.

The paragraph in which the absence of independent creation is invoked is separated from the preceding paragraph dealing with insufficient creativity: 'We note in passing ... for another reason' (Feist Publications, Inc. v. Rural Tel. Service Co., Inc., 1991, p. 363). However, it is more continuous with the subsequent paragraph. The subsequent paragraph opens, 'Nor can Rural claim originality in its coordination and arrangement' (Feist Publications, Inc. v. Rural Tel. Service Co., Inc., 1991, p. 362), with the opening '[n]or' implying some difference but also a continuity. A difference is revealed in the concern with collection and arrangement rather than selection and in the presence of independent creation – 'no one disputes that Rural undertook the task of alphabetizing the names itself' (p. 363). The subsequent paragraph is concerned with 'nothing remotely creative' (p. 363). Continuity must then reside in the concern with 'nothing remotely creative' (p. 363). The final summative clause of the current paragraph, 'dictated by state law' (Feist Publications, Inc. v. Rural Tel. Service Co., Inc., 1991, p. 363) can then be understood as characterizing 'nothing remotely creative' (p. 363) as well as the possible absence of independent creation.

The particular sense of 'dictated' can be inferred from its context and its occurrence elsewhere in the decision. '[D]ictated' is used elsewhere in the decision, again in connection with law, 'the statute dictates' (Feist Publications, Inc. v. Rural Tel. Service Co., Inc., 1991, p. 358). '[D]ictated' can then be understood as an intense form of specification, with intensity semantically contained within the primary term, *dictated*, rather than added by a qualifier, in contrast to the previous formulations. '[S]tate law' refers to law, state rather than federal, imposed on the process of selection, from outside that process. Law (p. 363) refers to a law or very

2 *Feist* had contended that, 'The listings do not evidence any selectivity. The white pages listings take the entire universe of data, and indeed, RTSC is required to publish all the data as part of its telephone service franchise' (*Feist*, 1990, p. 22).

strong rule imposed on a process from outside that process. 'Dictated ... by law' (p. 363) can then be understood as an intense form of specification, with intensity semantically contained within the primary term, dictated, rather than added by a qualifier. Both 'dictated' and 'state law' can then be understood in central ordinary discourse senses. Contained within a single clause, the relation between 'dictated' and 'state law' can be read as a conjunction (see Figure 4.5).

'[D]ictated' (p. 363) as a verb invokes a process rather than the product of selection, indicated by the verb form select in 'did not truly "select"' (Feist Publications, Inc. v. Rural Tel. Service Co., Inc., 1991, p. 363). The reference of the passage is clearly and strongly to the process rather than directly to the product of selection.

The relation of the clause, 'dictated by state law', to the 'so mechanical or routine' can be considered. The intensity of 'dictated' confirms the intensity conveyed by the 'so mechanical', whereas state law would exemplify the routine as commonplace, ordinary, or usual. '[S]tate' in 'state law' (p. 363) can be understood as an exemplification of the routine and as qualifying primarily the process and secondarily the product of selection. Rather than being associated primarily separately with either the 'so mechanical' or the 'routine', the clause as a whole can be understood as exemplifying, although not fully or exclusively occupying, the conjunction of the 'so mechanical' with the 'routine' within the umbra of the absence of creativity. Hence, the reading of 'so mechanical or routine' as a conjunction is supported. The 'so mechanical or routine' and the absence of creativity can now be further understood to include, as a centrally characteristic referent, the carrying out of a process in strict conformity with a well-known law externally derived and imposed.

The meaning of 'dictated by state law' is then consistent with the interpretation developed of the extreme absence of creativity, as so mechanical OR so ... routine with the expectation that the conjunction, or AND, will be substantially and significantly occupied. Applying to the process of selection for Rural's white pages as an exemplar, it also illustrates the most inclusive logical reading (a so mechanical AND so ... routine process AND a highly routine product) identified as the strongest form of the extreme absence of creativity.

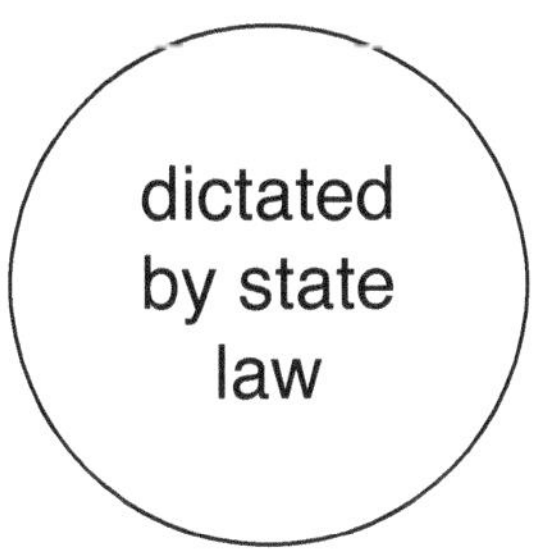

Figure 4.5 Logical representation of *dictated by state law*

In summary, then, the content bearing terms in 'dictated by state law' can be understood in their central ordinary discourse senses. '[D]ictated' and 'state law' are in conjunction with each other. The clause can be understood as referring to one instance of the conjunction of the 'so mechanical' with the 'routine'.

Age-old practice ... time-honored tradition

The concluding characterizes the alphabetical coordination and arrangement of the directory in a series of consecutive clauses.

> But there is nothing remotely creative about arranging names alphabetically in a white pages directory. It is an age-old practice, firmly rooted in tradition and so commonplace that it has come to be expected as a matter of course. ... It is not only unoriginal, it is practically inevitable. This time-honored tradition.
>
> (Feist Publications, Inc. v. Rural Tel. Service Co., Inc., 1991, p. 363)

'[N]othing remotely creative' (Feist Publications, Inc. v. Rural Tel. Service Co., Inc., 1991, p. 363) indicates a concern with the extreme antithesis to creativity, the extreme of 'the creative spark ... utterly lacking' (p. 359).

The initial clauses positively delineating the 'nothing remotely creative' from *age-old practice* to *expected as a matter of course* are, in contrast to previous passages, grouped directly and closely contiguous to one another, with the subsequent clauses, *practically inevitable* to *time-honored tradition*, similarly grouped. The clauses represent the most connected positive delineation of the absence of creativity in the decision. The crucial clauses can be extracted, with their sequence preserved.

> an age-old practice, firmly rooted in tradition and so commonplace that it has come to be expected as a matter of course ... practically inevitable ... time-honored tradition
>
> (Feist Publications, Inc. v. Rural Tel. Service Co., Inc., 1991, p. 363)

Collectively, the clauses constitute the most extensive resource offered by the decision for an exegesis of the antithesis to creativity.

The positive terms in the relevant clauses are not accompanied by immediate citations, or otherwise indicated to have technical or specialized meanings, and must then be understood in their ordinary discourse senses. The absence of other occurrences in the decision offers no immediate resource for elucidation. They are semantically dominated by a historical reference or resonance, incorporating a very extensive chronological reference. '[A]ge-old' refers to a very long duration, not confined to any particular historical period, and transcending historical variation and periods. The particular practice of alphabetic arrangement, to which reference is made, has a very long history, embodied in the term, alphabet (alpha, beta; Harris, 1986). '[A]ge-old' could then be understood as reaching to at least the emergence of written alphabetic literacy. '[F]irmly rooted in tradition' implies repeated over historical time and could even be read to imply the arbitrary nature of the ordering, in which the initially arbitrary becomes the traditional. '[S]o commonplace that it has come to be expected as a matter of course' reveals the historical becoming the everyday, a process which has been understood as naturalization (Berger and Luckmann, 1966). With 'practically inevitable', the historical is beginning to merge into the natural and the inescapable. The repetition of *tradition* and its presence in the concluding clause – 'time-honored tradition' – is suggestive of the significance attached to tradition for characterizing the absence of creativity. Long duration and transcendence of particular historical periods are then central to the characterization of the absence of creativity. Semantically, the clauses are complementary, although not identical to one another and could be conceived as overlapping.

The relation between clauses and their most appropriate logical translation also needs to be considered. The initial clauses are separated by a comma or by *and* and subsequent clauses are in separate sentences. The expressive structure is suggestive of parallelism between clauses, consistent with their similarity in meaning. The single referent, of the absence of creativity, continues. On the basis of their overlapping semantics, the suggestions of the parallelism conveyed by the expression, the continuity of a single referent, the relation between constituent clauses can be read as fully equivalent to logical OR, in the modern inclusive sense. Other passages in the decision containing clauses separated by commas can also plausibly be read as embodying an OR relation between constituent clauses. The single referent and the semantic overlap of the clauses yields the further expectation that real-world instances of the absence of creativity would be describable by more than one clause (corresponding to the conjunction, or AND, contained within inclusive OR; see Figure 4.6).

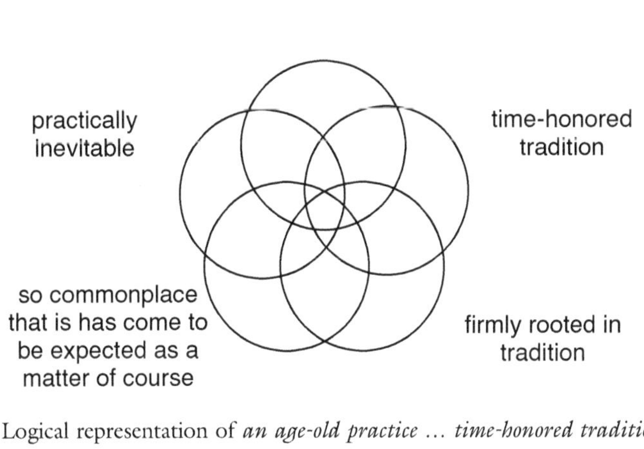

Figure 4.6 Logical representation of *an age-old practice ... time-honored tradition*

The relation of the clauses to the 'so mechanical or routine' can also be considered. Semantically, the clauses are closer to the routine than to the mechanical and can regarded as further amplifying 'routine', giving it a historical scope and resonance. In an analogy to the understanding established for the 'entirely typical ... the most basic information' the series of clauses, 'age-old practice ... time-honored tradition', can be regarded as a further, and still not necessarily exhaustive enumeration of species, conceived as overlapping rather than sharply differentiated, of the genus, routine. Their historical resonance exposes the 'entirely typical' and its associated clauses as semantically ahistorical although with a contemporary reference, in a standard directory.

The historical clauses in the opinion are separated from 'so mechanical' by 'routine' and by subsequent clauses, implying that they are indirectly connected to 'so mechanical' (Feist Publications, Inc. v. Rural Tel. Service Co., Inc., 1991, p. 362) and also may relate to 'so ... routine'. In terms of the order of words within the opinion, 'routine' in 'so mechanical or routine' mediates between 'mechanical' and the historical. The mediation could be understood as revealing how mechanical processes can become routine as commonplace.

The routine now emerges as mediating between the mechanical and the historical, with particular mechanical processes becoming routine through their recurrence over time. The mechanical, routine, and historical can then be understood as points along a continuum, counter to the commonly encountered opposition of the mechanical, conceived as industrial machinery and studied by engineering disciplines, to history, with history understood referentially to include preindustrial periods and as part of the human sciences. '[R]outine' (Feist Publications, Inc. v. Rural Tel. Service Co., Inc., 1991, p. 362) which combined with 'mechanical', can now be understood as mediating between the mechanical and the historical.

The concern of the paragraph is primarily with the process of alphabetization, with the concern with process revealed by the verb forms, 'alphabetizing' (p. 363) and 'arranging' (p. 363).

In summary, then, the conclusion to the characterization of the antithesis to creativity offers the richest resource for exegesis. Terms within clauses could be understood in their central ordinary discourse senses and had an extensive historical scope and very strong historical resonance. Clauses could be understood as complementary and overlapping. They primarily amplified 'routine' in 'so mechanical or routine' and could be understood as species of the routine. They exposed the ahistorical semantics and contemporary reference of the previous amplification of the routine. The routine further emerged as mediating from the mechanical to the historical and the primary concern was with process.

Synthesis

The *ratio decidendi*, then, substantively and extensively characterizes the 'creative spark ... utterly lacking' (Feist Publications, Inc. v. Rural Tel. Service

Co., Inc., 1991, p. 359). Five references within the *ratio decidendi* substantively characterize the level of creativity indicated by the earlier reference to the 'creative spark ... utterly lacking' (p. 359). Classically, this section of the judgment would be expected to rest on the principal distinctions previously established, in this instance, the requirement for independent creation and for a minimal degree of creativity, the existence of levels of creativity 'utterly lacking or so trivial as to be virtually nonexistent' (p. 359), and to bring these considerations to the issues under consideration, and this expectation is fulfilled. Some characterization is given of a specific instance of the possible absence of independent creation, although indirectly – 'for another reason' (p. 362) – but none for 'the creative spark ... so trivial as to be virtually nonexistent' (p. 359), consistent with the absence of any delineation of creativity within the decision. The extent of the delineation given of the creative spark utterly lacking, and the focus upon it, confirms is significance to the decision.

The passage as a whole consists of a consecutive sequence of connected paragraphs. It would be legitimate, based on the detectable structure, to regard the opening clause as strongly characterizing the absence of creativity, the intermediate passages as consistent and amplifying the initial themes, and the final sequence of clauses as a summative conclusion. A common rhetorical strategy for prose exposition consists of an indicative opening, which may be brief, but contains the kernel, and possibly the limits of what is to be expanded or developed; some intermediate observations; and a summative conclusion, fuller than the indicative opening, but without exceeding the initially established boundaries. The presence of a commonly used rhetorical structure is indicative of the cohesiveness of the delineation of creativity utterly lacking.

The significance to the decision of creativity utterly lacking compels, and the rhetorical cohesiveness of its presentation legitimates, the consideration of its delineation as a whole. A more concise, and, accordingly, more immediately intelligible, characterization of creativity utterly lacking can be constructed. Crucial descriptive clauses isolated can be recalled, in their entirety, with the distinctions between groups of clauses retained.

> 'so mechanical or routine'
> 'entirely typical ... end product ... garden-variety'
> 'could not be more obvious ... the most basic information'
> 'dictated by state law'
> 'an age-old practice, firmly rooted in tradition and so commonplace that it has come to be expected as a matter of course ... practically inevitable ... time-honored tradition'
>
> (Feist Publications, Inc. v. Rural Tel. Service Co., Inc., 1991, pp. 362–363)

Crucial terms within clauses were not specialized or technical, nor immediately amplified by citations to cases, statute law, or the Constitution or its interpretations, and could then be understood in their ordinary discourse meanings. The particular senses of terms could be elucidated from their immediate context, and where terms occurred elsewhere in the decision, this could be used as a further resource for explication. In all instances, the occurrence of terms within the crucial passages in central ordinary discourse senses was confirmed.

'[S]o mechanical or routine' (Feist Publications, Inc. v. Rural Tel. Service Co., Inc., 1991, p. 362) directly characterized 'no creativity whatsoever' (p. 362), opened the characterization, and was a general and comprehensive statement. Some priority was given to 'mechanical', by citing it first and with a qualifier directly conferring intensity upon it. The initial characterization as 'so mechanical or routine' applied to all of selection, coordination, and arrangement primarily as processes. The initial invocation of the 'so mechanical or routine' can be regarded as an encompassing statement that sets precise boundaries for the antithesis to creativity, but which still be further internally amplified or made fuller

The initial statement is then further developed.

- '[E]ntirely typical … end product … garden-variety … devoid of even the slightest trace of creativity' (Feist Publications, Inc. v. Rural Tel. Service Co., Inc., 1991, p. 362) adds the complementary possibility of reading the absence of creativity from the product, directly refers to the selection, coordination, and arrangement of Rural's directory, and invokes an antithesis to creativity consistent with the opening reference. The substantive terms of the delineation are cognate with the routine and not in tension or contradiction with the mechanical.
- '[C]ould not be more obvious … the most basic information … insufficient creativity' (pp. 362–363) are concerned with the selection, and not directly with the coordination and arrangement, of Rural's white pages and with a complement to creativity, 'insufficient creativity' (p. 363), contiguous with the boundary with creativity. The substantive terms of the delineation are primarily concerned with processes and belonged to the routine, while being consistent with the proximity of the routine to the mechanical.
- The clause, 'dictated by state law' (p. 363), could be understood as a single clause with differentiable aspects. '[D]ictated' directly amplified the 'so mechanical' and 'state law' the 'routine', while the clause as whole exemplified the 'so mechanical or routine' and could be connected with the subsequent reference to 'nothing remotely creative'(p. 363).

The further clauses are then directly concerned with Rural's directory and mold into the final general statement of 'nothing remotely creative' (p. 373). They can then be understood as intermediate characterizations between the opening and the conclusion.

The final sequence – 'an age-old practice, firmly rooted in tradition and so commonplace that it has come to be expected as a matter of course … practically inevitable … time-honored tradition' (Feist Publications, Inc. v. Rural Tel. Service

Co., Inc., 1991, p. 363) – was concerned with the process of alphabetical arrangement and with an extreme antithesis to creativity, 'nothing remotely creative' (p. 363). It historicized the routine. The historical resonance of the conclusion exposed the earlier sequence of clauses, from 'entirely typical' to 'most basic information', as a contemporary amplification of the routine. The routine, in its ordinary or not immediately historical sense, also mediated between the mechanical and the routine.

The delineation of the 'creative spark ... utterly lacking' (Feist Publications, Inc. v. Rural Tel. Service Co., Inc., 1991, p. 359) is, then, concerned with different levels of antithesis to creativity, all containable within creativity utterly lacking. The opening and dominant statement, 'so mechanical or routine as to require no creativity whatsoever' (p. 362), encompasses all levels of antithesis. The next is concern with the selection, coordination, and arrangement of Rural's white pages and with a potentially similar range of antithesis to creativity, 'devoid of even the slightest trace of creativity' (p. 362). The concern then turns to selection alone by Rural and with a complement to creativity, 'insufficient creativity' (p. 362), cognate with the routine and contiguous to a boundary with creativity. Rural's selection is then considered as 'required ... as part of its monopoly franchise' (p. 362), characterized as 'dictated by state law', and connectable with an extreme antithesis to creativity, 'nothing remotely creative' (p. 363). The final and concluding clauses were a general characterization of the process of alphabetization directly characterized as 'nothing remotely creative' (p. 363). The concern of the majority of the clauses was directly and implicitly with processes, while a single clause was explicitly concerned with the products of those processes. Subsequent clauses, then, amplified the initial characterization of the extreme absence of creativity as 'so mechanical or routine', without entering into tension or contradiction with the initial terms.

A formally logical account of creativity utterly lacking can now be synthesized, given verbally in this paragraph and paralleled by a sequence of logical statements and diagrammatic representation (see Figure 4.7). '[S]o mechanical or routine' is dominant with OR as the preferred relation between the constituent terms. '[E]ntirely typical ... garden-variety' are semantically cognate with the routine and qualify an 'end product', understandable as an AND relation. '[C]ould not be more obvious ... the most basic information', primarily amplify the routine, and can be considered as a more informative species, included within the routine. '[D]ictated by state law' belongs to the conjunction of the so mechanical and routine, which can be expressed as material implication (understood to be equivalent to inclusion, for these purposes). '[A]ge-old practice ... time-honored tradition' historicize the routine, and, for the purposes of a formal presentation, can be considered as includable within the scope of, *so mechanical OR routine*. All clauses, then, can be captured within a *so mechanical OR routine process*, with the exception of the explicit designation of an end product, which can be understood as in an AND relation to those processes.

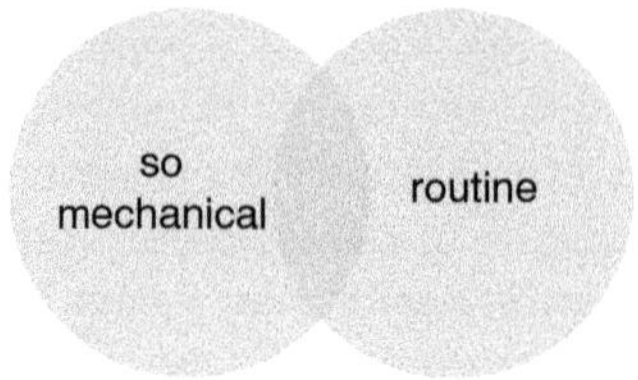

Figure 4.7a (so mechanical) OR (routine)

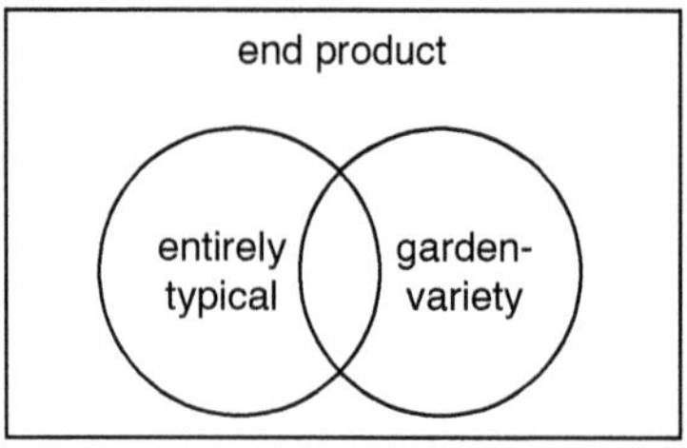

Figure 4.7b ((entirely typical OR garden-variety) AND end product) → so mechanical or routine

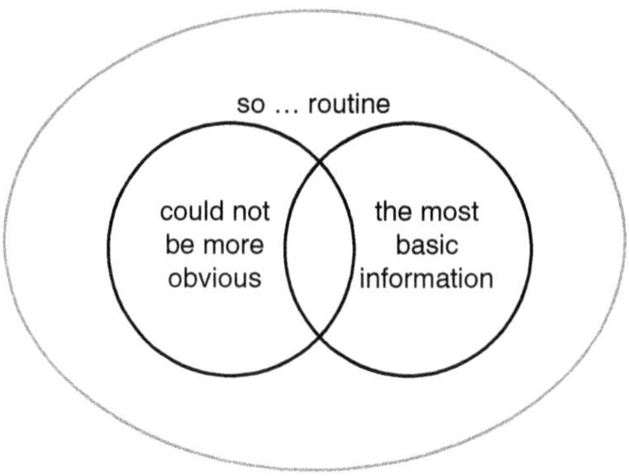

Figure 4.7c (could not be more obvious) OR (most basic information) → so … routine

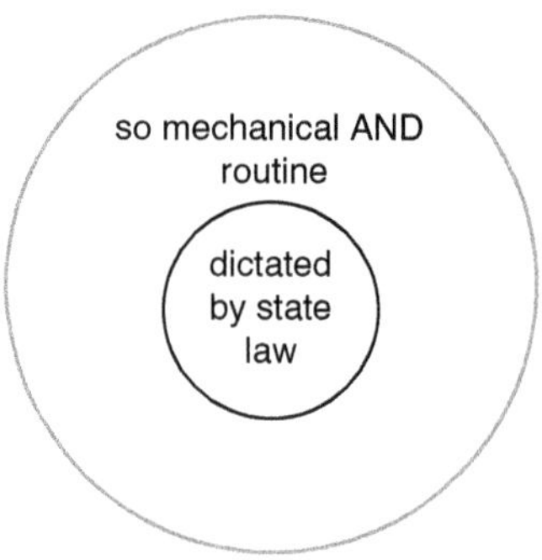

Figure 4.7d (dictated by state law) → so mechanical AND routine

Figure 4.7 Logical representation of the overall synthesis for creativity utterly lacking

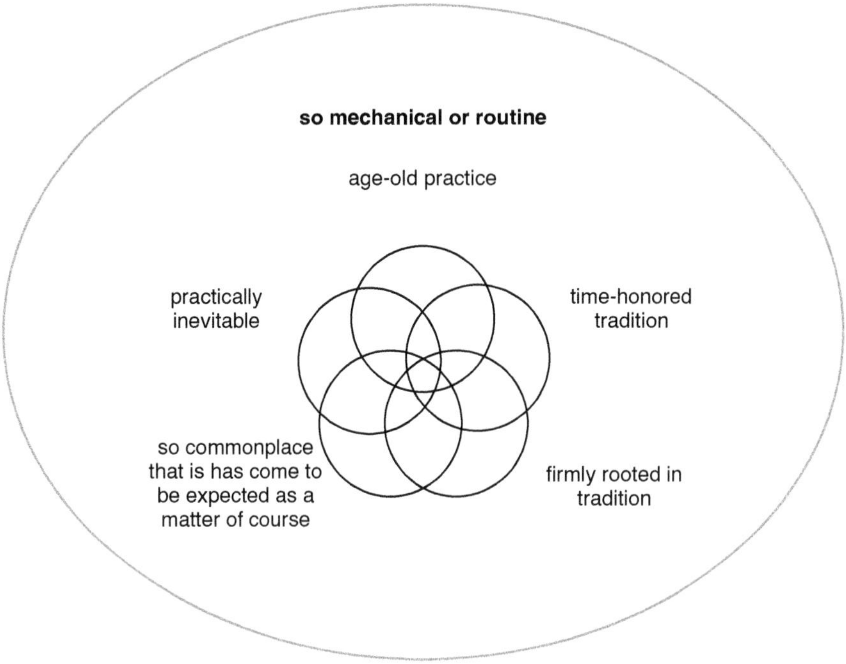

Figure 4.7e (((an age-old practice) OR (firmly rooted in tradition) OR (so commonplace that it has come to be expected as a matter of course) OR (practically inevitable) OR (time-honored tradition))) → (so mechanical OR routine)

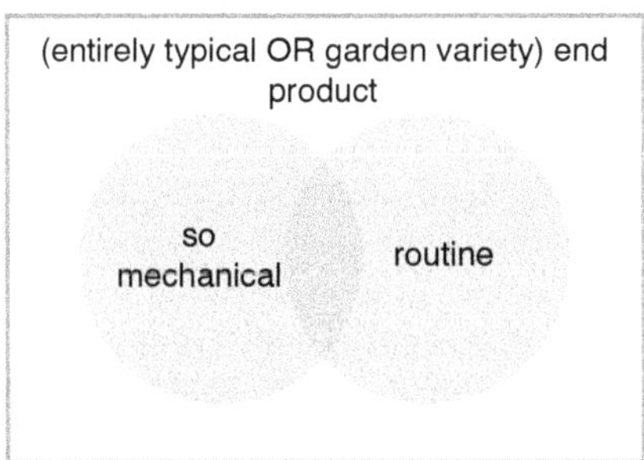

Figure 4.7f ((so mechanical) OR (routine) process)) AND ((entirely typical) OR ((garden-variety) end product))

Figure 4.7 (continued)

An understanding of creativity utterly lacking can then be formulated.

> A compilation has not the slightest trace of creativity if, and only if, it is constructed by a so mechanical or so … routine process and is an entirely typical or garden-variety end product.

The formulation for the antithesis to creativity explicitly incorporates the meaning of the two related clauses, of 'so mechanical or routine as to require no creativity whatsoever' (p. 362) and of an 'end product … devoid of even the slightest trace of creativity' (p. 363), and then applies, in the first instance, to those clauses, but should be consistent with the further clause, 'nothing remotely creative' (p. 363), from the potential subsuming of the meaning of its connected substantive terms within the scope of 'so mechanical or routine' (Feist Publications, Inc. v. Rural Tel. Service Co., Inc., 1991, p. 362). The qualification of a process by 'so mechanical or routine' (*Feist* Publications, Inc. v. Rural Tel. Service Co., Inc., 1991, p. 362) is raised to an explicit designation in the formulation, as, a so mechanical or routine *process*. The reading of the relation between the absence of creativity for compilations and the substantive terms of the characterization as, if, and only, if, is justified by the comprehensive capturing of all the delineated elements within the antithesis to creativity, within a set of references identified as exhaustive of creativity.

Relation to the European Union and other jurisdictions

We can consider to what extent the European Union and the rest of the world have also excluded the 'so mechanical or routine' (Feist Publications, Inc. v. Rural Tel. Service Co., Inc., 1991, pp. 362–363), as understood here, from copyright and other forms of protection.

Copyright in the European Union classically protected, and continues to protect, the products of *intellectual* labor (European Union, 2019). Intellectual labor can be provisionally understood as excluding 'so mechanical or routine' (Feist Publications, Inc. v. Rural Tel. Service Co., Inc., 1991, pp. 362–363) processes, but not as explicitly as *Feist*. Copyright in the European Union emerges then as potentially in broad congruence with *Feist* (1991), once the decision is fully understood.

Data protection in the European Union by contrast granted protection to the activities excluded from copyright by *Feist* (1991), which itself motivated the *European Union Database Directive*. However, the *sui generis* protection granted to databases by the directive was not strongly enforced in practice (Gupta, 2017) and has been recently further eroded (European Union, 2019).

The European Union then contains two, not necessarily contradictory but antithetical and intended to be complementary, elements. The mechanical and routine activities excluded from copyright by *Feist* would be protected in the European Union, not by copyright, but by the Database Directive, although judicial interpretation has tended to limit the scope of the Directive (Gupta,

2017). Activities corresponding to highly routine and to computational processes are excluded from copyright but admitted under *sui generis* database rights. The erosion of those *sui generis* rights implies a congruence, similar to *Feist* (Feist Publications, Inc. v. Rural Tel. Service Co., Inc., 1991, pp. 362–363), with underlying determining forces.

The rest of the world has tended to adopt a standard similar to that of *Feist* (1991) for exclusion from copyrightability (Gervais, 2002; Judge and Gervais, 2010). Adoption may have a dual motivation; first, explicitly from *Feist* (1991); and, second, through its correspondence to the underlying forces, the diffusion of the computer as the dominant instrument of mental labor, as exposed by the interpretation here.

Creativity utterly lacking: through the Wicket Gate: chapter summary

The extensive delineation of the creative spark utterly lacking, which implies creativity as its own antithesis, is carefully considered.

> 'so mechanical or routine'
> 'entirely typical … end product … garden-variety'
> 'could not be more obvious … the most basic information'
> 'dictated by state law'
> 'an age-old practice, firmly rooted in tradition and so commonplace that it has come to be expected as a matter of course … practically inevitable … time-honored tradition'
> (Feist Publications, Inc. v. Rural Tel. Service Co., Inc., 1991, pp. 362–363)

All the substantive terms in the delineation can be understood in their ordinary discourse senses. The *or* in the introductory clause, 'so mechanical or routine' (p. 358), could be understood in logical terms as an inclusive *OR*, which would contain the conjunction, *so mechanical AND routine*, as its most intense case. Subsequent clauses are semantically contained within so mechanical or routine. They were primarily concerned with processes and also gave some attention to the products of such processes.

A final understanding of the creative spark utterly lacking for compilations was obtained.

> A compilation has not the slightest trace of creativity if, and only if, it is constructed by a so mechanical or so … routine process and is an entirely typical or garden-variety end product.

Logically, this can be represented as

> (A compilation has not the slightest trace of creativity) $\leftrightarrow$ ((so mechanical $\vee$ so … routine) $\wedge$ (entirely typical $\vee$ garden-variety))

The distinction of process from product is retained, although not incorporated into the logical expression, to preserve simplicity. The *not* qualifying 'the slightest trace of creativity' can be transformed into negation of the clause as a whole, for simplicity and clarity.

> **~ (A compilation has the slightest trace of creativity) ↔ ((so mechanical ∨ so ... routine) ∨ (entirely typical ∨ garden-variety))**

We have therefore obtained a full, and formally logically formulated, understanding of the creative spark utterly lacking.

Narrative motif

We have then passed through the Slough of Despond, or despair at the complexity of the decision, and through the Wicket Gate (Bunyan, 1678/1985, pp. 12–25), the entrance to the narrow path to resolution.

Conclusion

What value can be attached to the exegesis established of the delineation of the levels of antithesis to creativity corresponding to the 'creative spark ... utterly lacking' (Feist Publications, Inc. v. Rural Tel. Service Co., Inc., 1991, pp. 359, 362–363)? A clear conception of the antithesis to creativity has then been established. The overall characterization of the antithesis to creativity is constituted by terms from ordinary discourse, used in unexceptionable senses, which promises the congruence desired by commentators between concepts from copyright with everyday understandings. Considerable progress has then been made in the exegesis.

We currently remain in the bottom right hand corner of the conceptual structure of the decision, but with the 'creative spark ... utterly lacking' (Feist Publications, Inc. v. Rural Tel. Service Co., Inc., 1991, p. 359) transformed into more fully understood ground from which to continue our journey (see Figure 4.8).

References

Aristotle (323BC/1989). Categories. In *Aristotle's Categories and De interpretatione*. Translated by J.L. Ackrill. Oxford: Clarendon Press.

Babbage C. (1989). *Science and reform: Selected works of Charles Babbage*. Edited with an introduction by A. Hyman. Cambridge: Cambridge University Press.

Berger, P.L. and Luckmann, T. (1966). *The social construction of reality*. Harmondsworth: Penguin.

Boole, G. (1854). *An investigation of the laws of thought, on which are founded the mathematical theories of logic and probabilities*. London: Walton and Maberly.

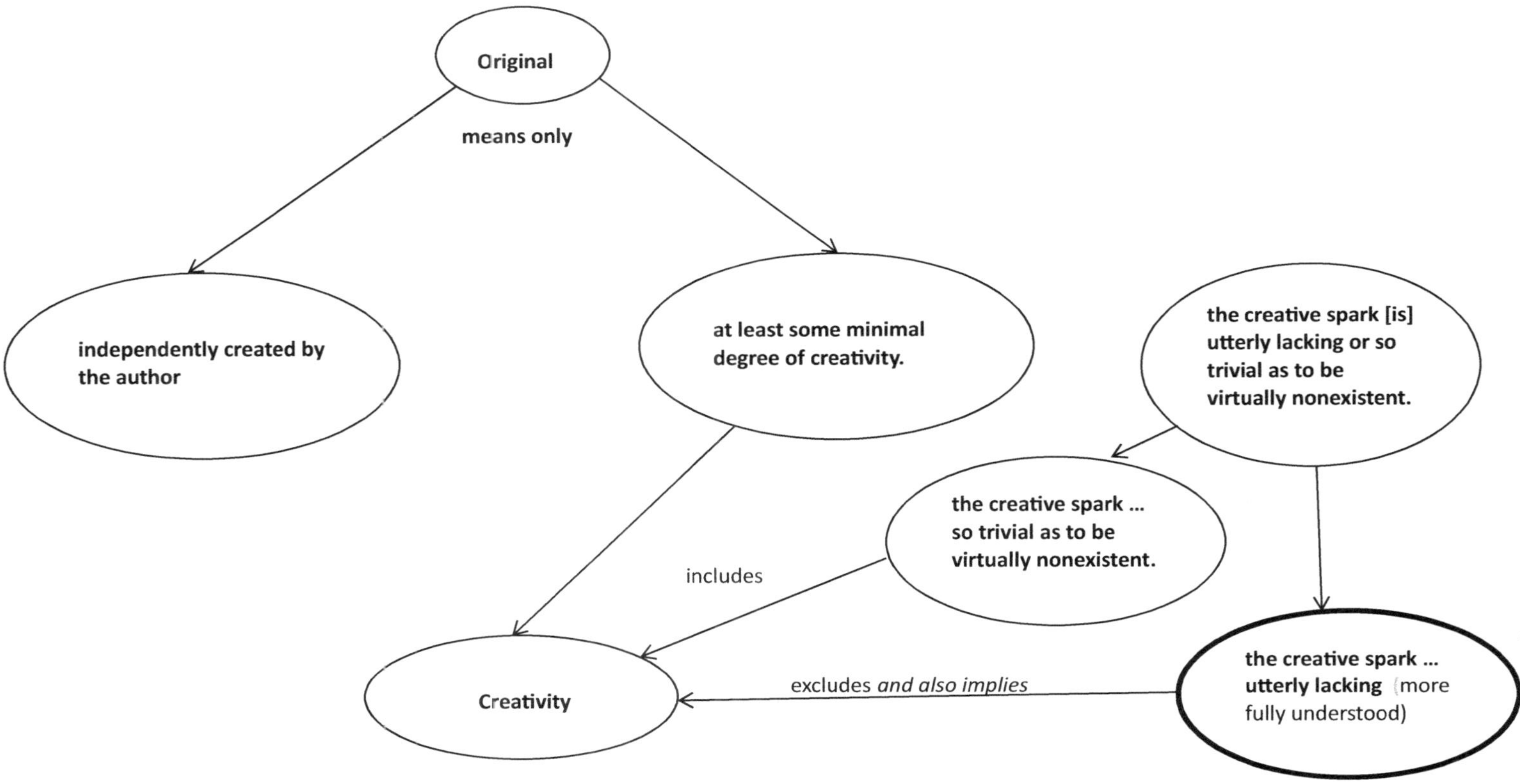

Figure 4.8 Location along the journey and progress made
Note. **Bold** is used for terms and phrases directly derived from the decision. The bold line indicates the substantiation of the current focus for the journey.

Bunyan, J. (1678/1985). *The pilgrim's progress.* Edited with an introduction and notes by R. Sharrock. London: Penguin.
Carroll, L. (1871/1998). *Through the looking glass, and what Alice found there.* In L. Carroll, *Alice's adventures in wonderland* and *Through the looking-glass and what Alice found there* (pp. 111–246). Edited with an introduction and notes by H. Haughton. London: Penguin Books.
Clifford, R.D. (2004). Random numbers, chaos theory, and cogitation: A search for the minimal creativity standard in copyright law. *Denver University Law Review.* 82, 259–299.
European Union (2019). Directive (EU) 2019/790 of the European Parliament and of the Council of 17 April 2019 on copyright and related rights in the Digital Single Market and amending Directives 96/9/EC and 2001/29/EC. *Official Journal of the European Union.* L 130/92.
Fallon, R.H. (2004). *The dynamic constitution: An introduction to American constitutional law.* Cambridge and New York: Cambridge University Press.
Feist (1990). Feist Publications Inc., Petitioner, v. Rural Telephone Service Company, Inc., Respondent. Brief for Petitioner. U.S. Lexis 602. At www.lexis.com (July 21, 2006).
Feist Publications, Inc. v. Rural Tel. Service Co., Inc. (1991). Feist Publications, Inc. v. Rural Tel. Service Co., Inc. 499 U.S. 340 (1991).
Gervais, D.J. (2002). Feist goes global: A comparative analysis of the notion of originality in copyright law. *Journal of the Copyright Society of the U.S.A.* 49, 949–981.
Ginsburg, J.C. (1992). No 'sweat'? Copyright and other protection of works of information after Feist v. Rural Telephone. *Columbia Law Review.* 92, 338–388.
Goldstein, P. (1991). Copyright. *Journal of the Copyright Society of the U.S.A.* 38, 109–122.
Greenberg, E. (1997). *The Supreme Court explained.* New York and London: W.W. Norton.
Greetham, D. (1996). The telephone directory and Dr. Seuss: Scholarly editing after Feist versus Rural Telephone. *Studies in the Literary Imagination.* 29, 53–74.
Gupta, I. (2017). *Footprints of Feist in European Database Directive: A legal analysis of IP law-making in Europe.* Singapore: Springer.
Harris, R. (1986). *The origin of writing.* London: Duckworth.
Jacobellis (1964). Jacobellis v. Ohio. 378 U.S. 184 (Stewart, J., concurring).
Judge, E.F. and Gervais, D. (2010). Of silos and constellations: Comparing notions of originality in copyright law. *Cardozo Arts and Entertainment.* 27, 373–407.
Metaphysics Research Lab, Stanford University (2008). Disjunction. In *Stanford encyclopedia of philosophy.* At http://plato.stanford.edu/entries/disjunction/#OrNatLang (January 3, 2020).
Narayanan, A.S. (1993–1994). Standards of protection for databases in the European Community and the United States: Feist and the myth of creative originality. *George Washington Journal of International Law and Economics.* 27, 457–500.
Nimmer, M.B. and Nimmer, D. (1978–2020). *Nimmer on copyright: A treatise on the law of literary, musical and artistic property, and the protection of ideas.* New York: Matthew Bender. Continually updated resource.
Raskind, L.J. (1991–1992). Assessing the impact of Feist. *University of Dayton Law Review.* 12, 331–344.
Resnik, D.B. (2003). Strengthening the United States' database protection laws: Balancing public access and private control. *Science and Engineering Ethics.* 9, 301–318.

Strong, W.G. (1994). Database protection after Feist v. Rural Telephone Co. *Journal of the Copyright Society of the U.S.A.* 42, 39–67.

VerSteeg, R. (1995). Sparks in the tinderbox: Feist, 'creativity', and the legislative history of the 1976 Copyright Act. *University of Pittsburgh Law Review*. 56, pp. 549–588.

VerSteeg, R. (2007). Originality and creativity in copyright law. In P.K. Yu (ed.), *Intellectual property and information wealth: Issues and practices in the digital age. Volume 1: Copyright and related rights* (pp. 1–31). *Westport,* CT and London: Praeger.

Webster (1981). *Webster's third new international dictionary of the English language. Unabridged*. Edited by P.B. Gove and others. Springfield, MA: Merriam.

5 Correlation

The key to Doubting Castle

Introduction

We have then made progress made along our path, by a full exegesis and analysis of creativity utterly lacking. It might still be objected that the terms characterizing the antithesis to creativity, so mechanical or routine, entirely typical, garden-variety, and end product, could themselves be subject to many different interpretations and do not constitute solid or final ground. The uncertainty indicated could be displaced by correlating creativity utterly lacking with something definitively known, a classic move in law.

In terms of our narrative motif, the journey towards salvation in *The Pilgrim's Progress* is interrupted and delayed by Giant Despair, who imprisons the pilgrim in Doubting Castle (Bunyan, 1678/1985, pp. 99–103). Our task then must be to escape from Doubting Castle, to resolve doubt, and to resume our journey on firm ground, a ground made stronger by the resolution of doubt.

A correlation is established between the antithesis to creativity in the judgment and classic conceptions of computability. A gestalt, or overall, sense of correspondence between the characterization of creativity utterly lacking and classic conceptions of computability is first revealed. Clauses from the decision are then progressively analyzed for their contribution to the gestalt effect. The term *mechanical* in '[S]o mechanical' in the characterization of creativity utterly lacking correlates verbally and conceptually with *mechanical* in a mechanical procedure or algorithm. '[S]o' implies a strong form of mechanical corresponding to an *automatic* mechanical procedure. The historical in the decision correlates with the natural in conceptions of computability (summary and informative accounts of concepts from computer science, such as that of computability, which may be familiar to some readers but less well known to others, will be given in text boxes). Connecting 'so mechanical' in the decision with an automatic mechanical procedure substantiates and confirms the gestalt effect of correspondence. Routine in the characterization of creativity utterly lacking is then differentiated from those elements which directly correlate with the mechanical and computability. Creativity utterly lacking, or the antithesis to creativity, is finally understood as residing in a so … routine automatic mechanical or computational procedure and also in highly routine, although not necessarily fully mechanical, processes which give rise to entirely typical or garden-variety products.

The correlation with classic conceptions of computability grounds the antithesis to creativity in a concept which is definitively known, of compelling contemporary significance, and which has acute practical relevance. We have then transcended from the possible questioning of terms in creativity utterly lacking, and we can resume our journey.

Overall correspondence

The full substantive content given to creativity utterly lacking can be recalled collectively, as a general characterization.

> so mechanical or routine
> entirely typical ... end product ... garden-variety
> could not be more obvious ... the most basic information
> dictated by state law
> an age-old practice, firmly rooted in tradition and so commonplace that it has come to be expected as a matter of course ... practically inevitable ... time-honored tradition.
> (Feist Publications, Inc. v. Rural Tel. Service Co., Inc., 1991, pp. 362–363)

'[S]o mechanical' obtains priority from its initial position. '[M]echanical' and all the other constituent terms of the characterization could all be understood in their central ordinary discourse senses.

The overall effect of the meanings of the substantive terms delineating the creative utterly lacking is analogous to a concept of compelling modern significance, to computability. The concept of computability was captured in a classic statement of its significance.

> It seems that this importance [of Turing's computability] is largely due to the fact that with this concept one has for the first time succeeded in giving an absolute definition of an interesting epistemological notion, i.e., one not depending on the formalism chosen. In all other cases treated previously, such as demonstrability or definability, one has been able to define them only relative to a given language, and for each individual language it is clear that the one thus obtained is not the one looked for.
> (Gödel, 1946/2004, p. 84)

The analogy rests primarily on an overall, or gestalt, effect of correspondence. The atomic fact, or primitive concept, with which creativity utterly lacking has been correlated, is of compelling contemporary significance, and, as instantiated in working computational processes, also of acute practical relevance (see also Box 5.1 on computability and its significance). A highly significant correlation has then been indicated.

Box 5.1 Computability and its significance

The working algorithms which form part of our everyday experience are equivalent to the computational processes modeled by Turing in 1936 (1936–1937/2004). Turing was concerned to give form to the concept of computability, to what would naturally be regarded as computable. As *Time* noted in 1999:

> everyone who taps at a keyboard, opening a spreadsheet or a word-processing program, is working on an incarnation of a Turing machine.
> (Quoted in Davis, 2000, p. 193)

The concept of a Turing machine would include the automatic operations of the spreadsheet or word-processing program but not necessarily direct human non-mechanical interaction with such processes (except as a choice machine, or, under some interpretations, as non-determinism). In everyday practice, an automatic mechanical procedure is represented by the automatic operations of spreadsheet or word-processing program, while human intervention would strongly tend to be non-mechanical.

Turing's model of the computational process has become dominant, since its formulation. The thesis that a process is computable, if and only if, it is Turing machine computable is regarded as still valid (Herken, 1994; Cockshott and Michaelson, 2007). Within the discipline of computer science, the thesis has a fundamental and largely unquestioned status (Cockshott and Michaelson, 2007, p. 232). It can be regarded as an absolute concept and as bedrock for our discussion.

Turing's model of computability also obtains wide current significance from its instantiation in practice, although the concept of computability itself may not necessarily be as widely explicitly diffused or fully publicly understood.

The concept of computability is, then, of compelling contemporary significance, both theoretically and practically, as instantiated in working computers and computational processes. It can be received as an absolute concept.

The clauses in the opinion and the particular characterization of computability have only one substantive word in common, *time* in 'time-honored' (Feist Publications, Inc. v. Rural Tel. Service Co., Inc., 1991, p. 363) in the judgment and 'for the first time' (Gödel, 1946/2004, p. 84) in the characterization of computability, but specific conceptual and verbal correlations can be found. '[M]echanical' in 'so mechanical' can be correlated with a mechanical procedure or algorithm, and 'so mechanical' (Feist Publications, Inc. v. Rural

Tel. Service Co., Inc., 1991, p. 362) as a whole with an automatic mechanical procedure or automatic computational process. Identifying specific correlations should have the effect of strengthening the overall analogy. The clauses in the opinion with a historical resonance, from 'an age-old practice' to 'time-honored tradition' (Feist Publications, Inc. v. Rural Tel. Service Co., Inc., 1991, p. 363), can be correlated with an element of the foundation for the concept of computability, with the natural in what would naturally be regarded as computable.

Specific correlations

The concern of this chapter, then, is with establishing, and also refining, the correlation of creativity utterly lacking with computability, by a progressively developed argument. We will focus on how each of the clauses contributes to the gestalt sense of correspondence and on the specific verbal and conceptual correlations between 'so mechanical' (Feist Publications, Inc. v. Rural Tel. Service Co., Inc., 1991, pp. 362–363) and an automatic mechanical procedure or algorithm.

So mechanical or routine

The opening clause of the delineation of creativity utterly lacking in the opinion, 'so mechanical or routine' (Feist Publications, Inc. v. Rural Tel. Service Co., Inc., 1991, p. 362), is consistent with the gestalt effect of correspondence with computability. It also contains a specifically correlating element, 'so mechanical' (p. 362), and a partially differentiating element, 'so ... routine' (p. 362).

So mechanical

'[S]o mechanical' is the first element of the clause and is then the dominant characterization of processes without any creativity. It can be correlated with a mechanical procedure (see Box 5.2 on mechanical procedure) through specific similarities.

Box 5.2 Mechanical procedure

Mechanical procedure is a classic term for an automatic computational process.

The computational process was classically characterized in mechanical terms. The concept and term mechanical procedure emerged from a model of a human computer acting mechanically.

> We may compare a man in the process of computing a real number to a *machine* which is only capable of a finite number of conditions.
>
> (Turing, 1936–1937/2004, p. 117 [emphasis added])

A mechanical procedure then corresponds to a computational process and includes a human acting mechanically or as a machine.

Classically, and in its origins, the modeling of the computational process in mechanical terms was concerned with automatic procedures: 'If at each stage the motion of a machine ... is completely determined by the configuration, we shall call the machine an 'automatic machine'. ... In this paper I deal only with automatic machines' (Turing, 1936–1937/2004, p. 118). In subsequent discussions, the deliberate limitation to automatic machines has been transformed into a primary focus. An automatic mechanical procedure has been widely regarded as the purest or most intense form of a computational process or a mechanical procedure from many perspectives, including discussions of computability (Turing, 1936–1937; Gödel, 1964/2004) and other disciplines, including classical experimental information retrieval and natural language processing (Wilks, Slator, & Guthrie, 1996). Mechanical procedure then refers primarily or exclusively to automatic computational processes, with automatic as the strongest or most intense form, and is a type of process.

The model of the computational process with which the term mechanical procedure is associated was intended to encompass preexisting terms and concepts, including algorithm, but to give them a more precise and materially definite form. The scope of the computational processes covered by mechanical procedure, algorithm, and effective procedure can be considered coterminous, for the analytical purposes here.

We will use *mechanical procedure* here as the preferred, although the not necessarily the exclusive, term, for its classical origins, precise description, and the direct verbal connection it offers with the opinion.

The most striking and immediate similarity subsists at the level of expression. '[M]echanical' in 'so mechanical' (Feist Publications, Inc. v. Rural Tel. Service Co., Inc., 1991, p. 362) is the identical verbal form to *mechanical* in mechanical procedure, if both occurrences are considered as sequences of characters from the given alphabet and written language. In formal logic, a good notation or symbolism can reveal relations between ideas, as Wittgenstein noted.

> Now we understand our feeling that we are in possession of the right logical conception, if only all is right in our symbolism.
>
> (Wittgenstein, 1922/1981, §4.1213)

In this instance, the identity in expression is a similarity in itself and a compelling suggestion of further similarities.

The common alphabet and language for mechanical are indicative of the contexts of use from which the term is derived. Mechanical in the opinion is not marked as a technical or specialized term by its alphabet or language nor by citation and is best understood as taken from ordinary discourse. Similarly, mechanical in mechanical procedure was derived from ordinary English language discourse. Although logical and mathematical notation was subsequently used in making more precise the concept of acting as a machine, the ordinary discourse term is still retained. Both occurrences of mechanical are then derived from a relatively common context of use in ordinary discourse.

The common derivation from ordinary discourse has implications for the meaning of mechanical adopted by the opinion and for a mechanical procedure. Classically, it was asserted that '[f]or a large class of cases – although not for all – in which we employ the word "meaning" it can be defined thus: the meaning of a word is its use in the language' (Wittgenstein, 1953/1968, §43). The relative commonality of the ordinary discourse context for derivation, 'the use in the language', then implies some commonality in the meaning adopted. The context for derivation further implies that the ordinary discourse meaning was adopted both by the opinion and for a mechanical procedure.

The question then arises of whether the ordinary discourse meaning of mechanical adopted is retained. For its occurrence in the opinion, no departure from its ordinary discourse meaning can be found. For a mechanical procedure, the history of the development of the concept indicates that the ordinary discourse meaning of mechanical has been retained as an essential basis while precision has been added to the idea of acting as a machine (Herken, 1994). The ordinary discourse meaning of mechanical must then be understood as fully retained, for both occurrences.

The meaning of mechanical in ordinary discourse includes both a human acting mechanically and the operations of a machine. For the opinion, this dual application of mechanical can be supported by reference to a definition taken from a culturally and chronologically proximate monolingual dictionary, 'done as if by machine' (Webster, 1981), where the qualification 'as if', can be read to indicate the inclusion of direct human activity. The concept of a mechanical procedure, from its preliminary scientific definition, similarly embraces both a human acting mechanically and the operations of a machine such as a computer. The different uses of the term, mechanical, then both have a comparable dual application.

The idea of acting mechanically implies an activity or process and this implication is realized in the opinion and for a mechanical procedure. '[S]o mechanical' in the opinion is contained within a paragraph introduced as concerned with 'selected, coordinated, or arranged' (Feist Publications, Inc. v. Rural Tel. Service Co., Inc., 1991, p. 362) where the verb form indicates reference to an activity or process. It also, and more immediately, characterizes the 'selection and arrangement of facts', which also can be read to invoke processes (Feist Publications, Inc. v. Rural Tel. Service Co., Inc., 1991). Procedure in mechanical procedure similarly refers to a type of process, from its definition. '[S]o mechanical' (Feist Publications, Inc. v. Rural Tel. Service Co., Inc., 1991, p. 362) in the opinion and in a mechanical procedure, then, have a further similarity in their reference to a process.

Processes are invoked by denotation. '[S]o mechanical' (Feist Publications, Inc. v. Rural Tel. Service Co., Inc., 1991, p. 362) in the opinion directly characterizes or denotes, rather than indirectly connotes, a type of process. A mechanical procedure also directly describes or denotes a process. Denotation is usually considered a stronger and more primary form than is connotation (Barthes, 1953/1984, pp. 149–150; Eco, 1976, pp. 55–86). The strength of the connection to the processes invoked is then conveyed by denotation, for both the opinion and for a mechanical procedure. The common use of denotation also constitutes a significant similarity between 'so mechanical' (Feist Publications, Inc. v. Rural Tel. Service Co., Inc., 1991, p. 362) in the opinion and mechanical in a 'mechanical procedure'.

The most intense sense of mechanical is at issue in the opinion and for a mechanical procedure. '[S]o' (Feist Publications, Inc. v. Rural Tel. Service Co., Inc., 1991, p. 362) in 'so mechanical or routine' (p. 362) directly qualifies mechanical and indicates that it is to be understood in its most intense sense. Mechanical in a 'mechanical procedure' is understood in an absolute sense, as matter of preliminary scientific definition, and this is occasionally marked by the additional term automatic in 'automatic mechanical procedure'. A similarity in intensity of meaning then has been established.

'[S]o mechanical' (Feist Publications, Inc. v. Rural Tel. Service Co., Inc., 1991, p. 362) is directly linked to the antithesis to creativity, 'no creativity whatsoever' (p. 362), which semantically encompasses both the extreme antithesis to creativity, 'nothing remotely creative' (p. 363), and its subsequent, less intense, complement, 'insufficient creativity' (p. 363). As the first and dominant term of 'so mechanical or routine' (p. 362), 'so mechanical' can be correlated with the extreme antithesis to creativity. A significant element directly correlated with computability is then linked to the extreme antithesis to creativity.

In summary, 'so mechanical' (Feist Publications, Inc. v. Rural Tel. Service Co., Inc., 1991, p. 362) and an automatic mechanical procedure can be highly correlated with each other. They have an identity in their expression and strong similarities in the derivation of mechanical from ordinary discourse, the adoption and retention of its ordinary discourse meaning, the inclusion of directly human and of machine activity, the invocation of a process, and the use of denotation. The most intense sense of mechanical is at issue in the opinion and for a mechanical procedure. The identity and similarities approach exhaustivity in their inclusion of aspects of possible resemblance which could be considered significant for correlation. '[S]o mechanical' (p. 362) in the opinion then can be definitively correlated with an automatic mechanical procedure. It can be linked to the extreme antithesis to creativity. The correlation of 'so mechanical' (p. 352) with an automatic mechanical procedure can be regarded as proven beyond reasonable doubt.

So … routine

'[S]o … routine' (Feist Publications, Inc. v. Rural Tel. Service Co., Inc., 1991, p. 362) in 'so mechanical or routine' (p. 362) can be considered in itself. Routine could be understood in its ordinary discourse sense, capable of qualifying both process and product, and as semantically distinct from, but not in tension, with 'so mechanical' (p. 362).

So mechanical or routine

We can now return to considering the clause 'so mechanical or routine' (Feist Publications, Inc. v. Rural Tel. Service Co., Inc., 1991, p. 362) as a whole, after having considered its significant constituent elements.

'[S]o mechanical or routine' (Feist Publications, Inc. v. Rural Tel. Service Co., Inc., 1991, p. 362) is directly linked to an antithesis to creativity, 'no creativity whatsoever' (p. 362). '[N]o creativity whatsoever' (p. 362) semantically includes both the extreme antithesis to creativity, 'nothing remotely creative' (p. 363), and its less intense complement, 'insufficient creativity' (p. 363). '[S]o mechanical or routine' (p. 362) thereby encompasses all levels of antithesis to creativity.

Entirely typical ... end product ... garden-variety ... could not be more obvious ... the most basic information

Entirely typical ... end product ... garden-variety

'[E]ntirely typical ... end product ... garden-variety' (Feist Publications, Inc. v. Rural Tel. Service Co., Inc., 1991, p. 362) were revealed to be close in meaning to 'so ... routine' (p. 362), although characterizing a product rather than a process. Their meaning was not in tension with 'so mechanical' (p. 362). The terms were connected to a clause, 'devoid of even the slightest trace of creativity' (p. 362), which implies the possibility of reading the absence of creativity from the product and which is concerned with a level of antithesis to creativity, at the boundary with the creative.

'[E]ntirely typical ... end product ... garden-variety' (Feist Publications, Inc. v. Rural Tel. Service Co., Inc., 1991, p. 362) can also be understood as characterizing the final product of established automatic mechanical procedures or of highly routine processes. The terms in the decision explicitly connected with an end product can then be absorbed into the correlation with computability and have a connection with the so ... routine.

Could not be more obvious ... the most basic information

'[C]ould not be more obvious ... the most basic information' (p. 362) were semantically cognate with the routine, although, again, not in tension with the mechanical. They directly linked to 'insufficient creativity' (p. 363), also understandable as an antithesis to creativity, on the boundary with creativity.

The hierarchy detected in the preceding chapter from raw data, through data, to information by processing for human interpretation is reminiscent of fully articulated and widely diffused understandings developed from computational contexts, where information is regarded as data organized to some purpose (Blair, 2002, pp. 1019–1020). The reminiscence of computational contexts then reinforces the appropriateness of computability theory as a resource for significant correlations.

Entirely typical ... end product ... garden-variety ... could not be more obvious ... the most basic information

The elements associated with 'so ... routine' (Feist Publications, Inc. v. Rural Tel. Service Co., Inc., 1991, p. 362) are then complementary to the correlation with computability established. As complementary, they also constitute a differentiating element, with the routine associated with areas semantically contiguous to creativity. Distinctively routine elements, which complement those directly correlated with computability, are, then, connected with a milder antithesis to creativity.

The differentiation of routinicity within the overall correlation with computability represents a significant analytic gain over the initial, undifferentiated, gestalt effect of correspondence.

Dictated by state law

'[D]ictated by state law' (Feist Publications, Inc. v. Rural Tel. Service Co., Inc., 1991, p. 363) is semantically contained within the conjunction of the 'so mechanical' (p. 362) and 'so ... routine' (p. 362). It is also directly connected to 'nothing remotely creative' (p. 363), the extreme antithesis to creativity.

'[D]ictated by state law' (Feist Publications, Inc. v. Rural Tel. Service Co., Inc., 1991, p. 363) implies an intense form of specification by an external law. As such, it is reminiscent of popular understandings of the automatic computational process and consistent with the understanding of the computational process within the theory of computability. '[D]ictated by state law' (p. 363) specifically and strongly contributes to the gestalt sense of correspondence with conceptions of computability.

A further element correlated with computability is then linked to the extreme antithesis to computability and the conjunction of the mechanical and the routine.

Age-old practice ... time-honored tradition

The sequence of clauses, from 'age-old practice' to 'time-honored tradition' (Feist Publications, Inc. v. Rural Tel. Service Co., Inc., 1991, p. 363), constitutes the most connected and extensive delineation of creativity utterly lacking in the opinion. The group of terms as a whole has a historical resonance, although the particular term *history* is not used. The characterization of the process of alphabetical arrangement in the opinion in historical terms can be correlated with the understanding of computability in terms of the natural, with what 'would naturally be regarded as computable' (Turing, 1936–1937/1993, p. 249) (see also Box 5.3 on computability and the natural), through a number of similarities.

Box 5.3 Computability and the natural

Conceptions of computability have repeatedly and consistently appealed to the natural.

Turing's (1936–1937/2004) own formulation of the concept of computability as what 'would *naturally* be regarded as computable' (p. 135) [emphasis added] drew on preceding thought in mathematics and mathematical logic and also was rooted in ordinary discourse and everyday experience. This characterization of computability has been accepted in subsequent logical and mathematical discourse and theoretical computer science. *Natural[ly]* is the specific and the dominant term.

Other terms for the concept of computability, analogous to the natural or even descending or derived from it, include particularly 'intuitive' (Boolos and Jeffrey, 1989, p. 20; Church, 1936/2004, p. 90; Davis, 1982, p. 10: Davis, 1994, p. 154; Minsky, 1967, p. 136; Rosen, 1994, p. 524; Turing, 1939/2004, p. 160) and 'appeals to intuition' (Turing, 1936–1937/2004, p. 135).

Conceptions of computability are, then, characterized as natural, with some further incorporation of the intuitive, and these characterizations are widely diffused within relevant scholarly spheres.

The primary similarity lies directly in meaning. The constituent substantive terms of the passage in the opinion – 'an age-old practice, firmly rooted in tradition and so commonplace that it has come to be expected as a matter of course … practically inevitable … time-honored tradition' (Feist Publications, Inc. v. Rural Tel. Service Co., Inc., 1991, p. 363) – indicate long duration and transcendence of particular historical periods, approaching the natural. One clause, 'practically inevitable' (p. 363), reveals the historical terminologically converging with the natural. Computability has been consistently conceived in terms of the natural, with what would naturally be regarded as computable. The terms in the opinion and the natural in conceptions of computability are then similar to each other in their meaning.

The historical in the opinion and the natural in the concept of computability both invoke a set of processes conceived as objects for characterization. That a set of processes is at issue in the opinion is indicated by the gerund, or noun form of the verb, 'arranging' (Feist Publications, Inc. v. Rural Tel. Service Co., Inc., 1991, p. 363). The natural in the concept of computability also is concerned with sets of processes conceived as objects for characterization. The common invocation of sets of processes conceived as objects for characterization constitutes a further similarity.

The mode of characterization of processes is indirect with elements of connotation. The historical reference and resonance of the clauses in the opinion function as an indirect description of processes. The conception of computability as natural which preexisted the formulation of satisfactory models of the computational process could be regarded as a concept or an indirect description awaiting an object which fully corresponded to the conception. With the formulation and publication of models of the computational process, and their acceptance as absolute definitions, conceptions of computability as natural have tended to be reduced to connotations of a primary and more clearly articulated denotation. Both the clauses in the opinion and the natural in computability are, then, similar in functioning as indirect descriptions of processes, approaching connotation rather than denotation.

A contrast in meaning also emerges directly between the historical resonance implied by the extensive chronological reference and references to 'tradition' in the opinion (Feist Publications, Inc. v. Rural Tel. Service Co., Inc., 1991, p. 363) and the natural explicit in conceptions of computability. The contrast runs counter to the similarity established and could disturb the correlation being developed.

The contrast's potential significance for disturbing the correlation can be reduced. The apparent sharpness of the difference immediately conveyed by the opposition of the historical to the natural is mollified when the long duration involved in the constituent terms of the opinion resonating with the historical is recalled. The independent status of the contrast is lessened by noting that the particular opposed elements are rooted in the underlying disciplinary bases from which different perspectives emerge. Law would have a humanistic and historical basis (Holmes, 1881/1991), corresponding to the historical resonance and reference of the terms in the opinion. *Naturally regarded*, and in its supporting role, *intuitive*, are resonant of a Platonist conception of mathematics, reflecting the disciplines from which the articulated concept of computability emerged. The disruptive potential of the contrast in meaning has then been reduced, by indicating its lack of sharpness and of independent status. A residual contrast between the historical and the natural remains.

In summary, then, the characterization of the antithesis to creativity in historical terms in the opinion can be correlated with the concept of computability, through a similarity in meaning, the common invocation of processes conceived as objects for characterization, and the indirect, approaching connotative rather than denotative, characterization of sets of processes. A contrast in meaning also emerged, between the historical and the natural. The extensive similarities constitute a strong correlation between the most extensive delineation of the extreme antithesis to creativity in the opinion and the concept of computability.

The clauses with a historical resonance which have been correlated with computability as natural characterize the extreme antithesis to creativity, 'nothing remotely creative' (Feist Publications, Inc. v. Rural Tel. Service Co., 1991, p. 363). They are also semantically reminiscent of 'so … routine' (p. 362) and were mediated to the mechanical by the routine. The elements connected with computability, are, then linked to the extreme antithesis to creativity and to the routine mediating to the mechanical.

Synthesis

All the constituent terms of the delineation of creativity utterly lacking in the decision correlate or differentiate, in complementary and mutually reinforcing ways, with computability.

- '[S]o mechanical or routine' (Feist Publications, Inc. v. Rural Tel. Service Co., Inc., 1991, p. 362) was consistent with the gestalt effect of correspondence and also contained a directly correlating and a complementary, and differentiating, element. '[S]o mechanical' (p. 362) conceptually and verbally correlated with an automatic mechanical procedure. '[S]o routine' (p. 362) signaled a complementary and differentiating element, of routinicity.
- '[E]ntirely typical … end product … garden' (Feist Publications, Inc. v. Rural Tel. Service Co., Inc., 1991, pp. 362–363) could be understood as the product of established mechanical procedures and highly routine processes.
- '[C]ould not be more obvious … the most basic information' was semantically cognate with the routine and also reminiscent of computational contexts.
- '[D]ictated by state law' (Feist Publications, Inc. v. Rural Tel. Service Co., Inc., 1991, p. 362) was reminiscent in its meaning with widely diffused understandings of the computational process.
- The sequence of clauses with a historical resonance – 'an age-old practice, firmly rooted in tradition and so commonplace that it has come to be expected as a matter of course … practically inevitable … time-honored tradition' (Feist Publications, Inc. v. Rural Tel. Service Co., Inc., 1991, pp. 362–363) – correlated with what would naturally be regarded as computable and with the absolute in the theory of computability, which is primarily concerned with automatic processes.

The initial gestalt effect of an analogy between creativity utterly lacking and computability has been rendered specific, by linking the historical in the opinion with the natural in understandings of computability and 'so mechanical' (Feist Publications, Inc. v. Rural Tel. Service Co., Inc., 1991, p. 362) with an automatic mechanical procedure.

Considering the correlating elements of the decision together can enhance the conviction to be attached to each correlation and to the correlation considered as a whole. The correlation of the historical in the opinion with the natural in understandings of computability complements and, by complementing, reinforces the correlation of 'so mechanical' (Feist Publications, Inc. v. Rural Tel. Service Co., Inc., 1991, p. 362) with an automatic mechanical procedure. The term, 'information' (p. 363), and its consistent differentiation from raw data and data, supported the relevance of the theory of computability. The correlation of creativity utterly lacking in the decision with an automatic mechanical procedure is, then, strengthened.

Considering the correlations as a whole also exposes parallels between the internal configuration of each body of thought. In the opinion, a direct description of type of process – as 'so mechanical' (Feist Publications, Inc. v. Rural Tel. Service Co., Inc., 1991, p. 362) – merges into a more indirect description of set of process conceived as objects for description, as 'an age-old practice … time-honored tradition' (p. 363), with denotation moving toward connotation. Analogously, the direct description or denotation of the computational process as a mechanical procedure is founded on a more indirect characterization of a set of processes, as what would naturally be regarded as computable. Denotation of a type of process and indirect denotation moving toward connotation of a set of processes are, then, parallel between the opinion and understandings of the computational process and of computability (see Figure 5.1). The movements are thematically complementary, although chronologically (understood as linear progression through a written text and as over historical time) reverse. In the opinion, the mechanical merges into the historical through the routine; for the theory of computability, historically established and routine procedures of calculation, characterized as natural, are rendered mechanical. The structural parallelism adds conviction to each of the separately established correlations and to the correlations considered as a whole.

The correlations considered together are comprehensive with regard to each correlated body of thought. All the elements in the opinion in the delineation of creativity utterly lacking (Feist Publications, Inc. v. Rural Tel. Service Co., Inc., 1991, pp. 362–363) have been accounted for, as correlating and differentiating elements. Centrally significant elements of understandings of the computational process and of computability are similarly all included, at the level of concepts – of an automatic mechanical procedure or algorithm and of computability – and also including specific verbal formulations whose recurrence is indicative of their significance, 'naturally be regarded as computable' (Turing, 1936–1937/2004, p. 135). The comprehensiveness of the correlations indicates that the two bodies of thought have been fully matched.

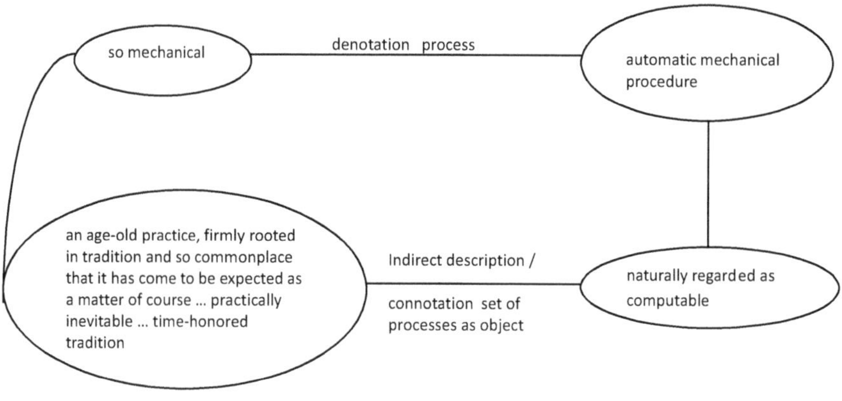

Figure 5.1 Parallels between the judgment and computability

The elements from the opinion directly and individually correlated with computability and routinicity, as contrasted with the more solely routine, are connected to different levels of antithesis to creativity. '[S]o mechanical', 'entirely typical … end product … garden-variety' (pp. 362–363), 'dictated by state law', and the sequence of clauses with a historical resonance (Feist Publications, Inc. v. Rural Tel. Service Co., Inc., 1991, pp. 362–363) could be directly correlated with computability. The directly supporting elements of the correlation, then, exist exclusively within, and fully occupy, the clauses corresponding to the extreme antithesis to creativity, to 'no creativity whatsoever' and 'nothing remotely creative' (Feist Publications, Inc. v. Rural Tel. Service Co., Inc., 1991, pp. 362–363). They can all be directly connected with the extreme antithesis to creativity and also be considered to encompass its complement. The more solely routine elements are connected with a milder antithesis, or the complement, 'insufficient creativity' (p. 363). The distribution can be graphically illustrated (see Table 5.1).

Combining the recognition of the pattern of distribution by levels of antithesis to creativity with the differentiation of the routine can yield a further analytic gain. An automatic computational process emerges as the extreme antithesis to creativity, while routinicity can be regarded as a less extreme antithesis. Routinicity, in addition to being 'could not be more obvious … the most basic information' (Feist Publications, Inc. v. Rural Tel. Service Co., Inc., 1991, p. 362), can also be

Table 5.1 Computability and routinicity and levels of antithesis to creativity

Clause in the decision	*Correlation with computability and with routinicity*	*Level of intensity of antithesis to creativity*
so mechanical or routine	Constituent elements directly correlating with computability and with routinicity.	as to require no creativity whatsoever
entirely typical … end product … garden-variety	Correlating with so … routine and consistent with the product of a routine mechanical process.	devoid of even the slightest trace of creativity
could not be more obvious … the most basic information	Semantically cognate with the routine and also reminiscent of computational contexts.	insufficient creativity
dictated by state law … nothing remotely creative	Correlating with computability and with the routine in combination together.	nothing remotely creative
an age-old practice, firmly rooted in tradition and so commonplace that it has come to be expected as a matter of course … practically inevitable … time-honored tradition	Correlating with computability and with the routine in combination together.	

consistently understood as semantically contiguous to computability and to the extreme absence of creativity and as possibly mediating to the creative.

We can consider how far the correlation established is widely acceptable, by turning to widespread discourse and practice. Some evidence of a parallel position developing in ordinary discourse is offered by a judgment of the Court of Appeals for the Second Circuit, which itself cites the *Feist* (Feist Publications, Inc. v. Rural Tel. Service Co., Inc., 1991) standard of originality.

> West concedes that the pagination of its volumes ... is determined by an automatic computer program, and West does not seriously claim that there is anything original or creative in that process.
>
> (West, 1998, p. 12)

The citation supports the correlation (although it does not amount to an exploration of the significance of the correlation, as conducted in this work). The phrasing, 'does not seriously claim' (West, 1998, p. 12), further suggests that idea of a computational process as being without creativity is entering ordinary discourse. Correspondence to ordinary discourse indicates that the correlation is grounded in our collective consciousness.

The diffusion of the computer can account for the emergence of the correlation in ordinary discourse. The computer has become the dominant instrument of mental labor in the twenty-first century, on a global basis. We could further say that processes have first been routinized and then mechanized, further accounting for the contiguity of routinicity to computability within creativity utterly lacking. The concept of computability is regarded as a bedrock concept, which has not been disproved (Cockshott and Michaelson, 2007). Global diffusion of the computer and the foundational status of computability give global and deep value to the correlation.

Relation to the European Union and other jurisdictions

From the diffusion of the computer and the emergence of the correlation between automatic computational processes in ordinary discourse, we might expect other jurisdictions to be in broad congruence with the correlation established here. The standard for the absence of copyrightability, 'so mechanical or routine' (Feist Publications, Inc. v. Rural Tel. Service Co., Inc., 1991, pp. 362–363) has begun to diffuse globally and was previously revealed as broadly implicitly congruent with the European Union's requirement for intellectual labor for copyrightability (see Chapter 4 on creativity utterly lacking). Other jurisdictions, not directly governed by *Feist*, would then be amenable to being assimilated to the correlation established here.

Narrative motif

In terms of our narrative motif, Bunyan's pilgrim was trapped by Giant Despair in Doubting Castle. Yet, Bunyan's pilgrim recalls that he has 'a key in my bosom, called promise, that will ... open any lock in Doubting-Castle' (Bunyan 1678/1985, p. 103). Bunyan's pilgrim then escapes from imprisonment with the aid of the key of promise which can open any lock in Doubting Castle. In terms of the analogy with *The Pilgrim's Progress*, we have then escaped from Doubting Castle, through correlation, and can return to the king's highway, to resume our journey.

Conclusion

The initial gestalt effect of an analogy between creativity utterly lacking in the decision and classic and continuing understandings of computability has been strengthened, and refined, by identifying and making fully explicit the correspondences informing, but subsumed, in the initial gestalt. The historical in the decision has been correlated with the natural in discussions of computability, the meaning of 'dictated by state law' (Feist Publications, Inc. v. Rural Tel. Service Co., Inc., 1991, p. 363) with popular conceptions of the computational process, 'so mechanical' (p. 362) conceptually and verbally correlated with an automatic mechanical procedure, enhanced conviction has been obtained from the mutual support of elements in the decision, a parallelism has been revealed between two bodies of thought, and they have been comprehensively combined. The extreme antithesis to creativity has been entirely correlated with computability in its strictest or purest sense where it is concerned with automatic mechanical procedures, while routinicity has been differentiated and understood as semantically contiguous. A gestalt effect, as a pattern or structure which transcends its constituent individual elements, is intrinsically not necessarily easily subjectable to decomposition without loss of conviction. Decomposition, and then recomposition, with enhanced conviction then confirm the strength of the initial gestalt.

The demonstration of the analogy and its constituent correlations, and the combination of the correlated elements with the highly routine in the opinion, amounts to as strong a proof as can be reasonably expected or demanded outside of logical and mathematical domains, where further propositions can be tautologically generated from axioms (Wittgenstein, 1922/1981). The existence of the correlation with computability has then been proven, beyond reasonable doubt.

The extreme antithesis to creativity has, then, been precisely identified, primarily through a careful and exhaustive process of correlation. The identification fulfills a rigorous test for knowledge, as 'an ideal reproduction of the external world serviceable for cooperative action thereon' (Childe, 1956, p. 54). The potential for cooperative action emerges from the correlation of the extreme antithesis to creativity with something capable of being known and from its implication of creativity.

The value of the correlation, and the further potential for cooperative action, as distinct from its existence, arises from the enhanced intersubjectivity of the formulation for the antithesis to creativity. The understanding obtained of creativity utterly lacking can be recalled.

> A compilation has not the slightest trace of creativity if, and only if, it is constructed by a so mechanical or so … routine process and is an entirely typical or garden-variety end product.

The formulation can be transformed, by substituting ***an automatic mechanical procedure*** for 'so mechanical' (Feist Publications, Inc. v. Rural Tel. Service Co., Inc., 1991, p. 362).

> **A compilation has not the slightest trace of creativity if, and only if, it is constructed by an automatic mechanical procedure or so … routine process and is an entirely typical or garden-variety end product.**

The transformation offers the possibility of a further elucidation of creativity utterly lacking, by referring it to something more definitively understood. The substitution of correlated external standard adds a strongly intersubjective element to the formulation, in a classic process of legal advance (Holmes, 1881/1991, pp. 110–111). The delineation of creativity utterly lacking has then been correlated with an external standard, 'capable of being known' (Golding, 2005; Holmes, 1881/1991, pp. 110–111).

Correlation: the key to Doubting Castle: chapter summary

A full understanding of the creative spark utterly lacking was obtained in the previous chapter. However, the terms delineating the creative spark utterly lacking, and in the exegesis given of them, could still be subject to disputes over their interpretation. A further, and still firmer, rooting remained desirable.

The delineation of creativity utterly lacking can be recalled.

> so mechanical or routine
> entirely typical … end product … garden-variety
> could not be more obvious … the most basic information
> dictated by state law
> an age-old practice, firmly rooted in tradition and so commonplace that it has come to be expected as a matter of course … practically inevitable … time-honored tradition.
> (Feist Publications, Inc. v. Rural Tel. Service Co., Inc., 1991, pp. 362–363).

There is a strong analogy with the concept of computability.

> It seems that this importance [of Turing's computability] is largely due to the fact that with this concept one has for the first time succeeded in giving an absolute definition of an interesting epistemological notion, i.e., one not depending on the formalism chosen. In all other cases treated previously, such as demonstrability or definability, one has been able to define them only

relative to a given language, and for each individual language it is clear that the one thus obtained is not the one looked for.

(Gödel, 1946/2004, p. 84)

The analogy with the creative spark utterly lacking in the decision rests primarily on an overall, or gestalt, effect of correspondence. The overall correspondence of the extended delineation of the creative spark utterly lacking to concepts of computability corresponds to broad equivalence.

(so mechanical $\vee$ routine) $\approx$ computability

Computability is of compelling contemporary significance and of acute practical relevance to compilations.

The analogy can be more closely specified. Specifically, *mechanical* in 'so mechanical' (Feist Publications, Inc. v. Rural Tel. Service Co., Inc., 1991, p. 362) has an identity in expression with *mechanical* in a mechanical procedure, is similarly derived from ordinary discourse, with the ordinary discourse meaning adopted and retained, can refer to a human acting mechanically and to the operations of a machine, and invokes a process by denotation. Mechanical in 'so mechanical' (p. 362) can then be regarded as equivalent to mechanical in a mechanical procedure, or, in logical notation,

mechanical (so mechanical) $\equiv$ mechanical (automatic mechanical procedure)

So in 'so mechanical' (p. 362) implies intensity. An automatic mechanical procedure is generally regarded as the purest or most intense form of mechanical procedure. '[S]o mechanical' then corresponds to an automatic mechanical procedure, algorithm, or computational process, or, in terms of formal logic,

so mechanical $\equiv$ automatic mechanical procedure

We have then identified a specific correlation within the overall analogy.

The closer specification of the analogy also enables a refinement of the overall analogy. Elements of routinicity can be differentiated from the so mechanical. We can then refine the overall analogy to incorporate the direct correspondence of 'so mechanical' (p. 362) to computability and to recognize the remaining elements of routinicity. '[S]o mechanical or routine' (p. 362) then be understood to correspond to *an automatic mechanical procedure or so … routine process.*

On the basis of this correspondence, we can transform the conclusion of the previous chapter, on the opposite to creativity. We can substitute automatic mechanical procedure for *so mechanical* in the verbal statement

> A compilation has not the slightest trace of creativity if, and only if, it is constructed by a so mechanical or so … routine process and is an entirely typical or garden-variety end product, can now be further developed.

becomes

> **A compilation has not the slightest trace of creativity if, and only if, it is constructed by an automatic mechanical procedure or so ... routine process and is an entirely typical or garden-variety end product.**

The parallel logical formulations can be similarly transformed.

> ~ (A compilation has the slightest trace of creativity) ↔ ((so mechanical ∨ so ... routine) ∧ (entirely typical ∨ garden-variety))

becomes

> **~ (A compilation has the slightest trace of creativity) ↔ ((automatic mechanical procedure ∨ so ... routine) ∧ (entirely typical ∨ garden-variety))**

We have obtained the desired further rooting of the antithesis to creativity.

From the correlation and rooting established, we can move to an understanding of creativity, in its positive sense.

We have then linked the dominant components of creativity utterly lacking to something of compelling contemporary significance and practical relevance, capable of being known, and understood as absolute, signified by the anvil shape in the figure of progress made (see Figure 5.2). We have transcended from the possible questioning of terms in creativity utterly lacking, by drawing upon the compellingly significant and deeply rooted concept of computability, and we can resume our journey.

We must now traverse the implication of creativity, in the next chapter.

References

Barthes, R. (1953/1984). Elements of semiology. In R. Barthes (ed.). *Writing degree zero and Elements of semiology.* Translated by A. Lavers and C. Smith. London: Jonathan Cape.

Blair, D.C. (2002). Knowledge management: Hype, hope, or help? *Journal of the American Society for Information Science and Technology.* 53(12), 1019–1028.

Boolos, G.S. and Jeffrey, R.C. (1989). *Computability and logic.* (3rd edn). Cambridge and New York: Cambridge University Press.

Bunyan, J. (1678/1985). *The pilgrim's progress.* Edited with an introduction and notes by R. Sharrock. London: Penguin.

Childe, V.G. (1956). *Society and knowledge.* London: George Allen and Unwin.

Church, A. (1936/2004). An unsolvable problem of elementary number theory. In M. Davis (ed.). *The undecidable: Basic papers on undecidable propositions, unsolvable problems and computable functions* (pp. 89–107). Mineola, NY: Dover.

Cockshott, P. and Michaelson, G. (2007). Are there new models of computation? Reply to Wegner and Eberbach. *The Computer Journal.* 50, 232–247.

Davis, M. (1982). *Computability and unsolvability.* Mineola, NY: Dover.

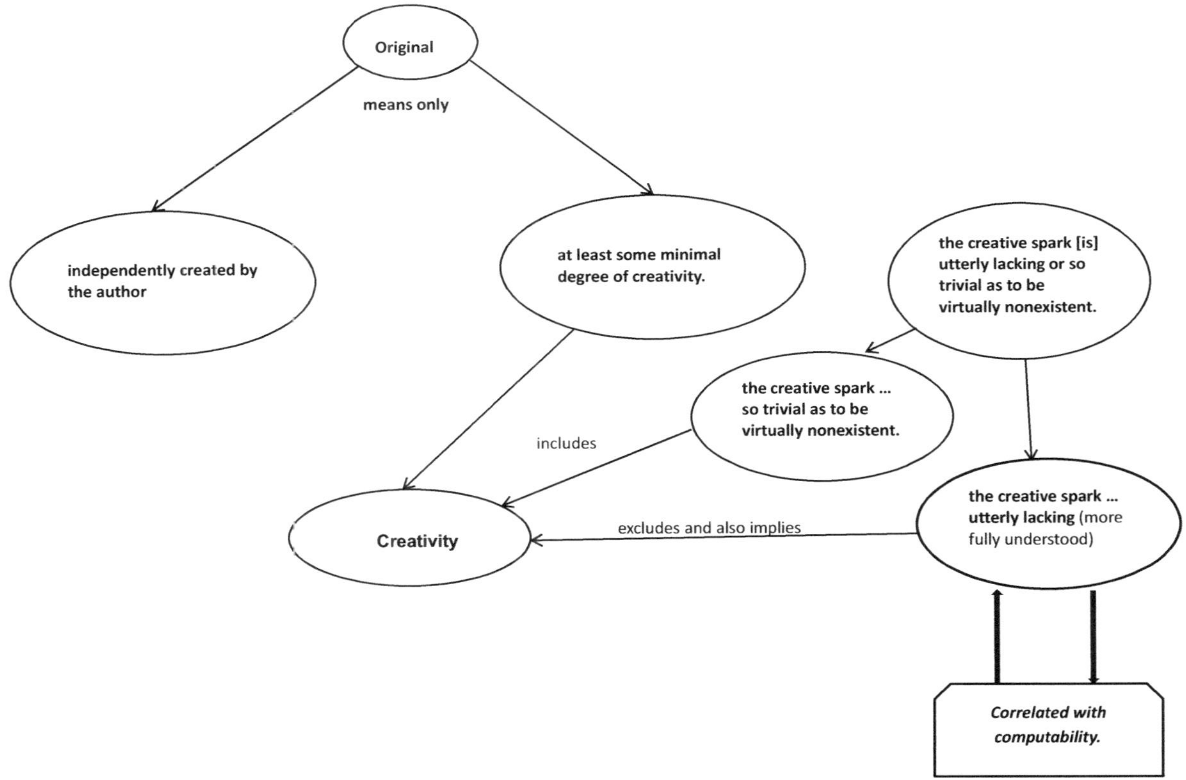

Figure 5.2 Location along the journey and progress made
Note: **Bold** is used for terms and phrases directly derived from the decision.

Davis, M. (1994). Mathematical logic and the origin of modern computing. In R. Herken (ed.). *The universal Turing machine: A half-century survey* (pp. 149–174). Oxford: Oxford University Press.

Davis, M. (2000). *The universal computer: The road from Leibniz to Turing*. New York: W. W. Norton.

Eco, U. (1976). *A theory of semiotics*. London and Bloomington, IN: Indiana University Press.

Feist Publications, Inc. v. Rural Tel. Service Co., Inc. (1991). Feist Publications, Inc. v. Rural Tel. Service Co., Inc. 499 U.S. 340 (1991).

Gödel, K. (1964/2004). Postscriptum [To 'On undecidable propositions of formal mathematical systems']. In M. Davis (ed.). *The undecidable: Basic papers on undecidable propositions, unsolvable problems and computable functions* (pp. 71–73). Hewlett NY: Raven Press.

Golding, M. (2005). Responsibility. In M.P. Golding and W.A. Edmundson (eds), *The Blackwell guide to the philosophy of law and legal theory* (pp. 221–235). Malden, MA: Blackwell Publishing.

Herken, R. (ed.). (1994). *The universal Turing machine: A half-century survey* (2nd edn). Vienna and New York: Springer.

Holmes, O.W. (1881/1991). *The common law*. With a new introduction by Sheldon M. Novick. New York: Dover.

Minsky, M.L. (1967). *Computation: Finite and infinite machines*. Englewood Cliffs, NJ: Prentice-Hall.

Rosen, M. (1994). Effective processes and natural law. In R. Herken (ed.). *The universal Turing machine: A half-century survey* (pp. 523–537). Oxford: Oxford University Press.

Turing, A.M. (1936–1937/2004). On computable numbers, with an application to the Entscheidungsproblem. Paper read November 12, 1936. In M. Davis (ed.). *The undecidable: Basic papers on undecidable propositions, unsolvable problems and computable functions* (pp. 116–151). Mineola, NY: Dover.

Turing, A.M. (1939/2004). Systems of logic based on ordinals. In M. Davis (ed.). *The undecidable: Basic papers on undecidable propositions, unsolvable problems and computable functions* (pp. 155–222). Mineola, NY: Dover. First published in *Proceedings of the London Mathematical Society*. Series 2, 45 (1939), 161–228.

Webster (1981). *Webster's third new international dictionary of the English language*. Unabridged. Edited by P.B. Gove and others. Springfield, MA: Merriam.

West (1998). Matthew Bender & Company, Inc., Plaintiff-Appellee, Hyperlaw, Inc., Intervenor-Plaintiff-Appellee, v. West Publishing Co.; West Publishing Corporation, Defendants-Appellants. United States Court of Appeals for the Second Circuit. March 16, 1998, Argued. November 3, 1998, Decided.

Wilks, Y.A., Slator, B.M. and Guthrie, L.M. (1996). *Electric words: Dictionaries, computers, and meanings*. Cambridge, MA: MIT Press.

Wittgenstein, L. (1922/1981). *Tractatus logico-philosophicus*. London and New York: Routledge and Kegan Paul.

Wittgenstein, L. (1953/1968). *Philosophical investigations*. Oxford: Basil Blackwell.

6 Creativity

Out of the labyrinth

Introduction

This chapter develops an explicit understanding of creativity, from the antithetical clauses in the decision which negatively imply it, which fully meets the requirements for creativity derived from the decision. Crucially, creativity must be understood consistently with its ordinary discourse sense and reach from the lowest to the highest possible levels. We have navigated to the antithetical and dead center of an apparently labyrinthine, but finally simple and compelling, argument – the computational process as the antithesis to creativity. We must now navigate outwards, from the dead center of the judgment to creativity.

For the move towards creativity, creativity utterly lacking is understood as implying creativity fully present as its own opposite or antithesis. Creativity utterly lacking was understood as residing in an automatic mechanical procedure or highly routine process which gave rise to an entirely typical or garden-variety end product. Conversely, creativity can be understood as *not* residing in an automatic mechanical procedure or highly routine process which gives rise to an entirely typical or garden-variety end product.

A not automatic mechanical procedure is then populated, first simply by meaning, supported by the established distinction of semantic from the syntactic in the theory of computation. Meaning and semantic are then specifically understood as direct human engagement with meaning. Direct human engagement with meaning can gather together items related in meaning, but syntactically, or as expressions, not especially similar, for instance, *oranges* and *lemons*. Gathering together captures central aspects of classic concepts of creativity and is also crucial to human indexing of data. Creativity is finally understood as human activity motivated by meaning, above a certain level of routinicity. This concept of creativity corresponds to ordinary discourse understandings of creativity, particularly gathering together, and does apply to very low and to the highest possible levels of creativity. It thereby meets the conditions for creativity derivable from the decision,

The chapter then establishes a fully grounded understanding of creativity, for the judgment. Reflection on the formal and substantive qualities of the argument indicates the understanding developed to be very strongly proven.

We must begin by traversing the path along which creativity is implied (see Figure 6.1).

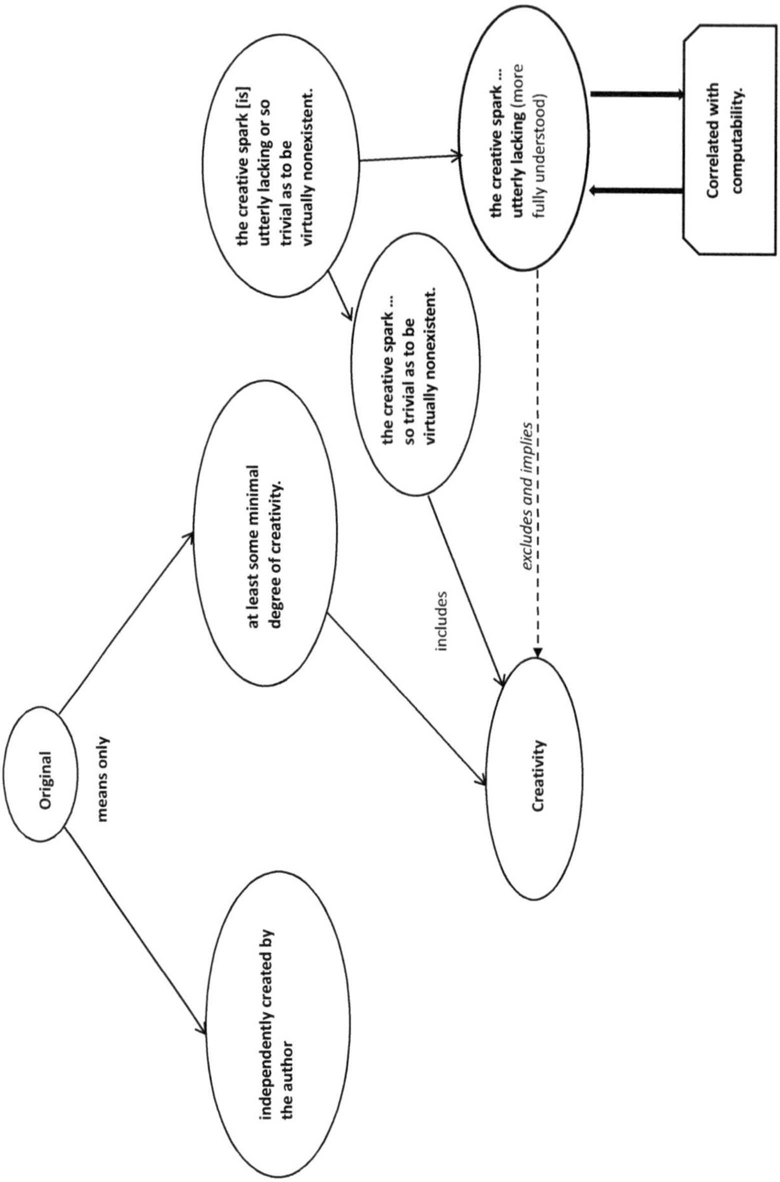

Figure 6.1 Path to be taken
Note: **Bold** is used for terms and phrases directly derived from the decision.

Transformation of negation

We can first transform the statement of the antithesis to creativity as given at the conclusion of the preceding chapter.

- A compilation has not the slightest trace of creativity if, and only if, it is constructed by an automatic mechanical procedure or so … routine process and is an entirely typical or garden-variety end product.

The statement can be transformed by the negation of the clauses connected by, if, and only, if, to yield a positive statement of creativity.

- A work *has* the slightest trace of creativity if, and only if, it is *not* constructed by an automatic mechanical procedure or so … routine process which results in an entirely typical or garden-variety end product.

The use of negation to derive the positive statement of creativity is legitimated by the antithetical character of 'utterly lacking' (Feist Publications, Inc. v. Rural Tel. Service Co., Inc., 1991, p. 359). The particular formulation is justified by the specific implication of the clause incorporated directly into it, by an end product with the slightest trace of creativity implied by an 'end product … devoid of even the slightest trace of creativity' (p. 362). Negation is also a widely accepted and deeply historically rooted technique of verbal and then more formally logical reasoning (Bochenski, 1961; Kneale & Kneale, 1962). In this instance, it is also compellingly simple.

A comprehensive collection of all the possible combinations for creativity can be displayed with a vertical ordering corresponding to the relative significance of elements to the opinion, descending from 'so mechanical' (Feist Publications, Inc. v. Rural Tel. Service Co., Inc., 1991, p. 362) or an automatic mechanical procedure to 'garden-variety' (p. 362) (Table 6.1), to reveal the overall distribution of the creative and the not-creative. The creative is concentrated in a major sequence of five rows at the head of the table, followed by a block of the not creative interrupted by two combinations for the creative. Creativity and the not-creative are then generally well separated from each other and strongly internally grouped, suggestive of the robustness and plausibility of the analysis.

The two interleaved combinations for the creative constitute exceptions to the overall pattern of distribution and could disturb the robustness of the analysis. The first encountered, on a downward reading of the table, is where an automatic mechanical procedure is used to construct an end product which is not entirely typical or garden-variety. The automatic mechanical procedure is not 'so … routine' (Feist Publications, Inc. v. Rural Tel. Service Co., Inc., 1991, p. 362), which could be novel or rarely used. It would then still be closely proximate to the non-mechanical activity normally involved in the production of significant automatic mechanical procedures. The combination can then be regarded as analogous to the highest placed combination for the creative, from which it differs by the one

Table 6.1 The creative and the not-creative

Process			*Product*			*Process and product*	*Creative or not-creative*	
automatic mechanical procedure	so … routine	**automatic mechanical procedure ∨ so … routine**	entirely typical	garden-variety	**entirely typical ∨ garden-variety**	(automatic mechanical procedure ∨ so … routine) ^ (entirely typical ∨ garden-variety)		
FALSE	FALSE	**FALSE**	FALSE	FALSE	**FALSE**	FALSE	Creative	
FALSE	FALSE	**FALSE**	FALSE	TRUE	**TRUE**	FALSE	Creative	
FALSE	FALSE	**FALSE**	TRUE	FALSE	**TRUE**	FALSE	Creative	
FALSE	FALSE	**FALSE**	TRUE	TRUE	**TRUE**	FALSE	Creative	
FALSE	TRUE	**TRUE**	FALSE	FALSE	**FALSE**	FALSE	Creative	
FALSE	TRUE	**TRUE**	FALSE	TRUE	**TRUE**	TRUE	not-creative	
FALSE	TRUE	**TRUE**	TRUE	FALSE	**TRUE**	TRUE	not-creative	
FALSE	TRUE	**TRUE**	TRUE	TRUE	**TRUE**	TRUE	not-creative	
TRUE	FALSE	**TRUE**	FALSE	FALSE	**FALSE**	FALSE	Creative	A novel mechanical procedure.
TRUE	FALSE	**TRUE**	FALSE	TRUE	**TRUE**	TRUE	not-creative	
TRUE	FALSE	**TRUE**	TRUE	FALSE	**TRUE**	TRUE	not-creative	
TRUE	FALSE	**TRUE**	TRUE	TRUE	**TRUE**	TRUE	not-creative	
TRUE	TRUE	**TRUE**	FALSE	FALSE	**FALSE**	FALSE	Creative	Tension between process and product.
TRUE	TRUE	**TRUE**	FALSE	TRUE	**TRUE**	TRUE	not-creative	
TRUE	TRUE	**TRUE**	TRUE	FALSE	**TRUE**	TRUE	not-creative	
TRUE	TRUE	**TRUE**	TRUE	TRUE	**TRUE**	TRUE	not-creative	

Note: The customary ordering for logical truth tables, from true to false, is reversed, to bring creativity to the upper levels of the ordering, in accord with the differentiation by levels of creativity within the opinion.

element of 'so mechanical' (p. 362), and regarded as substantively involving a not automatic mechanical procedure. The next met embodies a tension between a so mechanical and highly routine process and the absence of routinicity from the product. It could then be understood as formally possible and combinatorially produced but *a priori* unlikely. The possibility of disturbance to the analysis can then be reduced, both from the analogy of the first interleaved combination with an instance of the creative within the overall pattern and by recognizing the unlikely character of the second combination.

The possibility of further reduction of the formulation for creativity, to obtain a simpler or sharper differentiation of the creative from the not creative, can be pursued. The classic approach would be to be to search for a single element, from an automatic mechanical procedure, 'so ... routine', 'entirely typical', or 'garden-variety' (Feist Publications, Inc. v. Rural Tel. Service Co., Inc., 1991, pp. 362–363), or a subset of those elements, to discriminate the outcomes, the creative and the not creative, from each other. No single element or subset of elements discriminates in this way, even when the interleaved combinations are, respectively, assimilated and excluded. A simpler or sharper conception of creativity cannot then be obtained by further formal transformations on the identified elements.

The elements that constitute the creative can themselves be considered. The creative in the major sequence is both not 'so ... routine' and 'so ... routine', not 'entirely typical', and 'entirely typical', not 'garden-variety', and 'garden variety' (Feist Publications, Inc. v. Rural Tel. Service Co., Inc., 1991, p. 362), but invariantly not an automatic mechanical procedure (Table 6.1). The only invariant element then is a not automatic mechanical procedure. The interleaved combinations can be brought into accord with this invariance, in contrasting ways: The first, understood as substantively involving a not automatic mechanical procedure, can be positively assimilated; the second, fully mechanical but identified as unlikely, can, provisionally, be discounted. A not automatic mechanical procedure also characterizes some combinations for the not creative, as the impossibility of further reduction by formal transformations had implied. It must then be understood as invariant within, although not distinctive of, creativity. For further substantiating and developing creativity, then, we must focus on the not mechanical.

The not mechanical must intersect with the conditions for creativity derivable from the decision. From its inclusion in a minimal degree of creativity, creativity must occupy the 'extremely low' (Feist Publications, Inc. v. Rural Tel. Service Co., Inc., 1991, p. 345) level required for a minimal degree of creativity. It must also be sufficiently knowable to be incorporated into the possibility of obtaining knowledge of the level of creativity required for a minimal degree of creativity. As part of the 'creative spark ... so trivial as to be virtually nonexistent' (p. 359), creativity must occupy the level 'so trivial as to be virtually nonexistent' (p. 359), a level below the extremely low level required for a minimal degree. As a mediated constituent of originality, creativity must be applicable to all copyrightable works. Such works would exhibit very high and historically rare levels of creativity and creativity must then also comprehend the very highest possible level. In the absence of any specialized or technical conception of creativity, the conception of creativity must be consistent with ordinary discourse. Creativity must, then, occupy the level 'so trivial as to be virtually nonexistent' (p. 359), the 'extremely low' level required for a minimal degree of creativity, and the highest possible level. It should be knowable, applicable to all works, and consistent with ordinary discourse.

We can begin to populate the not mechanical.

The not mechanical and meaning

The not mechanical can be populated, from an established antithesis to an automatic mechanical procedure, specifically a contrast with meaning. Classic, although rather neglected, discussions of models of the theory of computability and models of the computational process have explicitly registered the exclusion of meaning from the models. The logician Kurt Gödel developed a distinction of mechanical processes from meaning.

> in the proofs we make use of insights, into these mental constructs, that spring not from the combinatorial (spatiotemporal) properties of the sign combinations representing the proofs [which are employed in mechanical procedures], but only from their *meaning*.
>
> (Gödel, 1958/1990, p. 241) [emphasis in original]

The emphasis – '*meaning*' – is indicative of the significance attached to meaning as contrasting with the 'combinatorial (spatiotemporal) properties of the sign' (Gödel, 1958/1990, p. 241) fundamental to mechanically conducted proofs. Gödel reiterates the contrast in a subsequent publication, which refers to and cites the previous paper.

> the question of whether there exist finite *non-mechanical* procedures not equivalent with any algorithm, has nothing whatsoever to do with the adequacy of any definition of 'formal system' and of 'mechanical procedure'. ... such as those which involve the use of abstract terms on the basis of their meaning.
>
> (Gödel, 1964/2004, p. 72) [emphasis in original]

A correspondence between non-mechanical procedures and the use of terms on the basis of their meaning is indicated. The emphasis, here given to '*non-mechanical*' (Gödel, 1964/2004, p. 72), indicates the intensity of the contrast between the mechanical and meaning. The exclusion of meaning from a mechanical procedure or algorithm, from the automatic computational process, would be generally accepted, if seldom emphasized, by relevant scholarly communities.

The population of the non-mechanical by meaning can be confirmed and reinforced by replacing the classic term, *mechanical*, with an alternative, and now widely accepted, term, which has a highly similar, if not identical scope, in a computational context, with *syntactic*.

> in the realm of formal systems ... the intuitive notion of 'effective process' [can be identified with] with the purely syntactic idea of string processing.
> (Rosen, 1994, p. 529)

Syntactic is embedded in a different set of contrasts and its customary complement or opposite would be *semantic*, corresponding to Gödel's *meaning*. Semantic would also normally be contrasted immediately with syntactic, in the sense that an intervening territory or intellectual space is not conceived. The distinction between syntactic and semantic is embedded in ordinary discourse, adding wider diffusion, and the implication of the robustness needed to survive wider diffusion, to Gödel's more deliberate theoretically formulated contrast between mechanical procedures and meaning.

A distinction of syntax from semantics was also made in a well-known and seminal critique of strong artificial intelligence (Searle, 1980). Formal symbol manipulations have a syntax but not a semantics and intelligence could not then be attributed to computers (Searle, 1980). The impact of the critique, as revealed in its subsequent reception, may be partly derived from its resonance with the ordinary discourse distinction of syntax from semantics.

The field of information theory, which has some analogies with the theory of computability, through its modeling of an information technology process, although of signal transmission rather than of computation, also excludes meaning from direct consideration, as a founding assumption.

> The fundamental problem of communication is that of reproducing at one point either exactly or approximately a message selected at another point. Frequently the messages have *meaning*; that is they refer to or are correlated according to some system with certain physical or conceptual entities. These semantic aspects of communication are irrelevant to the engineering problem.
> (Shannon, 1948/1993, p. 5) [emphasis in original]

The emphasis given to meaning indicates the significance of its exclusion and 'meaning' is directly correlated with 'semantic' (Shannon, 1948/1993, p. 5). In a later exposition of information theory intended for wider public dissemination, the exclusion of meaning is reiterated.

> Before we can consider how information is to be measured it is necessary to clarify the precise meaning of 'information' from the point of view of the communication engineer ... In any case, meaning is quite irrelevant to the problem of transmitting the information.
> (Shannon, 1968/1993, pp. 213–214)

The exclusion of meaning is again introduced as a founding, and preliminary, assumption. The exclusion of meaning from considerations of signal transmission in information theory corresponds to the contrast of mechanical procedures with meaning in computability, supporting the significance and fundamental nature of the distinction.

Meaning also has a specific application to compilations. The fundamental aim for compilations, across a historically and synchronically wide range of compilations, has been conceived as collocating common or related meanings, irrespective of their particular form of expression in the language of discourse. The involvement of meaning then includes a central form of activity for compilations.

The population of the not mechanical by meaning can admit the assimilation of the first interleaved combination for creativity to the major sequence. Activity in the construction of a mechanical procedure has been understood as human activity on meaning (Weizenbaum, 1976/1984). The first interleaved combination, in which creativity is immediately connected with a mechanical procedure but was revealed to have a deeper and substantive connection with non-mechanical activity, then also involves activity on meaning. It can then continue to be assimilated to the major sequence.

In summary and synthesis, then, meaning is understood as contrasting with the mechanical in a number of partly independent, although also interconnected, domains, in the theory of computability, ordinary discourse, a critique of artificial intelligence, and information theory. The contrast of syntax with semantics is conceived as fundamental, significant, and intense, and as immediate, without intervening territory. We therefore have very strong warrant for taking meaning as the immediate population of the not mechanical.

Meaning and direct engagement with meaning

A dual sense of meaning can be detected in its contrast with the mechanical. Explicitly, it is largely conceived as a different level of analysis, in accord with a familiar distinction inherited from historically embedded modes of thought. Implicitly, and emerging, it has also been understood as direct engagement with meaning.

Some of the sources indicate or imply a conception of meaning as connected with direct human activity. Meaning in the sense in which it is used by Gödel – 'insights ... only from their *meaning*' (Gödel, 1958/1990, p. 241), and, 'the use of abstract terms on the basis of their meaning' (Gödel, 1964/2004, p. 72) – implies, particularly by 'insights' (Gödel, 1958/1990, p. 241) and 'use' (Gödel, 1964/2004, p. 72), direct human engagement with meaning. Searle implicitly connects semantics with intentionality, a feature of 'mental states' (Searle, 1980, p. 424) or human consciousness, which could include direct engagement with meaning. Ordinary discourse would not be in contradiction with meaning as part of human consciousness, although the distinction of syntax from semantics is also used to differentiate levels of analysis.

A particular form of direct human activity on meaning, the linking together of words which have dissimilar expressions but some commonality in meaning, can be revealed to be humanly simple but not automatically computable, in a classic sense. Everyday activity can be exemplified by the utterance, 'Oranges and lemons say the Bells of St. Clements'. A human, including a human child, could give ostensive or linguistic evidence of understanding the meaning of oranges and lemons and the connection between them, by pointing to or naming other instances of the category, fruit. The process of recognizing the meanings of the words, oranges and lemons, is self-evidently simple for a human to conduct, as recognition and connection can normally be made by children raised in a society with the specific spoken language. Computationally, or mechanically or syntactically, we can only engage directly with the expression of the words. The expressions, oranges and lemons, have extensive commonalities, in their existence as part of the lexicon of written English, and, further, in their derivation from a single alphabet and the arrangement of their constituent letters in accord with conventions for combination of letters into words within the English language lexicon. They both exemplify and correspond to a sophisticated understanding of the word of printed English, which embodies a rigorous focus on the level of expression, as 'a cohesive group of letters with strong internal statistical influences' (Shannon, 1951/1993, pp. 197–198). However, their very commonality implies that they do not offer elements distinctive to the particular expressions which can separate them from other words of printed English and which would be amenable to automatic mechanical or computational detection, in the classic sense of a general process for determining the presence of the desired characteristic (Turing, 1936–1937/2004). As such, detecting a common meaning is noncomputable. Recognition of commonality of meaning between two dissimilar expressions, drawn from a common lexicon, has then been revealed to be noncomputable under certain conditions. We have then identified a form of everyday activity which is humanly simple as a semantic process, but resistant to computation.

The fundamental aim for compilations, of collocating common or related meanings, irrespective of their particular form of expression in the language of discourse, can involve syntactic procedures or direct engagement with meaning, and in some instances may necessitate direct engagement with meaning. Related meanings with syntactically similar expressions – for instance, *lemon, lemons*, and *lemony* – could be collocated either by considerations of meaning or by syntactic computational transformations. Related meanings with strongly different expressions may require direct human engagement with meaning, if they are to be linked or collocated. For instance, to give a fictional example, Raymond Chandler, Dashiell Hammett, and William Faulkner, understood as the names of writers associated with a particular genre of film, could all be gathered under the generic term 'film noir', but such a collocation would require direct human engagement with meaning and could not be produced by mechanical or syntactic procedures, in the classic sense. A crucial potential value for human activity on meaning for compilations which is not immediately realizable mechanically or computationally – the gathering together of items related in meaning but dissimilar in pattern – has then been isolated. We have then definitively begun to illustrate and isolate direct human activity on meaning, distinctive from syntactic procedures, as it could be manifested for compilations.

The potential value for human activity on meaning of compilations has been partly deductively derived, from an understanding of the constraints on computational processes, but it can be inductively supported, from real-world practices on data for compilations. Linking together terms related in meaning but contrasting in pattern would form a substantial part of classic relations for compilations: from genus to species (for instance, fruit to lemon), of broader term to narrower term, and term to related term, in thesauri, and see and see also cross-references in indexes. Human activity for databases has substantial costs (Hayes, 2000) and may have value not obtainable from mechanical procedures. Value, as perceived by consumers of compilations, can be evidenced by a continuing market for particular compilations (Swanson, 1980). Markets for the costly activity of linking syntactically different, but semantically related, terms together continue to exist, within such disparate compilations as library catalogs and e-Bay. Oranges and lemons, if made available for sale on e-Bay, could be covered by the, possibly fictional, generic term and category, fruit. We have then obtained very strong inductive support for a partly deductively derived argument, from practical developments.

In summary, then, meaning as direct human activity motivated by meaning can include a form of activity, the association of syntactically strongly different but semantically related expressions, which is distinctively not mechanical, in the specific sense of not being immediately amenable to automatic computation. Such activity can be humanly simple and is significantly realized for compilations. The idea of meaning as direct human engagement with meaning has not been in contradiction with meaning as a level of analysis, but complementary and enabling fuller development of the not mechanical, providing the least and sharpest difference from an automatic mechanical procedure.

Direct engagement with meaning and classic concepts of creativity

The linking of disparate things together to form a cohesive whole is central to high levels of creativity, on classic and widely diffused understandings of creativity. The eighteenth-century Italian philosopher Giambattista Vico understood the human faculty for ingenuity, which would include creativity, in this fashion.

> The power of ingenuity ... consists in the reciprocal joining of diverse things ... Indeed, in an acute saying, these three features are found – the things (*res*), the words (*verba*), and the joining or tying (*ligamen*) of things and words ... acumen consists in a rare and new aptness of two extremes happily joined in a certain saying.
>
> (Vico, 1711/1996, pp. 125–126)

Vico traces the joining together of diverse things as highly creative to Aristotle's work.

> in the *Rhetoric* he [states that] ... 'only creative and acute philosophers are capable of finding in things far removed from each other that similarity which can be contemplated'.
>
> (Vico, 1711/1996, p. 126)

A significant twentieth-century statement of synthesis and amalgamation as central to creativity can be found in T.S. Eliot's conception of the poet's mind.

> When a poet's mind is perfectly equipped for its work, it is constantly amalgamating disparate experience ... falls in love or reads Spinoza ... the noise of the typewriter or the smell of cooking; in the mind of the poet these experiences are always forming new wholes.
>
> (Eliot, 1921/1950, p. 247)

The notion of a 'knight's move', the discovery of previously unarticulated connections, can be found in ordinary discourse. In information science, creativity has been understood as the making of unprecedented connections between public knowledge, although it has been primarily computationally modeled rather than conceived as human activity directly motivated by meaning (Swanson, 1986). A concept of high levels of creativity, consistent with and continuous from creativity as human activity on meaning, is, then, historically well established and also sustained in modern discourse, including ordinary discourse and information science.

An example can be given which combines the procedures of selection, coordination, and arrangement, as understood to be involved in compilations, from the perspective of copyright, with very high levels of creativity. Written English could be conceived for analytical purposes, as a lexicon of words, broadly corresponding to a monolingual dictionary. A rhetorical task could then be conceived of taking the names of the 12 calendar months, selecting 17 words from the lexicon, and coordinating the names of the months and the words, with normal punctuation marks, to produce an interesting utterance. Very high, and extremely rare, levels of creativity are exhibited in the following utterance.

> October. This is one of the peculiarly dangerous months to speculate in stocks in. The others are July, January, September, April, November, May, March, June, December, August, and February. *Pudd'nhead Wilson's Calendar.*
>
> (Twain, 1894/1969, p. 177)

The interest of the utterance is evidenced by the continuing market for the work in which it is included, *Pudd'nhead Wilson* (Twain, 1894/1969), and the rarity of such creativity by the limited survival in current markets of works from the late nineteenth century. The passage obtains some of its effect from the contrast of the reversals and gaps in chronological order – 'June, December, August' (p. 177) – with the customary chronological sequence of the months, which could be syntactically generated, as well as from the contradiction between the meaning of 'peculiarly dangerous' (p. 177) and the exhaustive listing of the 12 months. A specific example has then been added to theory.

Creativity, including the highest levels of creativity, can then smoothly and progressively emerge within the not mechanical. The possibility of novelty contained within such high levels of creativity corresponds to the specific implications of the antithetical clause, 'nothing remotely creative' (Feist Publications, Inc. v. Rural Tel. Service Co., Inc., 1991, p. 363), that the fully creative should be not 'dictated by state law' nor 'an age-old practice, firmly rooted in tradition and so commonplace that it has come to be expected as a matter of course … practically inevitable … time-honored tradition' (pp. 362–363). The conception of creativity has then been extended to encompass the fully creative.

Creativity

The inclusion of novelty in the fully creative also implies a contrast with the 'so … routine', enabling a fuller understanding of the relation of creativity to the not mechanical. Routinicity in the process is explicitly designated as 'so … routine' and can also be revealed by being embodied in the product, as 'entirely typical' or 'garden-variety', both for processes designated as 'so … routine' (Feist Publications, Inc. v. Rural Tel. Service Co., Inc., 1991, p. 362), and those not so designated. Within the not mechanical, and reading upwards (Table 6.2), where routinicity is present in the process and revealed in the product, the compilation is not creative. Where a 'so … routine' process (p. 362) persists but the level of routinicity diminishes, as indicated by its embodiment in the product, creativity emerges when no routinicity is revealed in the product. Such compilations could be understood to have the slightest trace of creativity. Where 'so … routine' (p. 362) is not designated for the process and routinicity is increasingly less marked in the product, the process can be understood to reach progressively slightly higher levels of creativity. Where routinicity is not marked at all in the process or present in the product, the process can be understood as fully creative, for both the highest placed combination and the interleaved combination regarded as analogous to it. The not mechanical remains substantively invariant within creativity, across all the transitions in levels of routinicity. We can then understand not mechanical activity on meaning as becoming creative, first at a transitional level, then creative, and finally fully creative, as it passes certain levels of routinicity (Table 6.2).

The understanding of creativity meets all the conditions for creativity derived from the decision. The negation of the antithesis to creativity indicates that creativity begins immediately after the absence of creativity, at a transitional level corresponding to the level of creativity required for the 'creative spark … so trivial as to be virtually nonexistent' (Feist Publications, Inc. v. Rural Tel. Service Co., Inc., 1991, p. 359). The smooth movement between transitional and very high levels of creativity means that creativity necessarily includes the 'extremely low' (p. 345), but more than 'so trivial' (p. 359), level of creativity required for a minimal degree of creativity. Creativity can be read from the end product as something not devoid of the slightest trace of creativity, in a mode of reading warranted by the reading of the absence of creativity established by the opinion, as 'devoid of even the slightest trace of creativity' (Feist Publications, Inc. v. Rural Tel. Service Co., Inc., 1991, p. 362). Creativity is then knowable on the model of the treatment of the absence of creativity within the opinion. The connection to classic discourse about creativity gave it some

Table 6.2 Creativity

Process			*Product*			*Process and product*	*Creative or not-creative*			
automatic mechanical procedure	so … routine	**automatic mechanical procedure ∨ so … routine**	entirely typical	garden-variety	**entirely typical ∨ garden-variety**	(automatic mechanical procedure ∨ so … routine) ∧ (entirely typical ∨ garden-variety)				
FALSE	FALSE	**FALSE**	FALSE	FALSE	**FALSE**	FALSE	Fully creative	Absence of marked routinicity.	Not mechanical	Routinicity
FALSE	FALSE	**FALSE**	FALSE	TRUE	**TRUE**	FALSE	Creative	Decreasing levels of routinicity in the process as revealed in the product.		
FALSE	FALSE	**FALSE**	TRUE	FALSE	**TRUE**	FALSE	Creative			
FALSE	FALSE	**FALSE**	TRUE	TRUE	**TRUE**	FALSE	Creative			
FALSE	TRUE	**TRUE**	FALSE	FALSE	**FALSE**	FALSE	Slightest trace of creativity	Routinicity marked in the process but decreasingly 'so … routine' as revealed in the product.		
FALSE	TRUE	**TRUE**	FALSE	TRUE	**TRUE**	TRUE	not-creative			
FALSE	TRUE	**TRUE**	TRUE	FALSE	**TRUE**	TRUE	not-creative			
FALSE	TRUE	**TRUE**	TRUE	TRUE	**TRUE**	TRUE	not-creative			
TRUE	FALSE	**TRUE**	FALSE	FALSE	**FALSE**	FALSE	Fully creative	Absence of marked routinicity.		

(Continued)

Table 6.2 (Cont.)

Process			*Product*			*Process and product*	*Creative or not-creative*	
TRUE	FALSE	**TRUE**	FALSE	TRUE	**TRUE**	TRUE	not-creative	
TRUE	FALSE	**TRUE**	TRUE	FALSE	**TRUE**	TRUE	not-creative	
TRUE	FALSE	**TRUE**	TRUE	TRUE	**TRUE**	TRUE	not-creative	
TRUE	TRUE	**TRUE**	FALSE	FALSE	**FALSE**	FALSE	Creative	Tension between process and product.
TRUE	TRUE	**TRUE**	FALSE	TRUE	**TRUE**	TRUE	not-creative	
TRUE	TRUE	**TRUE**	TRUE	FALSE	**TRUE**	TRUE	not-creative	
TRUE	TRUE	**TRUE**	TRUE	TRUE	**TRUE**	TRUE	not-creative	

connections with ordinary discourse and the idea of creativity as constituted by a departure from routinicity, within the not mechanical, would be consistent with contemporary ordinary discourse. Creativity as involving direct engagement with meaning is also *prima facie* applicable to works other than compilations and the inclusion of all possible levels of creativity renders it fully applicable to all works. Creativity then occupies all required levels, is knowable on the given model, has a strong consistency with ordinary discourse, and is applicable to all works.

The formulation for creativity, that

> A compilation has the slightest trace of creativity if, and only if, it is not constructed by an automatic mechanical procedure or so … routine process which results in an entirely typical or garden-variety end product.

can then be transformed. The inclusion of the highest possible levels of creativity enables the replacement of *the slightest trace of creativity* by *creative*. The applicability of creativity to all works legitimates the replacement of compilation by work. The transformed formulation then reads.

> **A work is creative if, and only if, it is not constructed by an automatic mechanical procedure or so … routine process which results in an entirely typical or garden-variety end product.**

(In the formulation, *is* is substituted for *has the* as an acceptable simplification for the embodiment of creativity in the product). We have then obtained a formulation for creativity, by a transformation of its antithesis, which fully meets all the conditions for creativity derived from the decision.

The unexplained residue, noted in the previous chapter, of the contrast between the historical in the decision and the natural in classic conceptions of computability has also been effectively explained away, by insisting on the directly human, and thereby historical, nature of creativity. The unexplained residual contrast has then been transformed into a basis for explanation.

Relation to the European Union and other jurisdictions

Full comparison between the creativity requirement of *Feist* (Feist Publications, Inc. v. Rural Tel. Service Co., Inc., 1991) and more labor oriented standards in other jurisdictions must be delayed until we reach a minimal degree of creativity and, finally, originality itself. A minimal degree of creativity, and not just creativity, is the necessary component of originality as the final requirement for copyrightability. At this stage, we can note that the understanding of creativity developed for *Feist* does not exclude labor. The possibility of congruence of *Feist* with other jurisdictions has then been retained. The absence of exclusion of labor then holds the possibility for reconciliation (which will be obtained in Chapter 8, after considering the minimal degree of creativity which itself is needed for originality).

Narrative motif

Labyrinths have served as images or metaphors for creativity. We negotiated the labyrinth of the judgment to its negative or antithetical center, obtained an understanding of the antithesis to creativity, and established a compelling correlation with computability, giving an enhanced and deeply intersubjectively rooted understanding of the antithesis to computability. Routes out of the labyrinth in classic instances, such as the legend of Theseus, follow previously laid threads. In this instance, we did not simply return but followed an unknown, and largely unexplored, path to develop new concepts. In the legend of Theseus, navigation out of the labyrinth is part of becoming fully human (Vico, 1744/1976, §561, 565, 1028). The motif of the labyrinth thereby confirms the renewal of our humanity, consistent with creativity as directly human activity.

Creativity: out of the labyrinth: chapter summary

The conclusion of the previous chapter that, a compilation has not the slightest trace of creativity if, and only if, it is constructed by an automatic mechanical procedure or so … routine process and is an entirely typical or garden-variety end product, was transformed into its implication, by negation.

> A compilation has the slightest trace of creativity if, and only if, it is not constructed by an automatic mechanical procedure or so … routine process which results in an entirely typical or garden-variety end product.

The formally logical equivalent to this verbal statement can similarly be transformed.

> ~ (A compilation has the slightest trace of creativity) ↔ ((automatic mechanical procedure ∨ so … routine) ∧ (entirely typical ∨ garden-variety))

becomes first

> ~ ~ (A compilation has the slightest trace of creativity) ↔ ~ ((automatic mechanical procedure ∨ so … routine) ∧ (entirely typical ∨ garden-variety))

The double negation can then be eliminated to yield.

> **(A compilation has the slightest trace of creativity) ↔ ~ ((automatic mechanical procedure ∨ so … routine) ∧ (entirely typical ∨ garden-variety))**

The reasoning by negation is in close accord with the antithetical character of the formulations for the ‘creative spark … utterly lacking’ (Feist Publications, Inc. v. Rural Tel. Service Co., Inc., 1991, p. 359). The logical formulation is particularly valuable here, as it enables the construction of truth tables (see Tables 7.1 and 7.2).

The logical formulation cannot be further reduced by formal operations on its components and we must therefore attend to the formulation as a whole. On inspection, a not automatic mechanical procedure emerged as invariant within the creative. It therefore has potential discriminatory power to separate the creative from the not creative. However, it also appeared in the not creative. Its potential discriminatory power was not then immediately realized and the argument required further development to transform its potential into actual discriminatory power.

An automatic mechanical procedure is concerned with formal or syntactic operations and not with the meaning of the signs on which it operates, and this was acknowledged in classic discussions of computability. *Meaning* or semantics then emerges as populating a *not* automatic mechanical procedure. Meaning or semantics is often understood as a different level of analysis to syntax, but it can also be understood as direct human engagement with meaning and there are some implications of this understanding in the classic discussions. Direct human engagement with meaning also provided the least and sharpest contrast with syntactic operations.

Using direct human engagement with meaning, we could associate or bring together ideas and objects with no special commonality as expressions in language, such as *oranges* and *lemons.* Bringing ideas together corresponds to a central component of creativity as understood in ordinary and specialized discourses. High levels of creativity may involve unprecedented associations of ideas and this could also be accomplished by direct human activity motivated by meaning. The not automatic mechanical procedure, understood as direct human engagement with meaning, is then potentially creative.

The other elements of the formulation – 'so … routine … entirely typical or garden-variety' (Feist Publications, Inc. v. Rural Tel. Service Co., Inc., 1991, pp. 362–363) – could all be understood as connected with routinicity.

Creativity then emerged, progressively and smoothly, within a not automatic mechanical procedure, as routinicity diminishes, first directly in the process and then as revealed in the product. The understanding of creativity meets the conditions established for it, of application to all works, of extending from the lowest to the highest level, consistency with ordinary discourse, having level, and being knowable.

We arrive at a more and sufficiently definite understanding of creativity.

> **A work is creative if, and only if, it is not an entirely typical or garden-variety end product constructed by an automatic mechanical procedure or a so … routine process.**

Or, in logical notation.

> **Creativity ↔ ~ ((automatic mechanical procedure ∨ so … routine) ∧ (entirely typical ∨ garden-variety))**

Conclusion

The argument has had certain characteristics to commend it.

In relation to the decision, creativity was substantiated but not over-populated, in accord with a negative approach to its delimitation in the judgment. The treatment of an automatic mechanical procedure as the primary element of the creativity 'utterly lacking' (p. 359) corresponds to the priority accorded to 'so mechanical' (p. 362) within the opinion. The order of discrimination for originality for compilations embodied the relative priority given to each element in the decision, from 'so mechanical' (p. 362), through a further level and then an amount of creativity, to independent creation. These elements of parallelism between the argument and decision are suggestive of the appropriateness of the argument to its object, to the decision. Parallelism also suggests the capture of the decision's approach.

The argument has also had substantive and formal characteristics generally considered desirable. Substantive distinctions, for instance, of meaning from syntactic processes, are accepted as founding assumptions in the disciplines from which they were derived and are also present in ordinary discourse. The substitution of a correlated external standard to yield a conceptual gain of greater intersubjectivity is also a classic process of legal advance. Formally, the central components of the argument consisted only of the correlation and a major inferential step, of negation, revealing economy. Each subsequent step, from an automatic mechanical procedure to the not mechanical, from the not mechanical to meaning, from meaning to direct engagement with meaning, and from direct engagement with meaning to classic concepts of creativity, took the outcome of the previous stage as its basis, indicating a sequential argument connected as a single chain. Creativity was progressively developed from a transitional to the very highest level. Deep rooting in relevant discourses, economy, sequentiality, and progressiveness are often taken to indicate valid arguments, if their object has been fully comprehended.

In this instance, these qualities have been combined with a full capture of the conditions required for creativity. We can then regard the understanding of creativity as human action motivated by meaning, above a certain level of routinicity, as very strongly proven creativity (see Figure 6.2).

We have established a fully grounded understanding of creativity, for the judgment.

References

Bochenski, I.M. (1961). *History of formal logic.* Translated by I. Thomas. Notre Dame, IN: Notre Dame University Press.

Eliot, T.S. (1921/1950). The metaphysical poets. In T.S. Eliot. *Selected essays.* New York: Harcourt, Brace.

Feist Publications, Inc. v. Rural Tel. Service Co., Inc. (1991). Feist Publications, Inc. v. Rural Tel. Service Co., Inc. 499 U.S. 340 (1991).

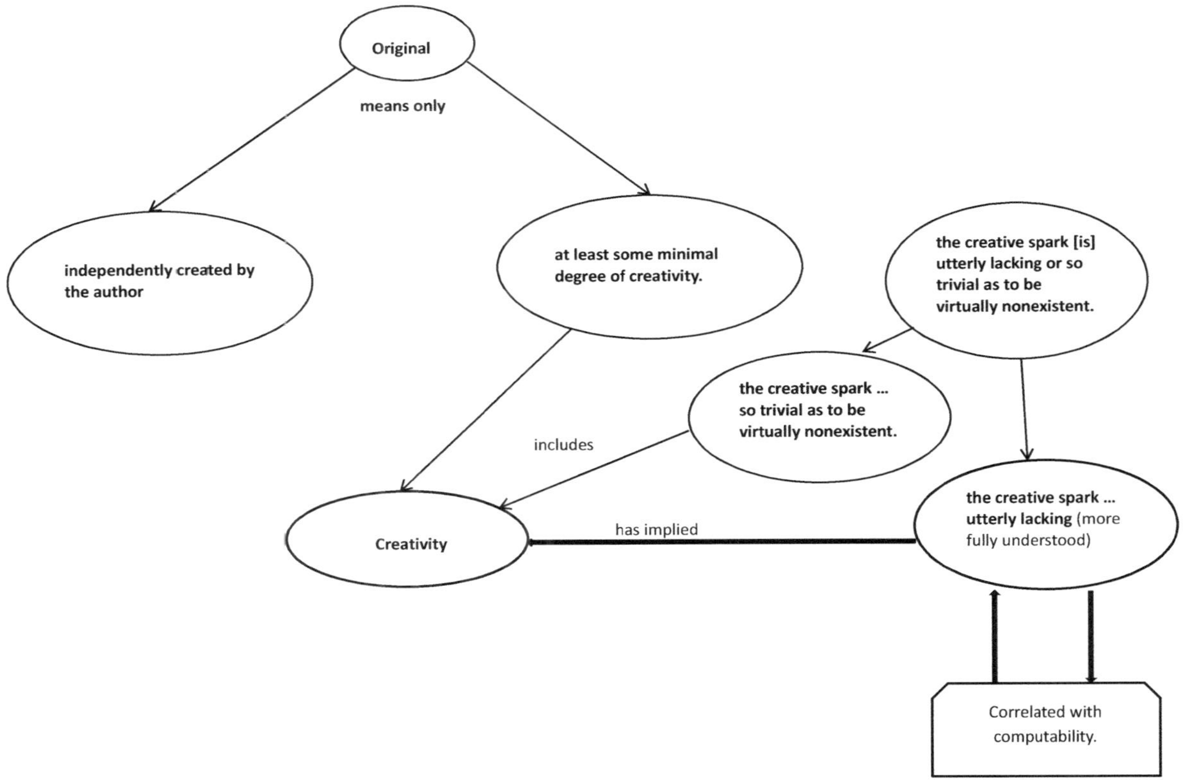

Figure 6.2 Progress made
Note: **Bold** is used for terms and phrases directly derived from the decision.

Gödel, K. (1958/1990). On a hitherto unutilized extension of the finitary standpoint. In K. Gödel. *Collected works. Volume II: Publications 1938–1974* (pp. 24–251). Edited by S. Feferman with J.W.Dawson Jr., S.C. Kleene, G.H. Moore, R.M. Solovay and J. van Heijenoort. New York and Oxford: Oxford University Press.

Gödel, K. (1964/2004). Postscriptum [To, On undecidable propositions of formal mathematical systems]. In M. Davis (ed.). *The undecidable: Basic papers on undecidable propositions, unsolvable problems and computable functions* (pp. 71–73). Hewlett, NY: Raven Press.

Hayes, R.M. (2000). Assessing the value of a database company. In B. Cronin and H.B. Atkins (eds). *The web of knowledge: A festschrift in honor of Eugene Garfield* (pp. 73–84). Medford, NJ: Information Today.

Kneale, W.K. and Kneale, M. (1962). *The development of logic.* Oxford: Clarendon Press.

Rosen, M. (1994). Effective processes and natural law. In R. Herken (ed.). *The universal Turing machine: A half-century survey* (pp. 523–537). Oxford: Oxford University Press.

Searle, J.R. (1980). Minds, brains and programs. *The Behavioral and Brain Sciences.* 3, 417–457.

Shannon, C.E. (1948/1993). A mathematical theory of communication. In C.E. Shannon. *Collected papers* (pp. 5–83). Edited by N.J.A. Sloane and A.D. Wyner. Piscataway, NJ: IEEE Press.

Shannon, C.E. (1951/1993). Prediction and entropy of printed English. In C.E. Shannon. *Collected papers* (pp. 194–208). Edited by N.J.A. Sloane and A.D. Wyner. Piscataway, NJ: IEEE Press.

Shannon, C.E. (1968/1993). Information theory. In C.E. Shannon. *Collected papers* (pp. 212–220). Edited by N.J.A. Sloane and A.D. Wyner. Piscataway, NJ: IEEE Press.

Swanson, D.R. (1980). Libraries and the growth of knowledge. In D. R. Swanson (ed.). *The role of libraries in the growth of knowledge* (pp. 112–136). Chicago, IL: University of Chicago Press.

Swanson, D.R. (1986). Undiscovered public knowledge. *Library Quarterly.* 56, 103–118.

Turing, A.M. (1936–1937/2004). On computable numbers, with an application to the Entscheidungsproblem (paper read 12 November 1936). In M. Davis (ed.). *The undecidable: Basic papers on undecidable propositions, unsolvable problems and computable functions* (pp. 116–151). Mineola, NY: Dover.

Twain, M. (1894/1969). *Pudd'nhead Wilson.* Harmondsworth: Penguin Books.

Vico, G. (1711/1996). *The art of rhetoric* (Institutiones oratoriae, 1711–1741). From the definitive Latin text and notes, Italian commentary and introduction by G. Crifo. Translated and edited by G.A. Pinton and A.W. Shippee. Amsterdam and Atlanta, GA: Rodopi.

Vico, G. (1744/1976). *The new science of Giambattista Vico.* Unabridged translation of the Third Edition (1744) with the addition of 'Practic of the New Science' by T. G. Bergin and M. H. Fisch. Ithaca, NY and London: Cornell University Press.

Weizenbaum, J. (1976/1984). *Computer power and human reason: From judgment to calculation.* Harmondsworth: Penguin.

7 A minimal degree of creativity

Introduction

We have traversed the implication of creativity (see Figure 6.2). The elucidation of creativity in the preceding chapter opens the way for developing an understanding of a minimal degree of creativity, understood as including creativity. Our understanding of a minimal degree of creativity must be continuous with the understanding established of creativity as human activity directly motivated by considerations of meaning, above a certain level of routinicity. We must now integrate the understanding of creativity obtained with a minimal degree of creativity, in this chapter, in our ascent towards originality (see Figure 7.1).

A minimal degree of creativity, and not just creativity, is required for copyrightability. A minimal degree of creativity includes creativity on an ordinary language reading, but is verbally different as an expression from creativity, by *a minimal degree of.* Substantive significance for the verbal difference is intimated by creativity also being included in the creative spark 'so trivial as to be virtually nonexistent', which does not give rise to copyright. Creativity is then present both in all the copyrightable and in part of the not copyrightable. Careful elucidation of *a minimal degree* is required to reveal its particular significance.

Different verbal forms in the judgment can be assimilated to a minimal degree of creativity. A review and synthesis of the references to a minimal degree of creativity reveals that it consists of a certain level of creativity and a certain amount at that level. An extremely low level is required. It correlates with the intellectual level classically required for copyrightability. It can be read from the product in question or, failing that, by a further enquiry into the circumstances of construction of the product. The amount needed at the required level is slight. A minimal degree, which combines of level and amount, can be detected from the exchange values connected with the product.

Conditions derivable from the judgment for a minimal degree of creativity – that it must have level, amount at that level, and be knowable – are then all met. Creativity itself is then integrated with the understanding of a minimal degree of creativity obtained. A definitive understanding of a minimal degree of creativity, which incorporates the understanding of creativity obtained, is then established, by the chapter.

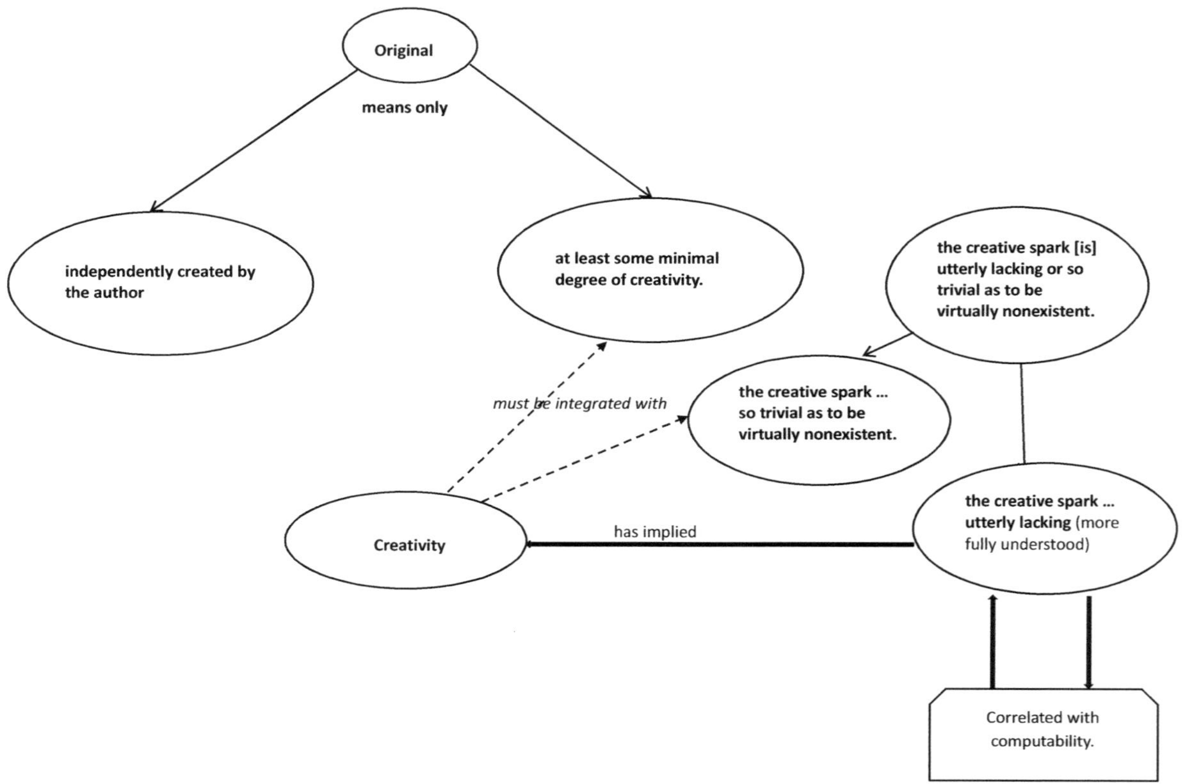

Figure 7.1 Paths for integration
Note: **Bold** is used for terms and phrases directly derived from the decision.

A minimal degree of creativity is elucidated, like creativity, by a close reading of the judgment. All readings, of both semantics and grammar, are ordinary language readings, unless otherwise indicated. Once a minimal degree of creativity has been fully elucidated, it can be reintegrated with creativity, to validate and test the understanding of both a minimal degree of creativity arrived at and that of creativity previously established. The relation of the requirement for a minimal degree of creativity for copyrightability to European and global requirements for copyrightability is also considered.

A minimal degree of creativity

All references to a minimal degree of creativity in the decision can be considered, in sequential order, for their implications.

Introduction of a minimal degree of creativity

A minimal degree of creativity is introduced as part of a passage concerned with the meaning of original.

> Original ... means only that the work ... possesses at least some minimal degree of creativity. To be sure, the requisite level of creativity is extremely low; even a slight amount will suffice. The vast majority of works make the grade quite easily, as they possess some creative spark, 'no matter how crude, humble or obvious' it might be. Originality does not signify novelty.
>
> (Feist Publications, Inc. v. Rural Tel. Service Co., Inc., 1991, p. 345) [citations omitted]

'To be sure' (p. 345) indicates a continuity from 'some minimal degree of creativity' (p. 345) and the subsequent transition to considering another aspect of originality, the absence of a requirement for novelty – 'Originality does not signify novelty' (p. 345) – implies the end of the continuity indicated. The passage from '[T]o be sure' to 'it might be' (p. 345) can then all be read as concerned with a minimal degree of creativity.

'To be sure' (Feist Publications, Inc. v. Rural Tel. Service Co., Inc., 1991, p. 345) then applies to all of the subsequent treatment of a minimal degree of creativity, in the passage. It implies both a strong degree of confidence in the statements and a basis in established practice for that confidence. The syntactic parallelism of the subsequent passage – 'the requisite level of creativity is extremely low; even a slight amount will suffice' (p. 345) [citations omitted] – with the immediately previous 'some minimal degree of creativity' implies a direct correspondence between the two passages. '[E]xtremely low level' and 'slight amount' (p. 345) can then be understood as corresponding to 'minimal degree' (p. 345). 'Extremely low' (p. 345) and 'slight' (p. 345) semantically correspond to 'minimal' (p. 345) and level and amount must then correspond to degree. The mention of level before amount implies that amount must be understood as amount at the given level. '[R]equisite', qualifying level, and 'suffice', governed by amount, indicates that the necessary level must exist in sufficient amount, to constitute to a minimal degree of creativity. A minimal degree of creativity then immediately disaggregates into level and amount and is constituted by an 'extremely low' (p. 345) requisite level and a sufficient 'slight amount' (p. 345).

The concern then turns to the proportion of works with at least a minimal degree of creativity.

> The vast majority of works make the grade quite easily
>
> (Feist Publications, Inc. v. Rural Tel. Service Co., Inc., 1991, p. 345)

'The vast majority of works' (Feist Publications, Inc. v. Rural Tel. Service Co., Inc., 1991, p. 345) indicates a proportion of works. 'Works' (p. 345) can be understood as referring to works conceived as separate entities. '[W]orks' (p. 345) would include compilations. 'The' in 'the grade' indicates reference to something immediately previously mentioned and 'make the grade' (p. 345) implies meeting the conditions for a minimal degree of creativity. '[G]rade' (p. 345) must then be understood as referring to 'some minimal degree of creativity' (p. 345). *Grade* is more cognate in its own meaning with level than amount and thereby emphasizes the difference in level, in accord with the priority of mention and of being previously given to level. '[Q]uite easily' in '[m]ake the grade quite easily' (p. 345) implies a significant and readily discernible interval between the level and amount at the level of creativity embodied in the vast majority of works and the required level and sufficient amount. A proportion of works not meeting the grade could be understood to be logically or arithmetically implied, although it is not explicitly stated.

The condition by which works make the grade is then given.

> as they possess some creative spark
>
> (Feist Publications, Inc. v. Rural Tel. Service Co., Inc., 1991, p. 345)

'[S]ome creative spark' (p. 345) in the continuation from 'grade' (p. 345) cannot directly correspond to 'grade' (p. 345), as ordinary language usage would not normally allow something possessing itself. However, the possession of some creative spark enables a work to make the grade. '[S]ome creative spark' (p. 345) must then be understood as the combination of required level and sufficient amount of creativity which constitutes minimal degree of creativity. '[S]ome' (p. 345) can be understood as indicating a certain level and amount.

'[S]park' in 'creative spark' (Feist Publications, Inc. v. Rural Tel. Service Co., Inc., 1991, p. 345) can be understood as an initiator of a creative process. It corresponds to the judgment's emphasis on progress as the constitutionally mandated purpose of copyright.

> The primary objective of copyright is … '[t]o promote the Progress of Science and useful Arts.' To this end, copyright assures authors the right to their

original expression, but encourages others to build freely upon the ideas and information conveyed by a work.

(Feist Publications, Inc. v. Rural Tel. Service Co., Inc., 1991, pp. 349–350) [citations omitted]

'[S]park' (p. 345), understood as initiating a process, is then consistent with a central theme of the judgment, the insistence on progress as the purpose of intellectual property.

Spark as an initiator, in the opening reference to a minimal degree of creativity (p. 345), can be primarily understood in a metaphorical, rather than immediately material, sense. The metaphorical sense of spark does have a material basis, as a spark of fire, which has a hitherto unexplored relevance to a minimal degree of creativity. The significance of the material basis for spark can then be raised to consciousness. A material spark combines illumination and duration in a single entity, with illumination usually perceived before duration, in ordinary human experience. Illumination can be understood as corresponding to level and duration to amount. The level of illumination of a spark can range from the very low to the highest conceivable level, from that obtainable from striking flints together to that conferred by lightning. The possibility of creativity at the very highest level which was implied by the applicability of a minimal degree of creativity to all works and allowed for by the introductory reference to 'at least some minimal degree of creativity' (Feist Publications, Inc. v. Rural Tel. Service Co., Inc., 1991, p. 345) is thereby metaphorically expressed. The occurrence of illumination before duration corresponds to the priority of level to amount in the decision, and also indicates the possibility of interpreting amount as duration. Duration of a material spark is necessarily brief, corresponding to 'slight' in a 'slight amount' (p. 345). '[S]park' (p. 345), then, when considered in its material sense, combines level and amount in a single entity, gives priority to level, allows for very low to unlimited levels, and compels a slight amount. Spark, then, in the sense which corresponds to its material basis, then has analogies to the division of a minimal degree into level and amount at that level. The priority of mention and emphasis given to level over amount has been further confirmed by the implications of the material basis of spark.[1]

1 Significant antecedents to spark as initiating a process which confirm its metaphorical sense but also explicitly contain its material basis can be found in Romantic and classical sources. A highly significant Romantic instance of the use the term, spark, occurs in Mary Shelley's account of the monster given life by Frankenstein.

> With an anxiety that almost amounted to agony, I collected the instruments of life around me that I might infuse a *spark* of being into the lifeless thing that lay at my feet. It was already one in the morning; the rain pattered dismally against the panes, and my candle was nearly burnt out, when, by the glimmer of the half-extinguished light, I saw the dull yellow eye of the creature open; it breathed hard, and a convulsive motion agitated its limbs.
>
> (Shelley, 1818/1998, pp. 38–39) [emphasis added]

The terms which follow and qualify 'some creative spark' (Feist Publications, Inc. v. Rural Tel. Service Co., Inc., 1991, p. 345) – 'no matter how crude, humble or obvious it might be' (p. 345) – are consistent in meaning with the combination of 'extremely low' (p. 345) level and 'slight' (p. 345) amount of creativity which constitute a minimal degree of creativity and readily applicable to level and amount in combination. They conclude the introductory explication of 'at least some minimal degree of creativity' (p. 345)

The passage immediately following the introduction of 'at least some minimal degree of creativity' (Feist Publications, Inc. v. Rural Tel. Service Co., Inc., 1991, p. 345) can then be read continuously and as a whole. A minimal degree of creativity is constituted by a required, 'extremely low' (p. 345), level and a sufficient 'slight' (p. 345) amount of creativity at that level. The degree of confidence with which works with a minimal degree of creativity can be discerned, the basis for that confidence in established practice, and the proportion of works expected to have a minimal degree of creativity, are all indicated. Priority of mention and emphasis of meaning is given to level over amount. The passage as a whole can be understood as an explication of 'at least some minimal degree of creativity' (p. 345).

The monster is made from dead human parts and brought to life by intervention from a living human. '[S]park' (Shelley, 1818/1998, p. 38) is used in both a directly material sense, as a spark of electricity, with a strong and explicit metaphorical connotation, of infusing life into inert thought or matter, reminiscent of the divine infusing of life into human forms in Genesis.

A material sense of *spark* emerges strongly from another well-known Romantic reference, by Coleridge on the actor Edmund Kean. 'Kean is original; but he copies from himself. His rapid descents from the hyper-tragic to the infra-colloquial, though sometimes productive of great effect, are often unreasonable. To see him act, is like reading Shakespeare by flashes of lightning. I do not think him thorough-bred gentleman enough to play Othello' (Coleridge, 1835, p. 44). '[F]lashes of lightning' (Coleridge, 1835, p. 44) is semantically cognate with spark, although without spark as a term. The formulation 'flashes of lightning' (Coleridge, 1835, p. 44) carries some literal and material, as well as metaphorical, implications. Some inconvenience in reading is implied, by the literal implication of 'flashes of lightning' and the insight given by Kean is transitory – 'not … thorough-bred gentleman enough to play Othello' (Coleridge, 1835, p. 44) – like a material spark, with its brief duration (Coleridge, 1835, p. 44). The material basis for the metaphorical sense then emerges strongly.

A significant classical instance occurs in Plato's expression of the value of spoken dialogue compared to the dissemination of thought by written language, without immediate dialogue, for the development of understanding, in the *Phaedrus*. 'It is only when all these things, names and definitions, visual and other sensations, are rubbed together and subjected to tests in which questions and answers are exchanged in good faith and without malice that finally, when human capacity is stretched to its limit, a *spark* of understanding and intelligence flashes out and illuminates the subject at issue' (Plato, 400 BC/1973, p. 140) [emphasis added]. In this passage, 'spark' is used in a metaphorical sense, 'a spark of understanding' (p. 140). Traces of a material sense, as a physical spark of fire, with reference both to the production of a spark, 'things … are rubbed together' (p. 140), and its effects, 'flashes out and illuminates the subject at issue' (p. 140), is also discernible.

In both the Romantic and the classical instances, the spark has a communicative function, is humanly made, and creates the possibility of further growth, by initiating a process.

Basis for the requirement for a minimal degree of creativity

The basis for the requirement for a minimal degree of creativity as part of originality is then found in the Constitution. The Constitution had authorized Congress to 'secure for limited Times to Authors … the exclusive Right to their respective Writings'. Crucial terms in this clause, authors and writings, were considered in two late-nineteenth-century decisions by the Supreme Court.

The first such decision, *The Trade-Mark Cases* (Trade-Mark, 1879), was concerned with the 'writings' in the constitutional clause.

> the Court addressed the constitutional scope of 'writings'. For a particular work to be classified 'under the head of writings of authors', the Court determined, 'originality is required'. The Court explained that originality requires … a modicum of creativity
>
> (Feist Publications, Inc. v. Rural Tel. Service Co., Inc., 1991, p. 346)

'[A] modicum of creativity' (p. 346) is required for originality. '[R]equires' (p. 346) can be understood to be semantically included in 'means' in the initial introduction of a minimal degree of creativity by '[o]riginal means only' (p. 345). A modicum of creativity is then assimilatable to a minimal degree of creativity. *Modicum* would normally be understood as a small amount, possibly of some good or abstract quality. It is then consistent with the requisite level and sufficient amount of creativity at that level, required for a minimal degree of creativity.[2] The decision then immediately quotes from the cited judgment to give the basis for the requirement for a modicum of creativity in the constitutional reference to writings.

> [W]hile the word *writings* may be liberally construed … it is only such as … are founded in the creative powers of the mind … which are to be protected.
>
> (Feist Publications, Inc. v. Rural Tel. Service Co., Inc., 1991, p. 346) [emphasis in original]

The reference to 'a modicum of creativity' (p. 346) syntactically parallels 'creative powers of the mind' (p. 346) in the quoted decision and is semantically cognate with it. A modicum of creativity can then be understood as developed by the creative powers of the mind. The 'creative powers of the mind' (p. 346) as implied by writings in the Constitution, then, forms one part of the basis for asserting the requirement for a minimal degree of creativity.

2 The formulation, modicum of creativity, has been used in some subsequent discussions to refer to the creativity requirement articulated by *Feist*, warranted, to some extent, by its presence in the decision and enabled by its capacity to stand alone as a reference. However, 'minimal degree of creativity' (Feist Publications, Inc. v. Rural Tel. Service Co., Inc., 1991, p. 345) is the formulation initially used, is directly explicated, and occurs more frequently in the decision. It therefore has a claim to be the preferred formulation and has been adopted here.

The second and subsequent late-nineteenth-century decision, *Burrow-Giles* (1884), was concerned with authors in the constitutional clause.

> the Court distilled the same requirement from the Constitution's use of the word 'authors'.
>
> (Feist Publications, Inc. v. Rural Tel. Service Co., Inc., 1991, p. 346)

'[T]he same requirement' (p. 346) must be understood to refer to the requirement for originality asserted in connection with immediately previously cited decision, *The Trade Mark Cases*. The judgment continues.

> As in *The Trade-Mark Cases*, the Court emphasized the creative component of originality.
>
> (p. 346)

'As' (p. 346) indicates that the 'creative component' (p. 346) must be assimilatable to the previously cited 'a modicum of creativity' (p. 346) and to a minimal degree of creativity.

Modern cases and commentaries are cited to confirm the continuity from nineteenth-century judgments.

> The originality requirement articulated in *The Trade-Mark Cases* and *Burrow-Giles* remains the touchstone of copyright protection today. ... It is the very 'premise of copyright law.' ... Leading scholars agree on this point. As one pair of commentators succinctly puts it: 'The originality requirement is constitutionally mandated for all works.' ... 'originality is a statutory as well as a constitutional requirement'.
>
> (Feist Publications, Inc. v. Rural Tel. Service Co., Inc., 1991, p. 347) [citations omitted]

The 'originality requirement' (p. 347) would include a minimal degree of creativity and 'touchstone' (p. 347) can then be understood to include the requirement for a minimal degree of creativity.

Different aspects of the Constitutional clause, writings and authors, are, then, adduced as the basis for the requirement for a minimal degree of creativity, by the citation of the nineteenth-century cases, and there is a continuity to current understandings.

Application to compilations

The understanding of a minimal degree of creativity as constituted by a required level and sufficient amount at that level of creativity, and the confirmation of its basis in the Constitution, enables the application of a minimal degree of creativity to compilations.

> Factual compilations … may possess the requisite originality.
> (Feist Publications, Inc. v. Rural Tel. Service Co., Inc., 1991, p. 348)

Factual compilations can, then, have a minimal degree of creativity, as part of the requirement for originality. The condition under which they can obtain originality is then indicated.

> The compilation author typically chooses which facts to include, in what order to place them, and how to arrange the collected data so that they may be used effectively by readers. These choices as to selection and arrangement, so long as they are made independently by the compiler and entail a minimal degree of creativity, are sufficiently original that Congress may protect such compilations through the copyright laws.
> (p. 348)

'[S]o long as' (p. 348), which connects 'a minimal degree of creativity' to 'originality' (p. 348) indicates that 'a minimal degree of creativity' (p. 348) is included in originality. It is also verbally identical in its substantive terms to the initial reference to 'some minimal degree of creativity' (p. 345). It must then be equivalent to 'some minimal degree of creativity' (p. 345).

Elements of compilations which are not additional written expression can embody a minimal degree of creativity.

> a directory that contains absolutely no protectible written expression, only facts, meets the constitutional minimum for copyright protection if it features an original selection or arrangement.
> (Feist Publications, Inc. v. Rural Tel. Service Co., Inc., 1991, p. 348)

For such elements a minimal degree of creativity is recognized as 'elusive' (p. 349). Elements of compilations without original expression can, then, have a minimal degree of creativity only through the selection and arrangement of data.

'[S]ome minimal level of creativity' (Feist Publications, Inc. v. Rural Tel. Service Co., Inc., 1991, p. 358) is distinguished for elements of compilations without original written expression.

> Originality requires … that it display some minimal level of creativity.
> (Feist Publications, Inc. v. Rural Tel. Service Co., Inc., 1991, p. 358)

The level of creativity referred to in 'some minimal level of creativity' (p. 358) can be understood as meeting the level required for a minimal degree of creativity, from the governing of the 'some minimal level of creativity' by 'originality' in, '[o]riginality requires' (p. 358). On an understanding of 'requires' (p. 358) as semantically included in 'means' in '[o]riginal … means' (p. 345), the reference here to a minimal level of creativity, rather than to a minimal degree of creativity (understood as a requisite level and sufficient amount at that level of creativity) is consistent with the meaning of originality as including a minimal degree of creativity. '[S]ome minimal level of creativity' (p. 358) then corresponds to the level required for a minimal degree of creativity (and not to the combination of requisite level and sufficient amount). Level alone is cited, not level and amount in combination, or amount alone. Priority is then again given to level over amount.

The proportion of compilations which can be expected to be above the level required is next specified.

> some minimal level of creativity ... Presumably, the vast majority of compilations will pass this test, but not all will.
>
> (Feist Publications, Inc. v. Rural Tel. Service Co., Inc., 1991, pp. 358–359)

The particular passage, as quoted immediately above, also closely verbally parallels, while varying, the previous passage treating works. The passage can be recalled.

> at least some minimal degree of creativity ... To be sure ... [t]he vast majority of works make the grade quite easily
>
> (p. 345)

It can also be placed in a revealing parallel with the current passage. Some significant contrasts emerge.

- Compilations (p. 359) are specified rather than 'works' (p. 345), which included compilations.
- For compilations the immediate reference is to the required level, not directly to the proportion with the requisite level and sufficient amount for a minimal degree of creativity.
- 'Presumably' (p. 359) implies a similar, although possibly not quite as strong, degree of confidence to '[t]o be sure' (p. 346), but leaves open the basis for that confidence rather than implying a basis in accepted practices.
- '[V]ast majority' (p. 359) can be read continuously in meaning with the previous reference to the 'vast majority' (p. 346), with compilations also considered as separate entities.
- '[T]est' in 'will pass this test' implies that the level of creativity must be testable, although the qualification by '[p]resumably' (p. 358) leaves open how the level is to be rendered testable. In contrast, 'make the grade quite easily' (p. 345) implied a readily discernible interval with regard to level and amount and did not specify a test.
- The proportion of compilations below the required level – 'not all' (p. 359) – is explicitly specified rather than left implied, as it had been for works.

There is then a concern with compilations rather than works, with level rather than level and amount combined, a similarity in the degree of confidence, a difference in the basis for that confidence, an identity in the proportion stated, and a contrast in the requirement for testability compared to the implication of an extensive and readily discernible interval, and an explicit statement that some compilations will be excluded from copyrightability (see also Box 7.1).

Box 7.1 Comparison of corresponding passages

some minimal **degree** of creativity	**To be sure**	the [v]ast majority of	**works**	**make the grade**	**quite easily** (p. 345).
some minimal *level* of creativity	*Presumably,*	the vast majority of	*compilations*	*will pass this test,*	*but not all will* (pp. 358–359)

Note: Clauses are placed in parallel with corresponding clauses: equivalent clauses are given in ordinary black, the more inclusive or positive sense of parallel clauses in **bold** and the weaker or less inclusive sense in *italics*.

The nature of the population with regard to creativity is then specified for works ('works' (p. 359) and not just compilations) which will not pass the test for the requisite level.

> There remains a narrow category of works in which the creative spark is utterly lacking or so trivial as to be virtually nonexistent. See generally *Bleistein v. Donaldson Lithographing Co.*, 188 U.S. 239, 251 (1903) (referring to 'the narrowest and most obvious limits'). Such works are incapable of sustaining a valid copyright.
>
> (Feist Publications, Inc. v. Rural Tel. Service Co., Inc., 1991, p. 359)

'[R]emains' in '[t]here remains' (p. 359) indicates an immediate transition between the levels without a boundary which occupies a significant interval. A further category of works with levels of creativity below the level of creativity required for a minimal degree is distinguished (pp. 358–359). '[S]park' in 'the creative spark' (p. 359) can continue to be understood as a level and amount of creativity, although at a level below that required for a minimal degree of creativity. From the implications of the material basis of spark for level and amount works below the required level could have amount in an ordinary discourse sense.

In summary, then, compilations without original written expression can have a minimal degree of creativity through their selection and arrangement of data. The 'minimal level of creativity' (p. 359) distinguished for such compilations corresponds to the level required for a minimal degree. The decision further indicates the possible proportion, 'the vast majority' (p. 359), of compilations above that level, with a discernible systematic variation on the treatment of the proportion of all works with a minimal degree of creativity. Compilations and works which cannot give rise to copyrightability are primarily differentiated by level from works which can be copyrightable.

Ratio decidendi

Within the *ratio decidendi*, in addition to the focus on the antithesis to creativity, the 'creative spark … utterly lacking' (Feist Publications, Inc. v. Rural Tel. Service Co., Inc., 1991, pp. 362–363), there is a further, and complementary, concern with the requirement for a minimal degree of creativity and its absence from Rural's directory.

> This [Rural's] is 'selection' of a sort, but it lacks the modicum of creativity necessary to transform mere selection into copyrightable expression.
>
> (p. 362)

The direct linking to 'copyrightable' in 'copyrightable expression' (p. 362) indicates that 'the modicum of creativity' (p. 362) corresponds to the minimal degree of creativity required for copyrightability. The 'the' (p. 362) also implies a cross-reference, which can be read as a reference to, and thereby identity with, the earlier, 'a modicum of creativity' (p. 346). The current reference to 'the modicum of creativity' (p. 362) can, then, be assimilated to a minimal degree of creativity. Immediately prior to the conclusion of the *ratio decidendi*, alphabetical ordering is further characterized.

> this time honored tradition does not possess the minimal creative spark required by the Copyright Act and the Constitution.
>
> (p. 363)

'[T]he' (p. 363) implies a reference to the previous occurrence, to 'some creative spark' (p. 345). Meeting the requirements for a minimal degree of creativity is also indicated by the direct link to the requirements of the Copyright Act and the Constitution. '[T]he minimal creative spark' (p. 363) can then be understood as corresponding to the level required and amount sufficient for a minimal degree of creativity. Two references within the *ratio decidendi* therefore correspond to the required level and sufficient amount for a minimal degree of creativity. The contrast, in both instances, with the absence of a minimal degree of creativity from Rural's directory is consistent with the emphasis on the level required for a minimal degree.

Conclusion to the judgment

The conclusion to the judgment contains a further reference to a minimal degree of creativity.

> As a constitutional matter, copyright protects only those constituent elements of a work that possess more than a *de minimis* quantum of creativity. Rural's white pages, limited to basic subscriber information and arranged alphabetically, fall short of the mark.
>
> (Feist Publications, Inc. v. Rural Tel. Service Co., Inc., 1991, p. 363)

The connection of 'more than a *de minimis* quantum of creativity' to a 'constitutional matter' (Feist Publications, Inc. v. Rural Tel. Service Co., Inc., 1991, p. 363) indicates that it must correspond to at least the required level and sufficient amount for a minimal degree of creativity.

'[M]ore than' (p. 363) is understood in its ordinary discourse meaning, where it is applicable to differentiation by level and by amount (contrast, *fewer than*, normally only applicable to differentiation by amount). '*[D]e minimis*' (Feist Publications, Inc. v. Rural Tel. Service Co., Inc., 1991, p. 363) can be understood with its ordinary discourse meaning, as *of the least*, and with the more technical legal sense of something of insufficient significance for legal purposes, given a Supreme Court judgment as the context of discussion. '[Q]uantum' (p. 363) can be understood as an irreducible or indivisible unit.

The continuation of the judgment emphasizes differentiation by level of creativity.

> Rural's white pages, limited to basic subscriber information and arranged alphabetically, fall short of the mark.
>
> (Feist Publications, Inc. v. Rural Tel. Service Co., Inc., 1991, p. 363)

'Rural's white pages' (p. 363), understood as 'devoid of even the slightest trace of creativity' (p. 362), are below the level required for a minimal degree of creativity. '[F]all short of the mark' (p. 363) then applies to differentiation by level and implies that the level of creativity required for a minimal degree can legitimately be envisaged as indicated by a mark on a vertically arranged surface. '[Q]uantum' (p. 363) is understood as an irreducible unit, between the level required for a minimal degree and a zero level of creativity. Within the judgment, the range of creativity corresponding to that unit is characterized in ordinary discourse terms, as the 'creative spark … so trivial as to be virtually nonexistent' (p. 359). The ordinary discourse sense of *de minimis*, which could include its legal sense, is then applicable. '[A] *de minimis* quantum of creativity' (p. 363) can then be understood as at an irreducible unit of creativity at a level below the level of creativity required for a minimal degree of creativity.

Differentiation by amount, as well as by level, is also implied by the correspondence of 'more than a *de minimis* quantum' (Feist Publications, Inc. v. Rural Tel. Service Co., Inc., 1991, p. 363) to a minimal degree of creativity, understood as a sufficient amount at or above the requisite level. A '*de minimis* quantum' (p. 363) would then be understood conversely as an indivisible amount of creativity, at the level required for a minimal degree, although not of sufficient amount. Such amounts of creativity are not characterized elsewhere in the judgment. They are then not immediately evidenced in ordinary discourse, taking for these purposes, the judgment as a significant instance of such discourse. Further, from an ordinary discourse perspective, such amounts of creativity, understood for instance in terms of duration, could be further subdivided, weakening the ordinary discourse applicability of a *de minimis* quantum. The legal sense of *de minimis* must, then, be primarily understood here.

The legal and ordinary discourse senses of 'a *de minimis* quantum' (p. 363) were fully applicable to discrimination by level. In contrast, for amount, the legal sense held but the ordinary discourse application had to be qualified. The combination of full technical and ordinary discourse senses can be considered stronger than the legal sense with some reservation on the ordinary discourse application. '[M]ore than a *de minimis* quantum of creativity' (p. 363) then primarily contrasts by level with 'a *de minimis* quantum' (p. 363), with a supplementary contrast by amount.

In summary, then, 'more than a *de minimis* quantum of creativity' (Feist Publications, Inc. v. Rural Tel. Service Co., Inc., 1991, p. 363) can then be understood as a legally significant amount of creativity at more than an irreducible unit of level. The differentiation of 'more than a *de minimis* quantum' (p. 363) from a '*de minimis* quantum' (p. 363) can be graphically represented (see Figure 7.2). An analytically useful conception of amount as extended along a horizontal axis is added to the judgment's implication of levels vertically arranged.

Review and synthesis

A minimal degree of creativity is progressively developed, from the requirement for it, its explication, its historical basis, through its application to compilations, to the application of established distinctions to the particular compilation under consideration in the *ratio decidendi*, with a further concluding passage. The

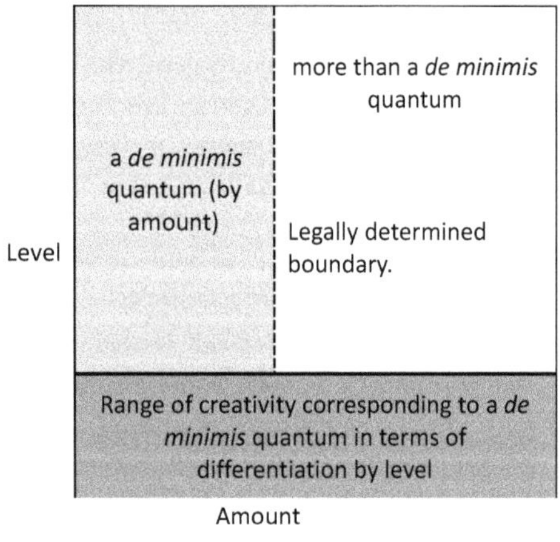

Figure 7.2 'more than a *de minimis* quantum' and '*de minimis* quantum' of creativity

development of the scope of a minimal degree of creativity is both restricted and cumulative: restricted in that further characterizations do not exceed the initial explication specifying the separation of level and amount or disturb the priority given to level; cumulative in that the characterizations develop specific characteristics of level and amount. The *ratio decidendi* draws on all the previously established distinctions, corresponding to classical requirement or expectation for this part of the judgment. The conclusion to the judgment is summative and integrating with regard to level and amount. In terms of rhetorical structure, then, there is a well-established pattern of introduction and progressive development, familiar from ordinary discourse and extra-legal texts, but also a degree of complexity of interaction, which may be less often encountered outside the text of Supreme Court opinions, together with conformity to the standard structure for a judgment. The rhetorical progression detected supports the validity of analysis.

Level and amount of creativity

A minimal degree of creativity is constituted by a 'requisite' (Feist Publications, Inc. v. Rural Tel. Service Co., Inc., 1991, p. 345) and 'extremely low' (p. 345) level and a sufficient and 'slight' (p. 345) amount at that level. The 'vast majority' (pp. 345, 359) of works and of compilations will have a minimal degree of creativity. '[T]he vast majority' (pp. 345, 359) is the only indication of proportion of works and compilations with a minimal degree of creativity. The level of creativity required for a minimal degree must be testable. A conception of levels as vertically arranged is warranted by the decision. The priority given to level at the initial introduction of a minimal degree of creativity is then matched by its development prior to amount in the opinion considered as a sequence, and by the relative emphasis given to it.

The requisite level and sufficient amount for a minimal degree of creativity are both specified and implied within its development and these can be isolated and reviewed. We can begin with the explicit specification of level, in accord with the priority accorded to it by the decision

Level

The level of creativity required for a minimal degree of creativity is explicitly designated. The requisite level need only be 'extremely low' (Feist Publications, Inc. v. Rural Tel. Service Co., Inc., 1991, p. 345), immediately more than the level 'so trivial as to be virtually nonexistent' (p. 358), and 'more than a *de minimis* quantum of creativity' (p. 363), with 'a *de minimis* quantum' understood as an indivisible unit immediately above the level of creativity 'utterly lacking' (p. 359). '[M]ore than' (p. 363) must be understood as indicating a Euclidean line, without significant breadth, separating the level required for a minimal degree of creativity from a *de minimis* quantum of creativity, to bring the meaning of 'more than' (p. 363) into accord with the implication an immediate transition by, '[t]here remains a narrow category of works in which the creative spark is ... so trivial as to be virtually nonexistent' (p. 359).

The requisite level of creativity is also deducible from correlations within the decision. References which could be assimilated to a minimal degree of creativity are connected, in the discussion of the historical basis for the requirement for a minimal degree, with terms potentially indicative of levels of creativity, in positively endorsed passages from previous judgments and commentaries. '[A] modicum of creativity' (Feist Publications, Inc. v. Rural Tel. Service Co., Inc., 1991, p. 346), which was assimilatable to a minimal degree of creativity, is connected with further terms.

> The Court explained that … 'only such [writings] as are *original*, and are founded in the creative powers of the mind … are to be protected are *the fruits of intellectual labor* (emphasis in original).'
>
> (Feist Publications, Inc. v. Rural Tel. Service Co., Inc., 1991, p. 346) [citation omitted]

Intellectual is the only term in the quotation with an immediate potential application to levels of creativity. '[T]he creative component of originality' (p. 346), similarly assimilatable to a minimal degree of creativity, is also correlated with further terms.

> the Court emphasized the creative component of originality. It described copyright as being limited to 'original intellectual conceptions of the author,' and stressed the importance of requiring an author who accuses another of infringement to prove 'the existence of those facts of originality, of intellectual production, of thought, and conception.'
>
> (Feist Publications, Inc. v. Rural Tel. Service Co., Inc., 1991, pp. 346–347) [citations omitted]

'[I]ntellectual conceptions … intellectual production … thought, and conception' (pp. 346–347) all correspond to 'the creative component' (p. 346). *Intellectual* is the only term which can be readily assimilated to a level of creativity. A quotation from a commentary, endorsed as produced by a '[l]eading scholar' (p. 347), also connects originality with 'intellectual'.

> 'originality is … a constitutional requirement' … 'a modicum of intellectual labor … clearly constitutes an essential constitutional element'
>
> (p. 347) [citations omitted]

Originality must be understood in its sense for copyright as requiring that the work has at least a minimal degree of creativity. '[I]ntellectual labor' (p. 347) must then correspond to a minimal degree of creativity, with *intellectual* again as the term which could be correlated with a level of creativity. Within the *ratio decidendi*, an earlier passage is reiterated in part, directly in connection with 'some minimal degree of creativity' (p. 362).

> As this Court has explained, the Constitution mandates some minimal degree of creativity ... and an author who claims infringement must prove the existence of ... intellectual production, of thought, and conception.
>
> (p. 362) [citations omitted]

The reiteration includes 'intellectual' as part of 'intellectual production' (p. 362) and *intellectual* can continue to be applied to a level of creativity. Intellectual occurs in nineteenth-century cases, within the opinion.

Intellectual, then, emerges as the only term which can be correlated with a level of creativity, from an exhaustive survey of all the references assimilatable to a minimal degree of creativity, in the decision. The term *intellectual* does not occur in connection with creativity below the level required for originality (or elsewhere in the opinion) and it thereby distinctively and uniquely characterizes the level required for a minimal degree of creativity. Intellectual must, then, be understood as corresponding to the level of creativity required for a minimal degree of creativity. Intellectual can be understood in its ordinary discourse sense, in the absence of contrary indications.

The relation between the explicit designation of level and the correlation established can be considered. The designation of the requisite level for a minimal degree of creativity is explicit and made directly in connection with a minimal degree of creativity, while the connection with intellectual is implied, occurs primarily in connection with references assimilatable to a minimal degree of creativity, and had to be deduced by a careful correlation. The explicit would normally have priority over the implicit and the explicit designation must be received as authoritative. The terms of the designation, 'extremely low' (Feist Publications, Inc. v. Rural Tel. Service Co., Inc., 1991, pp. 345), immediately more than 'so trivial as to be virtually nonexistent' (p. 358) and more than 'a *de minimis* quantum of creativity' (p. 363), can semantically absorb *intellectual*. The designation must then be received as authoritative and as capable of absorbing the inherited and previously articulated intellectual level.

The level of creativity required for a minimal degree of creativity has then been established, but the issue of how to determine this level remains. For levels of creativity below that required for minimal degree, warrant is given by the decision for reading the absence, and, by implication, the presence, of creativity from the end product. For the higher level of creativity required for a minimal degree, it could similarly be read from the product, or, if necessary established by enquiry into its circumstances of production and the processes which went into making the end product. The level of creativity distinguished then meets the condition indicated in the decision of being testable.

The level of creativity required for a minimal degree of creativity can be connected to the understanding of creativity previously established. The absence of routinicity from both the process and the product for the fully creative admits an intellectual level for both the highest placed and the interleaved combination for creativity (Table 7.1, first row). The fully creative would then correspond to the level required for a minimal degree of creativity. For the creative (Table 7.1, second to fourth rows), the level of creativity is increasingly unlikely (reading downwards from the second to the fourth row) to be intellectual if the routinicity in the product implies routinicity in the process. The creative, then, is below the required level. The routinicity designated in the process and revealed in the product for the slightest trace of creativity (Table 7.1, fifth row) renders it *a priori* unlikely to be intellectual in level. It is then necessarily below the required level for a minimal degree of creativity. Both the creative and the slightest trace of creativity correspond to a *de minimis* quantum of creativity, in its primary sense by level. Only the fully creative can then correspond to the level required for a minimal degree of creativity.

The level of creativity differentiated is also consistent with the 'vast majority of compilations' (p. 359) attaining this level. The vast majority was understood as referring to compilations conceived as separate works. *Google*, on this understanding, could be considered as a single or as a relatively small number of compilations, despite its size, scope, significance, and current dominance in searching

Works with the level of creativity required for a minimal degree require a sufficient amount of creativity, to be copyrightable. We can then move on to a consideration of amount of creativity, at or above the requisite level.

Amount

The amount of creativity at the requisite level which is sufficient for a minimal degree of creativity is also explicitly specified. A 'slight' (Feist Publications, Inc. v. Rural Tel. Service Co., Inc., 1991, p. 345) amount or 'more than a *de minimis* quantum' (p. 363) of creativity, with *de minimis* understandable in a specialized legal sense, is sufficient. '[S]light' (p. 345) and 'more than a *de minimis* quantum' (p. 363) are the only references to *amounts* of creativity at the requisite level and must then be received as exhaustive. For determining a sufficient amount of creativity at or above the required level, we are concerned with amount in combination with the level required for a minimal degree of creativity.

Level and amount

The combination of at least the level required and the amount of creativity sufficient for a minimal degree is explicitly indicated in the opinion, first directly and ostensively.

> if the compilation author clothes facts with an original collocation of words, he or she may be able to claim a copyright in this written expression. Others may copy the underlying facts from the publication, but not the precise words used to present them. In Harper & Row, for example, we explained that President Ford could not prevent others from copying bare historical facts from his autobiography, but that he could prevent others from copying his 'subjective descriptions and portraits of public figures.'
>
> (Feist Publications, Inc. v. Rural Tel. Service Co., Inc., 1991, p. 348)

Table 7.1 Creativity and a minimal degree of creativity

Process			*Product*			*Process and product*	*Creative or not-creative*	*A minimal degree of creativity*		*A minimal degree of creativity*	*Originality*
automatic mechanical procedure	so … routine	**automatic mechanical procedure v so … routine**	entirely typical	garden-variety	**entirely typical … garden-variety**	(automatic mechanical procedure v so … routine) ^ (entirely typical v garden-variety)		Requisite level of creativity	Sufficient amount of creativity		Original
FALSE	FALSE	**FALSE**	FALSE	FALSE	**FALSE**	FALSE	Fully creative	Yes	Potentially	Potentially	Potentially
FALSE	FALSE	**FALSE**	FALSE	TRUE	**TRUE**	FALSE	Creative	No	No	A *de minimis* quantum	Not original
FALSE	FALSE	**FALSE**	TRUE	FALSE	**TRUE**	FALSE	Creative				
FALSE	FALSE	**FALSE**	TRUE	TRUE	**TRUE**	FALSE	Creative				
FALSE	TRUE	**TRUE**	FALSE	FALSE	**FALSE**	FALSE	Slightest trace of creativity				
FALSE	TRUE	**TRUE**	FALSE	TRUE	**TRUE**	TRUE	not-creative	not-creative	not-creative	not-creative	
FALSE	TRUE	**TRUE**	TRUE	FALSE	**TRUE**	TRUE	not-creative	not-creative	not-creative	not-creative	
FALSE	TRUE	**TRUE**	TRUE	TRUE	**TRUE**	TRUE	not-creative	not-creative	not-creative	not-creative	
TRUE	FALSE	**TRUE**	FALSE	FALSE	**FALSE**	FALSE	Fully creative	Potentially	Potentially	Potentially	Potentially

(*Continued*)

Table 7.1 (Cont.)

Process			*Product*			*Process and product*	*Creative or not-creative*	*A minimal degree of creativity*		*A minimal degree of creativity*	*Originality*
TRUE	FALSE	**TRUE**	FALSE	TRUE	**TRUE**	TRUE	not-creative	not-creative	not-creative	not-creative	Not original
TRUE	FALSE	**TRUE**	TRUE	FALSE	**TRUE**	TRUE	not-creative	not-creative	not-creative	not-creative	
TRUE	FALSE	**TRUE**	TRUE	TRUE	**TRUE**	TRUE	not-creative	not-creative	not-creative	not-creative	
TRUE	TRUE	**TRUE**	FALSE	FALSE	**FALSE**	FALSE	Creative	Not	not-creative	not-creative	
TRUE	TRUE	**TRUE**	FALSE	TRUE	**TRUE**	TRUE	not-creative	not-creative	not-creative	not-creative	
TRUE	TRUE	**TRUE**	TRUE	FALSE	**TRUE**	TRUE	not-creative	not-creative	not-creative	not-creative	
TRUE	TRUE	**TRUE**	TRUE	TRUE	**TRUE**	TRUE	not-creative	not-creative	not-creative	not-creative	

The precise words, understood to be a product of President Ford's creative activity at an intellectual level, correspond to the combination of the level required and the amount of creativity sufficient for a minimal degree of creativity. The formulations, 'an original collocation of words', and, more intensely, 'the precise words' (p. 348), imply a definite order of words. The number of precise words then corresponds to a sufficient amount of creativity at the requisite level. Short (fewer than 10, for instance) sequences are known to be likely to be distinctive, even in very large corpora, from experience of using large collections of text searchable by phrase searching. The distinctiveness of such sequences is also theoretically explicable, from the understanding of the word as 'a cohesive group of letters with strong internal statistical influences' (Shannon, 1951/1993, pp. 197–198). A sequence of words would then be a linear concatenation of internally cohesive units, without the internal statistical influences between units. A sufficient amount of creativity, for compilations and other works with added written expression, can then definitively be read directly from the product, from a sufficient number of consecutive words.

The decision then indicates how this minimal degree of creativity is to be embodied in the process of creating compilations, without 'an original collocation of words' (Feist Publications, Inc. v. Rural Tel. Service Co., Inc., 1991, p. 349).

> Where the compilation author adds no written expression but rather lets the facts speak for themselves, the expressive element is more elusive. The only conceivable expression is the manner in which the compiler has selected and arranged the facts.
>
> (Feist Publications, Inc. v. Rural Tel. Service Co., Inc., 1991, p. 349)

The amount of creativity for compilations without additional written expression cannot be directly read from the number of consecutive words.

The equivalence to the minimal degree of creativity in the precise words can be discerned from an exchange value perspective. Amounts of creativity at the required, level can be understood as equivalent, when they can be fairly exchanged for each other, drawing on a deep sense of exchange value. The amount of creativity embodied in the precise words can be understood to be represented by the exchange, or monetary, values connected with them, from a related and surface, although not superficial, sense of exchange value. An equivalent amount of creativity embodied in compilations without additional written expression can then be understood to be similarly represented by exchange or monetary values closely comparable to those connected with the precise words. Such an understanding of amount is also consistent with a minimal degree of creativity as 'more than a *de minimis* quantum of creativity' (Feist Publications, Inc. v. Rural Tel. Service Co., Inc., 1991, p. 363). Quantum is still understood as an irreducible unit, continuous with its previous interpretation, but with reference to amount rather than to level, and *de minimis* can be restricted to its specialized sense, of below legal significance. The amount of creativity required, for both compilations with and without additional written expression, can then be understood to be indicated by more than a *de minimis* quantum of exchange values connected with the product and arising from creative activity at or above the required level.

Synthesis of level and amount

We have then obtained a full understanding of a minimal degree of creativity, first as constituted by a requisite level and sufficient amount of creativity at that level. The requisite level is 'extremely low' (Feist Publications, Inc. v. Rural Tel. Service Co., Inc., 1991, p. 345), more than 'so trivial as to be virtually nonexistent' (p. 359) and more than 'a *de minimis* quantum of creativity' (p. 363), and can absorb *intellectual* as a level. The sufficient amount of creativity at or above that level is 'slight' (p. 345) and 'more than a *de minimis* quantum' (p. 363). Robust and systematic means of determining the requisite level and sufficient amount have also been developed. The requisite level can be read from the product or by an enquiry into its processes of production. The combination of the requisite level and sufficient amount of creativity at that level, which constitutes a minimal degree of creativity, can then be read from the exchange values connected with the product.

The conditions for a minimal degree of creativity derived from the decision can be recalled. It was required to have a level and for that level to be knowable, from its specification as part of a test for originality. Creativity at the required level must also give rise to an amount significant for copyrightability and amount should be discernible. The identification of the level required as intellectual, and as readable from the product or by an enquiry into its conditions of production, fulfills the requirement for a testable, or sufficiently knowable to be testable, level. The possibility of determining the sufficiency of amount, from the exchange values connected with the combination of level and amount in the end product, renders amount discernible. A minimal degree of creativity, as realized in compilations, is then itself discernible. The understanding of a minimal degree of creativity then meets all the conditions derived from the decision and is thereby sufficient.

Integration of creativity

A minimal degree of creativity and the 'creative spark … so trivial as to be virtually nonexistent' (Feist Publications, Inc. v. Rural Tel. Service Co., Inc., 1991, p. 359) both include creativity, previously understood as human activity directly motivated by meaning above a certain level of routinicity. The levels of creativity required for a minimal degree of creativity and involved in the 'creative spark … so trivial as to be virtually nonexistent' (Feist Publications, Inc. v. Rural Tel. Service Co., Inc., 1991, p. 345) can all correspond to direct human motivation by meaning. Both a minimal degree of creativity and the 'creative spark … so trivial as to be virtually nonexistent' (p. 345) can have amount consistent with creativity understood as consisting of human activity, for instance as composed of human activity of a certain duration and intensity although at different levels.

The relation of the two interleaved combinations for creativity to the overall argument can be clarified (see Table 7.1). The first, understood as not mechanical activity in the construction of a significant and not so … routine automatic mechanical procedure admits an intellectual and specialized level and a sufficiency of amount of creativity, in addition to the common activity on meaning already identified. The level and amount of creativity can also be indicated by its exchange value. The analogy with the highest placed combination for creativity is then confirmed. The second, with a 'so mechanical or routine' (Feist Publications, Inc. v. Rural Tel. Service Co., Inc., 1991, p. 362), process necessarily falls below an intellectual level and can be definitively excluded from a minimal degree of creativity. The discounting of the combination, previously and provisionally made for creativity, is then rendered unnecessary and can be replaced by a definitive placing out of relevant scope in relation to a minimal degree of creativity. The possible disturbance to the argument has not then been realized and the integrity of the analysis has been sustained. The fully creative is confirmed as potentially corresponding to a minimal degree of creativity, for all the combinations.

The understandings obtained of a minimal degree of creativity and of the 'creative spark … so trivial as to be virtually nonexistent' (Feist Publications, Inc. v. Rural Tel. Service Co., Inc., 1991, p. 359) have then been integrated with the understanding of creativity previously established.

Relation to the European Union and other jurisdictions

The minimal degree of creativity required by *Feist* (1991) is also broadly potentially commensurate with European Union and global requirements for copyrightability (Gervais, 2002; Gupta, 2017). Intellectual as the level required for a minimal degree of creativity correlates with intellectual in the intellectual labor needed for copyrightability. Labor, and its significance, still need to be explained.

The potential commensurability reinforces the global applicability of the interpretation developed here of *Feist* (Feist Publications, Inc. v. Rural Tel. Service Co., Inc., 1991).

Narrative motif

In terms of the narrative motifs adopted, we have abandoned Ariadne, or the art of shore-based navigation through circuitous islands, and adopted Phaedra, or the sister art of ocean navigation (Vico, 1744/1976, §635), to understand a minimal degree of creativity and to move towards home. In the trans-oceanic journey, guided by Phaedra, we have moved more straightly and in less winding ways.

Conclusion

The substantive significance of *minimal degree* in 'a minimal degree of creativity' (Feist, 1991) was implied by the inclusion of creativity in the 'creative spark … so trivial as to be virtually nonexistent' (Feist, 1991), which does not give rise to copyright. The nature of that significance has now been fully revealed. The level of creativity required has been established, with an implementable test for that level. The combination of required level and sufficient amount is then determinable from the exchange values connected with the product.

The analysis has had certain qualities to commend it. All references to a minimal degree of creativity in the decision have been encompassed, indicating comprehensiveness in relation to the decision. The exhaustive identification of references to a minimal degree of creativity and to the creative spark below the level of creativity required for originality, demonstrated to contain the totality of consideration of creativity in the direct text of the decision, is indicative of comprehensiveness. Comprehensiveness indicates that the relevant substantive elements of the decision have been fully captured. References to the creative spark below the level for originality were then fully distributed between creativity 'utterly lacking' and 'so trivial as to be virtually nonexistent' (Feist Publications, Inc. v. Rural Tel. Service Co., Inc., 1991, p. 359), demonstrating a full depth of analysis. A minimal degree of creativity has been continuously differentiated along a single dimension of routinicity, from lower levels of creativity, revealing economy in the explanatory framework. The understandings of both a minimal degree of creativity and of 'the creative spark … so trivial as to be virtually nonexistent' (p. 359) can absorb the previously established conception of creativity. The understanding of creativity was further validated by integrating creativity, understood as human activity on meaning above a certain level of routinicity, primarily into a minimal degree of creativity but also into the creative spark 'so trivial as to be virtually nonexistent' (Feist Publications, Inc. v. Rural Tel. Service Co., Inc., 1991, p. 359), with a minimal degree of creativity and independent creation integrated into originality. Comprehensiveness, economy, and extensive self-consistency are indicative of a strong argument. We can therefore regard the understanding of a minimal degree of creativity as constituted by a required, extremely low level and sufficient, slight amount of human activity directly motivated by meaning, as both significant and very fully established.

Our progress can be marked along a map (see Figure 7.3) and a logical summary of the argument given.

A minimal degree of creativity: chapter summary

A minimal degree of creativity is required for originality and for copyright, under the Constitution. A minimal degree of creativity includes creativity or

> A minimal degree of creativity → creativity

A minimal degree of creativity was distinguished from the 'creative spark … utterly lacking or so trivial as to be virtually nonexistent' (p. 358), or

> A minimal degree of creativity ↔ ~ (creative spark … utterly lacking or so trivial as to be virtually nonexistent)

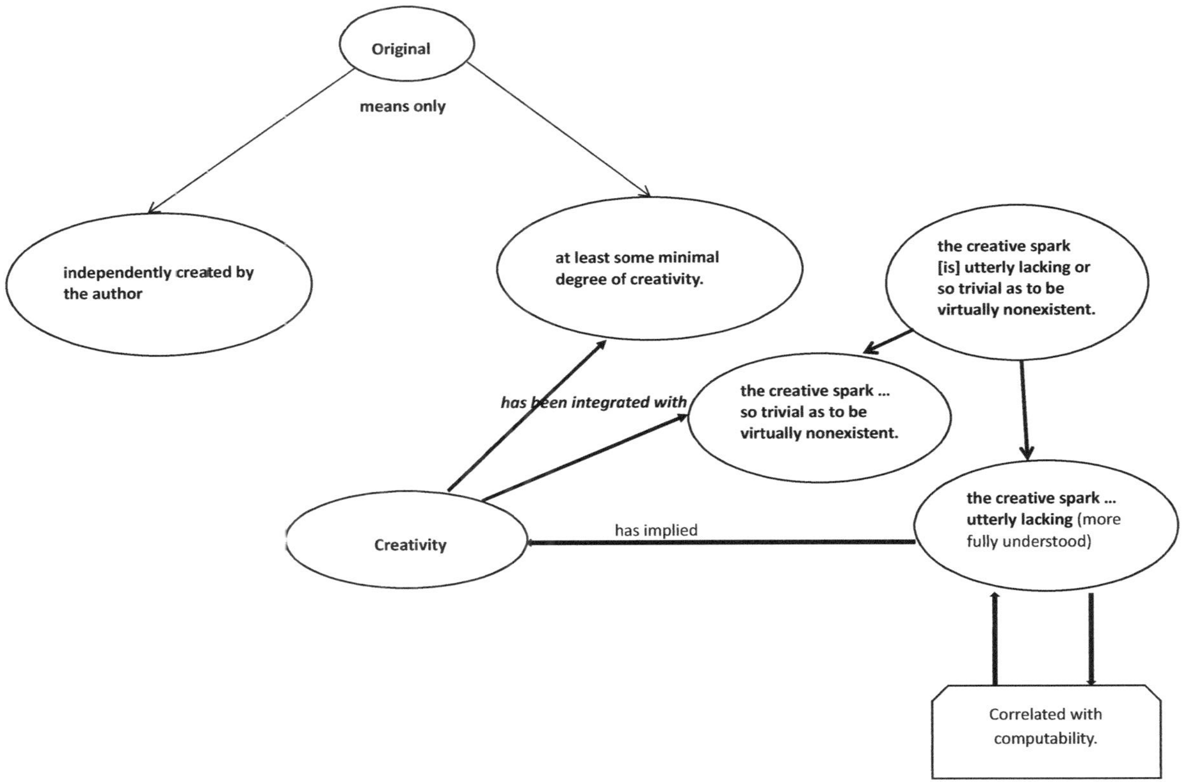

Figure 7.3 Progress made
Note. **Bold** is used for terms and phrases directly derived from the decision

The creative spark so trivial as to be virtually nonexistent, which cannot give rise to copyright also includes creativity

> creative spark so trivial as to be virtually nonexistent → creativity

Creativity is then part of a minimal degree of creativity, which can give rise to copyright, and of the creative spark so trivial as to be virtually nonexistent, which cannot give rise to copyright. The inclusion of creativity in a minimal degree of creativity and in the creative spark so trivial as to be virtually nonexistent can be combined in a single logical statement.

> (A minimal degree of creativity ∨ creative spark so trivial as to be virtually nonexistent creativity) → creativity

Crucially, creativity itself will not necessarily give rise to copyright and will not by itself distinguish the works which can give rise to copyright from those which cannot. The phrase, *minimal degree*, in a minimal degree of creativity must then be substantively significant. We must establish its particular substantive significance.

Degree in a minimal degree of creativity immediately disaggregates into a level of creativity and an amount at that level. The required level is 'extremely low' (Feist Publications, Inc. v. Rural Tel. Service Co., Inc., 1991, p. 345) and a sufficient amount at that level is 'slight' (p. 345), with 'extremely low' (p. 345) and 'slight' (p. 345) corresponding to *minimal.* Subsequent references which can assimilated to a minimal degree of creativity can be identified by their direct connection to originality or to the constitutional requirement for a minimal degree of creativity. They reiterate the requirement for certain level of creativity and a sufficient, although slight, amount at that level. Level is consistently given priority over amount.

The subsequent references also further specify the required level and sufficient amount. The combination of required level and sufficient amount at that level is finally explicitly specified as 'more than a *de minimis* quantum of creativity' (p. 363). *De minimis*, with regard to level, can be understood in a dual and strong sense as including both the legal and the ordinary discourse sense of *de minimis.* '[M]ore than a *de minimis* quantum' (p. 363), as the required level of creativity, can then be understood as more than a certain level of routinicity. The required level of creativity is also consistently and exclusively correlated with *intellectual* in quotations endorsed within the decision. We can then understand the level of creativity required to be explicitly specified as immediately more than a certain level of routinicity, with that level also corresponding to the historically established intellectual level. *De minimis*, with regard to amount at the required level, can be understood only in a legal, rather than ordinary discourse, sense, and does not then give rise to as strongly marked a boundary. It must continue to be understood as a 'slight' (p. 345) amount. A minimal degree of creativity can then be finally understood as more than a certain level of creativity, corresponding to an intellectual level, and more than a slight amount of creativity at that level.

The existence of such a minimal degree of creativity can be progressively determined.

- First, the required level can be read from the product, or, if necessary, by an enquiry into the circumstances of production.
- Second, the sufficient amount at that level can then be determined from the exchange values connected with the product.

We have therefore established an understanding of a minimal degree of creativity, which meets the conditions established for it, that it should consist of level and an amount at that level and that it should be knowable.

The creative spark so trivial as to be virtually nonexistent is differentiated from a minimal degree of creativity. It is further characterized as 'a *de minimis* quantum of creativity' (p. 363). As such, it can be understood to include levels of creativity below the required level. Such levels of creativity cannot give raise to copyright, whatever their amount. It must also be understood to include creativity at or above the required but of insufficient amount.

We have therefore substantiated the logical statement earlier.

A minimal degree of creativity ↔ ~ (creative spark … utterly lacking or so trivial as to be virtually nonexistent)

We now have a full understanding of the difference of a minimal degree of creativity from the creative spark so trivial as to be virtually nonexistent and the creative spark utterly lacking.

The understanding of creativity as direct human engagement with meaning, above a certain level of routinicity, could be integrated with the understandings established of both a minimal degree of creativity and the creative spark so trivial as to be virtually nonexistent.

(A minimal degree of creativity ∨ creative spark so trivial as to be virtually nonexistent creativity) → creativity

Similarly, we now have sufficiently full understanding of all the constituent terms.

References

Burrow-Giles Lithographic Co. v. Sarony, 111 U.S. 53 (1884) 111 U.S. 53.

Coleridge, S.T. (1835). *Specimens of the table talk of the late Samuel Taylor Coleridge.* Edited by H.N. Coleridge. London: John Murray.

Feist (1991). Feist Publications, Inc. v. Rural Tel. Service Co., Inc. 499 U.S. 340 (1991).

Feist Publications, Inc. v. Rural Tel. Service Co., Inc. (1991). Feist Publications, Inc. v. Rural Tel. Service Co., Inc. 499 U.S. 340 (1991).

Gervais, D.J. (2002). Feist goes global: A comparative analysis of the notion of originality in copyright law. *Journal of the Copyright Society of the U.S.A.* 49, 949–981.

Gupta, I. (2017). *Footprints of Feist in European Database Directive: A legal analysis of IP law-making in Europe*. Singapore: Springer.

Plato (400 BC/1973). Phaedrus. In *Phaedrus and the seventh and eighth letters*. Translated and introduced by W. Hamilton. Harmondsworth: Penguin.

Shannon, C.E. (1951/1993). Prediction and entropy of printed English. In C.E. Shannon. *Collected papers* (pp. 194–208). Edited by N.J.A. Sloane and A.D. Wyner. Piscataway, NJ: IEEE Press.

Shelley, M. (1818/1998). *Frankenstein or the modern Prometheus*. Oxford and New York: Oxford University Press.

Trade-Mark (1879). Trade-Mark Cases. 100 U.S. 82 (1879).

Vico, G. (1744/1976). *The new science of Giambattista Vico*. Unabridged translation of the Third Edition (1744) with the addition of 'Practic of the New Science' by T. G. Bergin and M. H. Fisch. Ithaca, NY and London: Cornell University Press.

8 Originality

Odysseus

Introduction

Originality is the direct requirement for copyrightability. It is simultaneously everything, in that it includes all the subordinate requirements for copyrightability, the summation of all its antecedents, and nothing in itself, in that it has no further qualities. Explicitly it is designated as meaning only that work is 'independently created ... and ... possesses a minimal degree of creativity' (Feist Publications, Inc. v. Rural Tel. Service Co., Inc., 1991, p. 345), is nothing in itself beyond these constituents. It has been rigorously understood in this way in the work to date and this understanding will continue. By implication, originality includes all antecedent activities, is everything in this sense.

The subtitle of the chapter refers to Odysseus, who is simultaneously everyman and, in the episode of Cyclops, adopts the name of Nobody. Analogously to originality, Odysseus is both no man and everyman. Explicitly, he adopts the name of Nobody and evades the one-eyed giant, Polyphemus, through cunning, knowledge, and insight, and strategy to evade a destructive and primitive giant, who is endowed with force without collective law. Implicitly, he is everyman – son, husband, father, warrior, and lover.

This chapter is concerned with originality, in its explicit aspect, as the direct requirement for originality, and implied aspect, as the summation of all antecedents. We confirm the requirement for and meaning of originality and also develop and substantiate the relation between the independent creation and minimal degree of creativity which constitute originality. We then address the implied summation of antecedent activities in the not original and the original – data collection and the selection, coordination, and arrangement of data. As part of the investigation of the implied summation of antecedents, we clarify the relation of the activities giving rise to copyright to those acknowledged in previous understandings of copyright, restoring the incentive function of copyright, and its broad consonance with natural justice. It also considers the practical implications of the understanding of a minimal degree of creativity for copyright in databases, its relation to natural justice, and to global standards for copyrightability.

We approach the topics of the chapter progressively. First, we address the explicit treatment of originality, both the requirement for it and its meaning, and the relation of independent creation to a minimal degree of creativity. Second, we demonstrate the implied summation of antecedent activities in the not original and the original, the significant similarities between those antecedents, and the implications of this for the relation to pre-existing conceptions of copyright.

The chapter, then, establishes a rigorous understanding of originality, which incorporates a minimal degree of creativity. It also brings the two constituents of originality, a minimal degree of creativity and independent creation, into a closer and better understood relation with each other. In addition, it correlates creativity with labor.

Originality requirement and meaning

Requirement

Originality is introduced as 'the *sine qua non* [without which nothing] of copyright' (Feist Publications, Inc. v. Rural Tel. Service Co., Inc., 1991, p. 345). In subsequent passages in the judgment, the embodiment of the *sine qua non* requirement for originality in the Constitution is noted – 'Originality is a constitutional requirement' (Feist Publications, Inc. v. Rural Tel. Service Co., Inc., 1991, p. 346). The constitutional requirement for originality was articulated in two late nineteenth-century decisions. The requirement for originality articulated in those decisions 'remains the touchstone of copyright protection today' … the 'very premise of copyright law' … 'constitutionally mandated' [and] 'a statutory as well as a constitutional requirement' (p. 347). Originality, as the 'constitutionally mandated prerequisite for copyright protection' (p. 350) was embodied in statute, in the 1909 Act, and, with greater clarity in the 1976 Act. Passages following the introduction of originality then reiterate the requirement for originality. There is a cumulative development, from *sine qua non*, to the Constitution and the judicial articulation of the Constitution, and then to statute, first the 1909 Act and then the 1976 Act. The requirement for originality is, then, asserted in the judgment in relation to ordinary understandings, the Constitution, and statute.

Meaning

The meaning of originality for copyright is given, immediately after the introduction of the requirement for originality.

> Original, as the term is used in copyright, means only that the work was independently created by the author (as opposed to copied from other works), and that it possesses at least some minimal degree of creativity.
>
> (Feist Publications, Inc. v. Rural Tel. Service Co., Inc., 1991, p. 345)

The meaning of originality, as distinguished from the requirement for originality, is only given once in the decision. Originality means only that the work has a minimal degree of creativity and that it is independently created (that is, not copied).

A closely subsequent passage indicates that originality, in the meaning established, 'does not signify novelty' (p. 345). '[S]ignify' (p. 345) can be understood as concerned with the implications of the meaning indicated and 'not' (p. 345) as indicating a negative implication, removing a potential confusion. The passage can then be understood as not significantly adding to, or subtracting from, the meaning of originality for copyright, although clarifying it

A further reference to '[o]riginality requires' (Feist Publications, Inc. v. Rural Tel. Service Co., Inc., 1991, p. 358) can be revealed to be consistent with the meaning of originality.

> Originality requires only that the author make the selection or arrangement independently ... and that it display some minimal level of creativity.
>
> (pp. 358–359)

Making the selection and arrangement independently corresponds to independent creation and 'some minimal *level* of creativity' (pp. 358–359) [emphasis added] would be part of the minimal *degree* of creativity, composed of level and amount, included in the meaning of originality. '[R]equires' (p. 358) can then be read as semantically included in 'means' (p. 345), consistent with the relation between means and requires in their ordinary discourse senses.

The meaning of originality is not, then, further developed, by subsequent references. The subsequent treatment of originality in the judgment is concerned with the application of originality requirement to compilations.

In summary, then, the treatment of originality in the judgment is concerned with the requirement for it and its meaning. The requirement is cumulatively developed and this renders it unambiguous and firmly rooted. The meaning of originality for copyright is given only once and is not subsequently modified. The initial statement of the meaning of originality is thereby confirmed as unique and authoritative. The understanding of originality used in the work here has been kept in rigorous accord with the meaning of originality for copyright, as constituted solely by a minimal degree of creativity and independent creation.

On the basis of a full confirmation of the requirement for and meaning of originality, we can now move to a consideration of its yet unexamined constituent, independent creation, and its relation to the other constituent of originality, to a minimal degree of creativity.

Independent creation and a minimal degree of creativity

Independent creation is parenthetically explicated at its introduction – 'independently created by the author (as opposed to copied from other works)' (Feist Publications, Inc. v. Rural Tel. Service Co., Inc., 1991, p. 345). The initial explication of independent creation is subsequently extended to apply specifically to the selection and arrangement involved in compilations: 'Originality requires only that the author make the selection or arrangement independently (i.e., without copying that selection or arrangement from another work)' (p. 346). The understanding of independent creation as not copied is thereby confirmed as applicable to compilations but is not itself modified.

The relation of independent creation to a minimal degree of creativity is given as part of the meaning of original.

> [O]riginal ... means only that the work was independently created by the author ... *and* that it possesses at least some minimal degree of creativity.
>
> (Feist Publications, Inc. v. Rural Tel. Service Co., Inc., 1991, p. 345) [emphasis added]

The 'and' (p. 345) can be read in its ordinary discourse sense of conjoining the two terms it connects. The relation of independent creation to a minimal degree of creativity is subsequently formulated as 'plus' (p. 346), which can be read as corresponding in meaning to the initial 'and' (p. 345). The relation is also reiterated as 'and' (pp. 348, 358) and these references can be understood as equivalent in meaning to the initial 'and' (p. 345). The necessity for both independent creation and a minimal degree of creativity for originality, then, is signaled by the *and* which connects them at their first introduction (p. 345), at subsequent iterations (pp. 348, 358), and by the alternative verbal form, 'plus' (p. 346). The relation of independent creation to a minimal degree of creativity can then be understood as conjunction.

Conjunction implies some further relation between the conjoined terms. Independent creation and a minimal degree of creativity cannot be in necessary and full contradiction, as otherwise no work could be original. The absence of necessary contradiction could extend to a substantive similarity. There should also be some distinction between the conjoined terms, from the perspective of both ordinary discourse and formal logic – 'Roughly speaking: to say of two things that they are identical is nonsense' (Wittgenstein, 1922/1981, §5.5303) – otherwise their separate specification would be redundant. Absence of contradiction, possibly extending to similarity, and difference must then both exist.

Some specific similarities and contrasts between independent creation and a minimal degree of creativity can be discerned within the judgment. Independent creation and a minimal degree of creativity also have an underlying similarity in terminology, between the root or stem *creat* in 'independently *creat*ed' (p. 345) and in 'a minimal degree of *creat*ivity' (p. 345) [emphases added], revealing a connection in etymology and possibly implying some semantic commonality. Analogously, to the implication of creativity in a minimal degree of creativity from its own antithesis, from the 'creative spark utterly lacking' (p. 358), independent creation is negatively delimited – 'as opposed to copied' (Feist Publications, Inc. v. Rural Tel. Service Co., Inc., 1991, p. 345). In contrast to a minimal degree of creativity, independent creation is fully explicated in parentheses at its introduction and is less extensively treated, implying that it is more easily delimited and less complex than a minimal degree of creativity. Some semantic commonality with a minimal degree of creativity and the lesser complexity of independent creation and is then implied, although neither implication is fully developed.

A particular similarity and difference and can be identified. In relation to the possible semantic commonality, the extreme antithesis to creativity has been identified with an automatic mechanical procedure or computational or syntactic process. Copying, negatively opposed to independent creation, would be one highly significant, if not archetypal, instance of a mechanical or syntactic process. Independent creation and a minimal degree of creativity then both exclude a syntactic process. Independent creation could have a semantic character, corresponding to the semantic character of creativity. The implied commonality of connection with creation has been made fully explicit. A difference also emerges. The exclusion of only one form of syntactic activity, of copying, from independent creation would also allow it to include other syntactic processes. It could also include semantic processes below the level required for a minimal degree of creativity. A significant difference has also been revealed. A minimal degree of creativity remains the broader concept, with creativity counterposed to other syntactic activities, as well as to copying, sustaining the less complex character of independent creation. We have therefore revealed a substantive connection and identified a specific difference.

Independent creation as not copied is the negation of copying, or of a routine and automatic mechanical activity. As such it is consistent with and also complementary to a minimal degree of creativity, as the companion constituent of originality. We have therefore deepened the connection between the two components of originality.

On the basis of a full understanding of the requirement for and the meaning of originality, and the relation between independent creation and a minimal degree of creativity within originality, we can move to a consideration of the relation of the requirement for originality to pre-existing understandings of copyright.

Originality and previous understandings of copyright

The requirement for originality has been understood to place the judgment in tension with classic, and long historically endorsed, understandings of copyright. Specifically, the requirement for a modicum of creativity, as part of originality, and the denial of protection to work solely the product of industrious collection, has been thought to place the judgment at odds with the classic understanding that copyright protected and rewarded the intellectual labor of authors. The tension was noted at an early date (Greetham, 1996, p. 59) and regarded as 'moot' (Greetham, 1996, p. 59). Some uncertainty as to the degree of dissonance was thereby implied and this remains unresolved. The uncertainty does leave scope for reconciliation and reintegration. Any reconciliation must be compatible with, and, if possible, account for, the simultaneous clear dismissal of industrious collection alone as giving rise to copyright.

We can begin by progressively characterizing the activities involved in the not original and those which are essential to originality, in relation to labor.

Originality and labor

The judgment does refer directly to *labor*.

> It may seem unfair that much of the fruit of the compiler's *labor* may be used by others without compensation.
>
> (Feist Publications, Inc. v. Rural Tel. Service Co., Inc., 1991, p. 349). [emphasis added]

'[F]ruit' (p. 349) in 'the fruit of the compiler's labor' (p. 349) can be more formally understood as corresponding to the *product* of processes. Classically, processes are congealed in the product. On this understanding, the fruit, or product, of the compiler's labor would embody all the antecedent activities, of data collection and the selection, coordination, and arrangement of data collected, required for a compilation. '[M]uch' (p. 349) indicates that such labor does not necessarily give rise to originality and copyrightability, but also negatively implies that the remaining activities can be comprehended as labor and may give rise to copyrightability. All the antecedent activities which result in the 'fruit', or product, of labor, both those which are not original and those which are required for originality, can then be subsumed as labor and thereby understood as labor, in the ordinary discourse sense in which the term 'labor' (p. 349) is used within the judgment. Both those activities which give rise and do not give rise to copyright can, then, be subsumed as labor.

The antecedent activities required for the compilation as a product, and which can be subsumed as labor, are also directly characterized within the judgment and we can consider how those characterizations relate to common understandings of labor. We can move progressively from those excluded from copyright, to those both excluded from copyright and also antithetical to creativity, through those below the level of creativity required for a minimal degree of creativity, to a minimal degree of creativity itself.

Sweat of the brow or industrious collection cannot give rise to copyrightability. Industrious collection is introduced as a judicially developed and mistaken theory under which the work involved in making compilations would by itself confer the 'right to copyright' (Feist Publications, Inc. v. Rural Tel. Service Co., Inc., 1991, p. 353). The work includes the collection of data as well as its selection, coordination, and arrangement. The theory was '[k]nown alternatively as "sweat of the brow" or "industrious collection"' (pp. 352–353). Sweat of the brow has a biblical connotation — 'In the sweat of thy face shalt thou eat bread' (Genesis, 3:17–19). The phrase in Genesis can be understood to refer to the work, which can be interpreted as the agricultural work which was to be man's curse, and responsibility: after being expelled from Eden. The implied emphasis then is on hard physical labor and its value. Industrious in industrious collection can be understood in its ordinary discourse sense, connoting industriousness, with the term, 'industriousness' (p. 360), occurring in a quoted and endorsed opinion. The justification which was given for the judicially developed theory – 'that copyright was a reward for the hard work that went into compiling facts' (Feist Publications, Inc. v. Rural Tel. Service Co., Inc., 1991, pp. 352–353) – refers to hard work, which can similarly be read in its ordinary discourse sense. *Sweat of the brow* and *industrious* are semantically reminiscent of labor and suggestive of physical labor, understood as difficult and demanding activity, and excluded from the possibility of giving rise to copyright.

The 'creative spark utterly lacking' (Feist Publications, Inc. v. Rural Tel. Service Co., Inc., 1991, p. 358) is both excluded from copyright and antithetical to creativity. The terms which qualify processes in the extended characterization of it – 'so mechanical or routine ... dictated by state law ... an age-old practice, firmly rooted in tradition and so commonplace that it has come to be expected as a matter of course ... practically inevitable ... time-honored tradition' (pp. 362–363) – are consistent with an ordinary discourse sense of labor. Those which qualify the directory as product – 'entirely typical ... garden variety ... the most basic information' (pp. 362–363) – reflect the expected products of highly routine or mechanical labor. The clause which qualifies both process and product, 'could not be more obvious' (p. 362) is consistent with the ordinary sense of labor and with being the product of highly mechanical or routine labor. The characterization of the 'insufficient' or zero level of creativity 'expended' by Rural – 'could not be more obvious ... the most basic information' (pp. 362–363) – is also consistent with the level of routinicity as the intervening dimension between the mechanical and the creative, within human activity motivated by meaning. The labor involved in the creative spark utterly lacking is then characterized as highly mechanical or routine and gives rise to products consistent with such forms of labor. '[S]o mechanical' (p. 362), or automatically computed, emerged as the extreme form of the creative spark utterly lacking and the 'so ... routine' (p. 362) as the less extreme dimension and this understanding is continued.

The 'creative spark ... so trivial as to be virtually nonexistent' (Feist Publications, Inc. v. Rural Tel. Service Co., Inc., 1991, p. 359) was understood as intermediate in level between the 'creative spark ... utterly lacking' and the level required for a minimal degree of creativity. The 'creative spark ... so trivial as to be virtually nonexistent' (p. 359) is not directly characterized, consistent with the absence of positive development of creativity within the judgment. The absence of direct characterization renders it not in contradiction with the ordinary discourse sense of labor. The creative spark below the level of creativity required for copyright was understood as the beginning antithesis to the 'creative spark utterly lacking' (p. 359), as opposed to the 'so mechanical or routine'. As such it was definitely not mechanical but remained routine, although progressively less so. The 'creative spark ... so trivial as to be virtually nonexistent' (p. 359) can then be understood as a routine form of labor.

A minimal degree of creativity can, together with independent creation, give rise to originality and copyrightability. Creativity within a minimal degree of creativity is not directly characterized in the judgment and remains not in contradiction with being understood as labor. A minimal degree of creativity is, however, connected with labor in quotations endorsed within the judgment. The writings to be protected are characterized as '*the fruits of intellectual labor*' (emphasis in original) (Feist Publications, Inc. v. Rural Tel. Service Co., Inc., 1991, p. 346) and the necessity for 'a modicum of intellectual labor' (p. 347) is also noted. '[*T*]*he fruits of intellectual labor*' (emphasis in original) (p. 346) correspond to the product required for a minimal degree of creativity and 'a modicum of intellectual labor' (p. 347) directly to a minimal degree of creativity. Creativity at or above the level of creativity required for a minimal degree of creativity can, then, be regarded as connected with *intellectual labor*. Intellectual is then necessarily equivalent to 'extremely low' (p. 345) level required for a minimal degree of creativity. Both intellectual and extremely low can also be understood as routine, although a lesser extent of routinicity than for the creative spark 'so trivial as to be virtually nonexistent' (p. 358) or, further, 'utterly lacking' (p. 358). The level of creativity required for originality is confirmed as labor, and, more specifically, as intellectual labor.

We can now more directly and empirically consider the activities subsumed and confirmed as labor. The activities specifically included in industrious collection – 'The man who goes through the streets of a town and puts down the names of each of the inhabitants, with their occupations and their street number acquires material of which he is the author' (Feist Publications, Inc. v. Rural Tel. Service Co., Inc., 1991, pp. 352–353) – would qualify as labor, on ordinary discourse understandings. '[G]o[ing] through the streets of a town' (p. 353) could be further understood as physical labor and 'put[ting] down the names of each of the inhabitants, with their occupations and their street number' as mental, predominantly clerical, labor (although the term *clerical* is not used within the judgment). The activities included in industrious collection can be categorized as physical, and mental labor.

The activities involved in both the 'creative spark utterly lacking' and 'so trivial as to be virtually nonexistent' (Feist Publications, Inc. v. Rural Tel. Service Co., Inc., 1991, p. 359) and in a minimal degree of creativity – the collection, selection, coordination, and arrangement of data – can also be more directly and empirically considered. They could be conducted by direct human labor, both at the levels of creativity below that required for copyrightability and for those above it. They can, then, all be understood as potentially varieties of labor, in a strong ordinary discourse sense of the term, as organic human activity subjectively experienced as labor. As activities, they can be mechanical or routine, with the routine extending to intellectual. The activities involved can, then, be understood as routine or mechanical mental labor with a physical component.

In summary, then, of the characterization and activities considered as forms of labor, industrious collection or sweat of the brow is excluded from the possibility of giving rise to originality, is characterized in terms strongly reminiscent of hard labor, and includes activities understandable as routine forms of physical and mental labor. The 'creative spark utterly lacking' (Feist Publications, Inc. v. Rural Tel. Service Co., Inc., 1991, p. 359) is antithetical to, as well as excluded from, the creative component of originality and is characterized in terms consistent with mechanical or routine forms of labor. The 'creative spark … so trivial as to be virtually nonexistent' (p. 359) is left uncharacterized, except by antithesis, and can be consistently understood as a routine, although not mechanical, form of labor. The characterization of the activities subsumed as labor confirms their nature as labor. We can also discern a progression from those activities excluded from and antithetical to copyright, through those with creativity below the requisite level of creativity, to a minimal degree of creativity, from the physical, mechanical, and highly routine, through the routine, to the less routine.

We can now synthesize our findings to characterize progressively the not original to the potentially original as forms of labor. The characterization within the judgment of the activities which result in compilations – the collection of data, and its selection, coordination, and arrangement– is then consistent with, and, to some extent, suggestive of these processes being understood as labor, for both processes lacking creativity and those at the level of creativity required for copyright. A continuum can be detected, from intellectual to 'so mechanical or routine' and sweat of the brow. Within the so mechanical or routine, we can also consistently differentiate so routine, so mechanical, and so mechanical and routine, in accord with their conceptual distance from creativity.

A further justification for the dimension, and an explanation for the occurrence of the judgment in 1991, can be found if we distinguish human labor from machine process. The forms of labor excluded, in the collection and arrangement of data, were strongly tending to become machine processes rather than direct human labor, at the time of the judgment. Labor, particularly as a verb, cannot accept a machine as its grammatical subject – *the machine was laboring* – except under certain specialized conditions where a machine is struggling, like a tired human. The processes excluded from copyright were then ceasing to be labor, and becoming machine processes, as they were excluded from copyright.

The labor theory of copyright, limited to *intellectual* labor, has then been renewed. If we allow the excluded processes to drop away, we see that intellectual or copyrightable labor occupies a larger proportion of labor than previously. We can therefore understand the labor theory of copyright, in this sense, to be intensified.

The identification of the activities which can give rise to originality and to copyright as labor defuses the tension with the conception of copyright as rewarding the labors of the mind. The distinctions within labor, between the forms of labor involved in the not original and the potentially original, account for the simultaneous definite exclusion of industrious collection and selection and coordination, and arrangement lacking the requisite level of creativity, from copyrightability. The identification of all the antecedent activities involved in the not original and the original as labor, and the progressive differentiation within labor, is consistent with the conclusion of the judgment, that 'copyright rewards originality, not effort' (Feist Publications, Inc. v. Rural Tel. Service Co., Inc., 1991, p. 363). Under this formulation, effort, or lower level of labor, would not confer copyrightability, although the required intellectual labor could include effort in its ordinary discourse sense.

We can attempt some understanding of the relation of creativity to labor. They have been revealed to be not antithetical, as critiques of the judgment had presumed or implied, but as complementary, with creativity involving labor. This position can be supported by previous significant copyright decisions, for instance, in the insistence that copyright extended to 'any physical rendering of the fruits of creative intellectual or aesthetic labor' (*Goldstein v. California*, 1973, p. 247). Creativity and labor have then been mutually reintegrated.

The recognition of the activities involved in originality as labor enables the incentive role of copyright to be explicitly restored.

Incentive role

Critiques of the decision considered that it grossly neglected the incentive function of copyright and that an incentive to prompt the production of databases may still be required (Ginsburg, 1992, pp. 341, 350). On the interpretation established here, that a minimal degree of creativity necessarily involves intellectual labor, the incentive role of copyright for intellectual labor is fully restored. More routine and also mechanical forms of mental labor, which both on the *Feist* decision and in other widely diffused understandings, would not by themselves have given rise to property pre-*Feist*, are deliberately excluded from originality and copyrightability (a copyright owner could still exercise those forms of labor, in addition to intellectual labor, without endangering their claim to property). Restoring the incentive role of copyright for intellectual labor provides incentives or protection adapted to a significant source of experienced real costs.

We can then regard the incentive role of copyright as restored and turn our attention to the consonance with natural justice, which tended to flow from that incentive role.

Consonance with natural justice

Critiques had also, both for copyright and specifically in relation to *Feist*, observed that the law needs to be in accord with natural justice, if it is to survive, and to be enforced by the courts. For copyright, natural justice rested strongly on the protection offered to the products of an author's intellectual labor. Restoring the incentive role of copyright for intellectual labor then brings the decision into accord with pre-existing conceptions of natural justice.

The understanding of originality obtained can be revealed to be consistent with informal judgments of ownership of intellectual property, derived from conceptions of natural justice. For instance, if a text was spell checked by a different individual from its original author, the original author would normally be considered the natural owner of property in the text, on the basis of their higher level and greater amount of creativity.

We can then regard consonance with natural justice as largely restored.

We can now consider how this understanding can be applied to compilations.

Application to compilations

The practical implications of the understanding of originality obtained can be considered. In relation to compilations, humanly constructed database and bibliographic records emerge as realizations of a minimal degree of creativity. In contrast, mechanical or computational procedures do not endow creativity on their products. In addition, highly routine, although not necessarily solely mechanical, activity in the construction of compilations may not reach the level required for a minimal degree of creativity (as in the case of Rural). Such activity may still have significant costs and could even – possibly, for instance, in the editing of a database – have creativity, but not at the level required for a minimal degree of creativity. The implications for practice of the distinction of a minimal degree of creativity from creativity have been revealed.

A humanly created bibliographic record then emerges as one possible correlate to, or, at least, constituent of, the combination of level required and amount sufficient for a minimal degree of creativity. The level of creativity involved in compilations can be understood as intellectual – independent references to the 'intellectual labor of cataloging and indexing' (Wilson, 2001, p. 203) can be found – and also to require specialized training. The combination of level and amount of creativity embodied in a bibliographic record has been connected with certain exchange and monetary values.

> Any proper accounting would assign a cost of at least $30 to the work in creating just one of those records [for OCLC World- Cat].
>
> (Hayes, 2000, p. 76)

The cost indicated would correspond or readily aggregate to more than a *de minimis* quantum of exchange values, in the legal sense of *de minimis*. Other correlates would then include semantically transformed indexes or other records constructed by human intellectual or specialized activity. Compilations could be protected, under this interpretation where the selection, coordination, or arrangement involves significant interpretation or direct consideration of meaning, which could be revealed in verbal transformations of an indexing language.

The differentiation of a minimal degree of creativity by degree of routinicity from the 'creative spark ... so trivial as to be virtually nonexistent' (Feist Publications, Inc. v. Rural Tel. Service Co., Inc., 1991, p. 359), and, further, from direct human engagement with meaning which does not rise to creativity could have significant practical implications. The 'creative spark ... so trivial as to be virtually nonexistent' (p. 359) was understood as a real level and amount of creativity below the level required for a minimal degree. Elements of works with creativity below the required level could have amounts of creativity in an ordinary discourse sense, consistently with the implications of 'spark' (pp. 346, 359, 363) for amount, but do not become copyrightable, whatever their amount of creativity, as they do not have the requisite level of creativity. Similarly, at further and lower degree of routinicity, Rural's nonmechanical, but highly routine, activity in the construction of their white pages had significant amount but did not rise to the requisite level of creativity.[1] Extensive editorial work on compilations, then, may not rise to the level of creativity required for copyrightability, whatever its extent or amount.

In its application to compilations, the understanding obtained of originality then promises to discriminate, by copyrightable status, compilations which embody the required level and sufficient amount of human activity motivated by meaning, from compilations with a level corresponding to a *de minimis* quantum of creativity and from so routine or mechanically generated descriptions without creativity, which would not be copyrightable.

Relation to the European Union and other jurisdictions

Recognizing that creativity and labor are not antithetical but becoming complementary is crucial. We previously (see Chapter 7) correlated the intellectual level of creativity required for a minimal degree of creativity with intellectual in intellectual labor. We can now further integrate with labor in intellectual labor.

The minimal degree of creativity required by *Feist* (1991) was broadly commensurate with global and European requirements for copyrightability (Judge and Gervais, 2010; Gupta, 2017). Understanding the originality required for copyrightability as labor enables precise equivalence to be added to the broad commensurability of a minimal degree of creativity with European Union and other jurisdictions' thresholds for copyrightability conceived in terms of labor.

In conclusion to our consideration of the relation of *Feist* to the European Union and the rest of the world, *Feist* (1991) was chronologically first, has then had an exemplary and leading role, with both parallel and partly antithetical developments in jurisdictions outside the United States. In containing considerations within copyright, rather than creating *sui generis* provisions, *Feist* is economical in its actions and thereby preferable. Its economy is fully revealed by the

1 Linking together different expressions with a common meaning, realized as reference, occurs in the oral hearing.

> MR. CAPLINGER: Communities. We decided to include business listings within this. We decided that in some communities we only put the town where in other communities we put the full address. We also decide what name, because my full name might be a fact. But I go by several names, James, Jim, Jay, JR, et cetera. And –
> QUESTION: I'm not stunned by the originality so far.
> (Laughter).
>
> (*Feist*, 1991)

James, Jim, Jay, JR would be the not immediately syntactically similar expressions and the speaker, Mr. Caplinger, the common referent or meaning. The reconciliation of the differing expressions with the single meaning (of James, Jim, JR et cetera with Mr Caplinger) could be understood as a highly routine process resulting in a routine product and thereby as not creative.

interpretation developed here. In common with other jurisdictions, interpretations of *Feist* (1991) have had to correspond to broader determining forces.

Narrative motif

Odysseus, has to become No Man in order to be fulfilled as everyman. Odysseus has, then, been, enabled to return home and re-establish the firmly founded bed on which copyright rests. Odysseus has to be Nobody in order to become everyman fully again, to return to Ithaca, to resume being everyman, in reverse chronological order, progressively father, husband, and son. We have also begun to dismiss the mist, or lack of recognition of the familiar, which obscured Odysseus's recognition of Ithaca on his return.

Conclusion

In conclusion, then, we have examined the requirement for originality and the meaning of originality, comprehensively with regard to the decision. Originality continues to be constituted by independent creation and a minimal degree of creativity. For independent creation, not previously fully studied here, we have outlined the understanding explicitly given of it, as not copied, and indicated the stated relation to a minimal degree of creativity, as conjunction. The understanding of independent creation and its relation to a minimal degree of creativity has an acute practical value. It can inform the order of a process of discrimination. We can first establish whether a work has a minimal degree of creativity and then consider independent creation. We then substantiated and deepened that relation and thereby established an economical order of discrimination for determining originality, from a minimal degree of creativity to independent creation. We have transformed the meaning of originality into a discriminatory process.

A discriminatory process for determining originality (which would apply to all works, including, but not confined to, compilations) can be outlined.

First we establish the existence, or not (as in the case of Rural's white page listing) of a minimal degree of creativity. The existence of the required level of creativity can be tested by two consecutive discriminations.

- Are there elements of the work not produced by an automatic mechanical procedure?
- Do those elements embody creativity at the required intellectual level?

We can then determine whether a sufficient amount of creativity exists at the requisite level.

- Do the elements at the required level embody a sufficient amount of creativity (as revealed by the exchange values associated with the product)?

Each discriminatory step takes the outcome of the previous discriminations as its exclusive object.

Second, if a minimal degree of creativity is confirmed to exist (which was not the case with Rural's listing), independent creation can then be determined.

- Who originated the elements of the work with a minimal degree of creativity?

The discriminatory step from a minimal degree of creativity also takes the overall outcome of the preceding steps within the determination of a minimal degree of creativity, as its exclusive object.

Originality, understood as solely constituted by a minimal degree of creativity and independent creation, is then discernible from a more than a ***de minimis*** quantum of exchange values arising from creative activity at, or above, the requisite level.

In many instances, the existence of originality will have to be read from the product. Reading copyrightability from the product has an analogy with established processes of determination of copyrightability, although primarily in connection with works which transgress property in other works, specifically, as an indication that copying has occurred.

> courts have taken strong showing of similarity, particularly for complicated works, as evidence of derivation which need be only weakly supported by evidence for the defendant's access to the original work.
>
> (Landes and Posner, 1989, p. 347)

Reading from the product avoids inquiry into the process of copying, to which direct and reliable access is difficult – '[i]t is generally not possible to establish copying as a factual matter by direct evidence' (Nimmer and Nimmer, 1978–2020, 13.01[b]). Discrimination from the product is then well warranted by the preceding history of the application of copyright.

The relation of the requirement for originality to pre-existing understandings of copyright has also been clarified. Intellectual labor and rewarding intellectual labor, continues to be the basis of copyright. In that respect, we have returned to, and renewed, a classic understanding of copyright – that if something is worth copying, it is worth protecting.

> if they command the interest of any public, they have a commercial value, – it would be bold to say that they have not an aesthetic and educational value, – and the taste of any public is not to be treated with contempt. It is an ultimate fact for the moment.
>
> (Bleistein, 1903, p. 252)

The approach to *Feist* and to copyright here has, then, had a strongly integrative effect in relation to previous understandings of copyrightability.

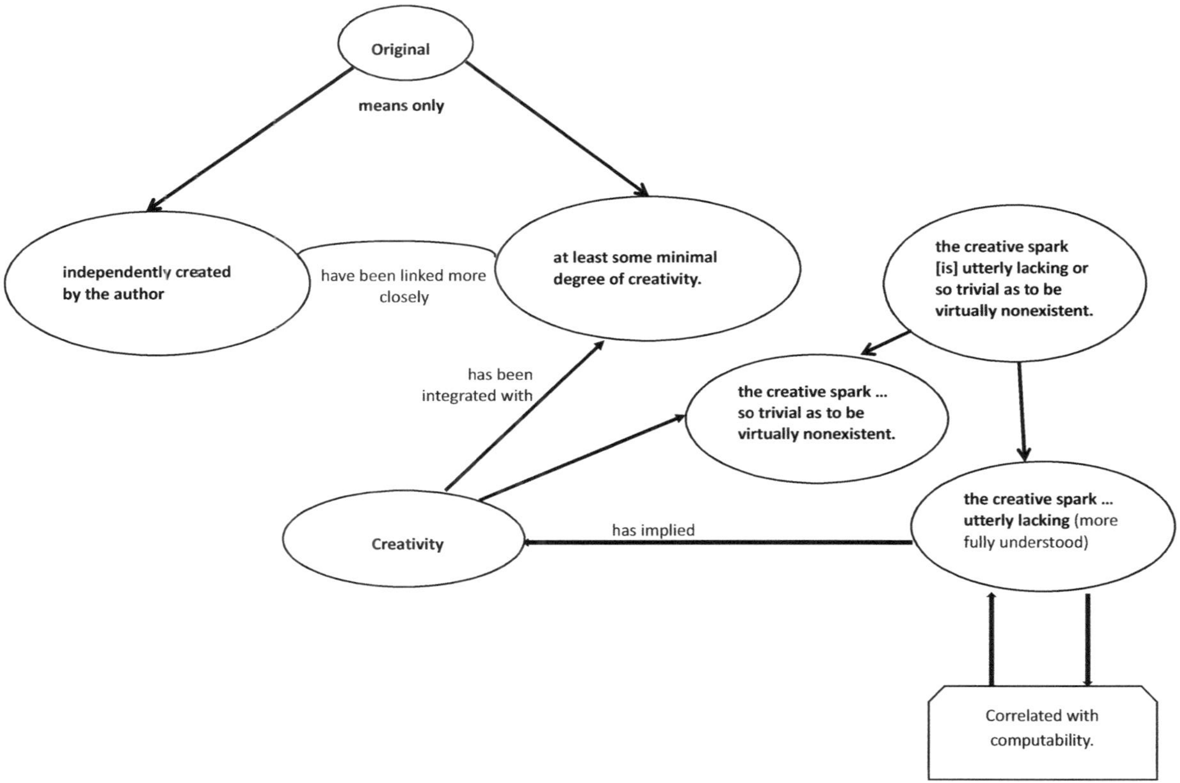

Figure 8.1 Progress made
Note: **Bold** is used for terms and phrases directly derived from the decision.

In relation to our previous analysis, we have further integrated the understanding of creativity established as human activity directly motivated by meaning, above a certain level of routinicity, which was previously sustained through a minimal degree of creativity, into originality. We have also both linked creativity to, and differentiated a minimal degree of creativity from, the independent creation contained within the meaning of originality. In summary, then, we have progressively integrated creativity into a minimal degree of creativity and into originality, further validating our understanding of creativity (see Figure 8.1).

A summary, including a logical summary, of the chapter is given.

Originality: Odysseus: chapter summary

The chapter returns to the starting point of the analysis, to originality, but with a deeper understanding of the constituents of originality and giving fuller attention to originality itself. The requirement for originality is substantiated as constitutional, articulated in judicial interpretations of the Constitution, and embodied in statute. The meaning of originality is confirmed as that a work must have at least some minimal degree of creativity and be independently created.

A minimal degree of creativity and independent creation are both required, as a matter of definition, for originality. Independent creation is parenthetically explicated at its introduction, as 'opposed to copied from other works' (Feist Publications, Inc. v. Rural Tel. Service Co., Inc., 1991, p. 345). The copying opposed to independent creation could be understood as a significant, if not archetypal, potentially automatically computational activity. Creativity in a minimal degree of creativity is also opposed to automatic computational activities. However, it is also opposed to computational processes other than copying and a minimal degree of creativity also excludes highly routine activities. Independent creation and a minimal degree of creativity are, then, similar as antithetical to computational processes, but differ in the extent of their antithesis to other computational activities and in the exclusion of highly routine, but not necessarily automatically computational, processes from a minimal degree of creativity. A minimal degree of creativity is then the more inclusive concept. The relation of a minimal degree of creativity to independent creation has then been substantiated and closened.

We can return to our initial logical representation of the meaning of originality.

Original ↔ ((at least some minimal degree of creativity) ^ (independently created))

And rewrite it as

((at least some minimal degree of creativity) ∧ (independently created)) ↔ Original

The statement is logically equivalent, but we now have a deeper, and sufficient, understanding of a minimal degree of creativity and independent creation, and of their conjunction as constituents of originality. The reversal of order of terms reflects the current direction of understanding.

We can establish a progressive order of discrimination. First, for a minimal degree of creativity.

- Are there elements of the work not produced by an automatic mechanical procedure?
- Do those elements embody creativity at the required intellectual level?
- Do the elements at the required level embody a sufficient amount of creativity (as revealed by the exchange values associated with the product)?

If a minimal degree of creativity exists, independent creation can be determined.

- Who originated the elements of the work with a minimal degree of creativity?

Each discriminatory step takes the outcome of the previous discriminations as its exclusive object.

The term labor in 'fruit of the compiler's labor' (p. 349) subsumes all the antecedent activities, of industrious collection and the selection, coordination, and arrangement of data which went into the making of that *fruit* or product, for both original and not original products. They are also characterized as labor and can be empirically understood to correspond to labor. A progressive differentiation emerges, for both industrious collection and the selection, coordination, and arrangement of data, from the physical and the mechanical, through the highly routine, which cannot not give rise to copyright, to intellectual labor, which is protected by copyright. They can then be considered to be fully labor. Industrious collection, excluded from copyright, and selection, coordination, and arrangement without creativity, excluding creativity but also antithetical to it, can then be seen to be deeply connected with each other.

Creativity and labor can be understood as broadly parallel.

The recognition of creative activities as labor, and the protection accorded to intellectual labor, dissolves the tension between the requirement for originality and the preexisting understanding that copyright protected and rewarded the intellectual labor of authors. The incentive role of copyright for intellectual labor is restored and copyright brought into broad consonance with natural justice.

We can then return to our initial proposition, that copyright requires originality or

$$\vdash \text{copyright} \leftrightarrow \text{originality}$$

but with a fuller understanding of the requirement as constitutional, as embodied in statute, and consistent with the pre-existing understanding of copyright, and with a full and sufficient understanding of originality and its constituents.

$\vdash$ **copyright $\leftrightarrow$ originality**

Finally, then, we have obtained a full understanding of originality, as the head concept, completed our journey, in this sense, returning to the locale from which we departed. The clarity, definiteness, and testability of the understanding of originality have the potential to bring to an end the otherwise potentially continuing proposals for *sui generis* legislation (Trosow, 2004–2005, p. 109). Such proposals have not insignificant deliberation costs. The discriminatory power of the understanding obtained and the possibility of ending unproductive debates give great value to the reading. Copyright can be regarded as restored to its historical basis, while incorporating modern practice.

References

Bleistein (1903). Bleistein v. Donaldson Lithographing Co., 188 U.S. 239 (1903).

Feist (1991). Feist Publications, Inc. v. Rural Tel. Service Co., Inc. 499 U.S. 340 (1991).

Feist Publications, Inc. v. Rural Tel. Service Co., Inc. (1991). Feist Publications, Inc. v. Rural Tel. Service Co., Inc. 499 U.S. 340 (1991).

Ginsburg, J.C. (1992). No 'sweat' copyright and other protection of works of information after Feist v. Rural Telephone. *Columbia Law Review*. 92, 338–388.

Goldstein v. California (1973). Donald Goldstein et. al., Petitioners v. State of California 412 U.S. 546 (1973).

Greetham, D. (1996). The telephone directory and Dr. Seuss: Scholarly editing after Feist versus Rural Telephone. *Studies in the Literary Imagination*. 29(2), 53–74.

Gupta, I. (2017). *Footprints of Feist in European Database Directive: A legal analysis of IP law-making in Europe*. Singapore: Springer.

Hayes, R.M. (2000). Assessing the value of a database company. In B. Cronin and H.B. Atkins (eds). *The web of knowledge: A festschrift in honor of Eugene Garfield* (pp. 73–84). Medford, NJ: Information Today.

Judge, E.F. and Gervais, D. (2010). Of silos and constellations: Comparing notions of originality in copyright law. *Cardozo Arts and Entertainment*. 27, 373–407.

Landes, W.M. and Posner, R.A. (1989). An economic analysis of copyright law. *Journal of Legal Studies*. 18, 325–363.

Nimmer, M.B. and Nimmer, D. (1978–2020). *Nimmer on copyright: A treatise on the law of literary, musical and artistic property, and the protection of ideas*. New York: Matthew Bender. Continually updated resource.

Trosow, S.E. (2004–2005). Sui generis database legislation: A critical analysis. *Yale Journal of Law and Technology*. 7, 1–109.

Wilson, P. (2001). Review of E. Svenonius, The intellectual foundations of information organization. *College and Research Libraries*. 62, 203–204.

Wittgenstein, L. (1922/1981). *Tractatus Logico-Philosophicus*. London and New York: Routledge and Kegan Paul.

9 Qualities of reading

Introduction

Critiques of the judgment identified issues which still required resolution, particularly its complexity and lack of substantiation of creativity (see Chapter 2). The intensive scrutiny the judgment had received had not revealed self-contradiction. We were therefore entitled to presume self-consistency. A satisfactory reading had to reveal the particular form of self-consistency, hidden behind the surface complexity, substantiate creativity and address the further issues identified from critiques.

In addition, it would be desirable for the reading to have further qualities of economy, comprehensiveness, final simplicity, and potential for practical implementation.

We can therefore review the reading established against the criteria identified from the critiques and consider the extent to which it embodies further desirable qualities.

Themes of critiques

The reading established can be systematically compared with the criteria for elucidation developed in Chapter 2, again considering issues in broadly descending order of significance and conceptual dependence.

Complexity

The self-consistency of the decision, which was earlier presumed, has been made specific and revealed, through careful verbal analysis. A self-consistent conceptual structure was revealed and used consistently and effectively for the subsequently analysis.

The primary analytic method used was the deeply historically rooted process of exegesis, or close reading. The analysis then rests on well-established methods. The results of exegesis were synthesized, in a discursive presentation and also diagrammatically with a parallel exposition as formal logic (a single, progressively developed diagram was used). The congruence between discursive and formal modes of presentation implies a robust analysis. Methods of analysis and of development then indicate that the argument is firmly rooted.

From the self-consistency revealed and used, and the deep rooting of the argument we can regard the concern of critiques with the complexity of the decision as fully resolved.

Creativity

A lack of substantiation of creativity was identified by critiques.

Creativity has been substantiated, as human action motivated by meaning, above a certain level of routinicity. It has not been over-populated, in accord with the resistance to final delimitation implied by the absence of direct explication of creativity in the judgment.

The argument is deeply rooted substantively and formally. Substantively, fundamental distinctions from the theory of computation, from information theory, and from ordinary discourse supported the identification of the not automatically computational with a strong sense of semantic, as direct human engagement with meaning. The concept of creativity arrived at was consistent with significant ordinary discourse. The extreme antithesis to creativity was tied to a bedrock concept, to that of an automatic mechanical procedure or automatic computational process. The concept is both bedrock and historically variable in its instantiation, if there are advances in implementation.

Formally, the technique of negation, used to derive an understanding of creativity from its antithesis, is deeply historically rooted. The argument held in discursive and formally logical form. The congruence in results between two methods of expression and of thought sometimes considered antithetical to or in tension with each other, of ordinary discourse and reasoning with symbolic logic and purely logical transformations, adds conviction to the result obtained. In this instance, logic is being used to give a slightly more definite expression to the result of a verbally conducted argument (Holmes, 1881/1991, p. 219). The understanding of creativity developed rests, therefore, on a very strong substantive and methodological basis.

The presence of a mechanical procedure or highly routine process in the processes which give rise to the end product directly considered for its copyrightability can be determined from a reading or inspection of the product, or, if necessary, by an enquiry into its circumstances of production. The degree of absence of routinicity required for creativity gives rise to a less sharp boundary than that between the mechanical or automatically computed and the not mechanical. The boundary is broadly congruent with the previous distinction of intellectual from clerical labor (clerical labor, by itself, would not normally have given rise to copyrightability). It is also analogous in not being an entirely sharp boundary. We then have a discriminatory principle for creativity which centrally contains a concept, of computability, which is both bedrock and flexible in its instantiation, and amenable to being known. The further dimension, of routinicity, is not more complex than historically inherited distinctions, most notably between intellectual and clerical. Creativity is then amenable to being known.

We can therefore regard the understanding of creativity as very strongly and usefully proven. The lack of substantiation of creativity, identified by critiques, has been addressed and resolved.

Dissonance

A tension with existing understandings of copyright was also detected.

The tension has been resolved, by dissolving the tension between creativity and labor and revealing the role of the author's intellectual labor in conferring property. An underlying continuity with a broad labor theory of copyright was also thereby revealed.

We can regard the dissonance detected with previous understandings of copyright as fully resolved.

Incentive role

The incentive role of copyright was also thought to have been neglected. The incentive role of copyright has been restored, for intellectual labor.

We have therefore resolved reservations concerned with the neglect of the incentive role of copyright.

Appeal to nineteenth-century precedents

It can be recognized that the cases cited were prompted by the diffusion of information technologies, specifically with late nineteenth-century technologies for data processing, such as a system of bookkeeping and photography. A continuity with the computer as a data processing technology is thereby exposed.

The appeal to nineteenth-century precedents by the Supreme Court can then best be understood as consistent with the judicial treatment of earlier information technologies. A deep historical awareness is implied.

Consonance with natural justice

A reading of the decision had to be consonant with natural justice.

Restoring the incentive role for intellectual labor was consistent with a long established justification for copyright, as rewarding the author's intellectual labor.

Consonance with natural justice has been reestablished.

Feist *and the digital age*

A specific relation to the digital age needed to be revealed.

We can confirm the relation of *Feist* (Feist Publications, Inc. v. Rural Tel. Service Co., Inc., 1991) to the digital age – the correlation of creativity utterly lacking with classic concepts of computability and the implied conception of the creative as residing within the not computable. *Feist* is then precisely situated in relation to the digital age. A pervasive component of digital technology processes, the automatic computational process, has been absorbed as the antithesis to creativity.

European Union

The dissolving of the tension between creativity and labor enables the approach taken within the United States to be correlated with that of the European Union, which has continued directly to emphasize intellectual labor for copyright.

Copyright in other jurisdictions, in so far as they continue to hold labor-oriented standards, can similarly correlated.

Conclusion

The reading established has, then, been systematically compared with the criteria for elucidation developed in Chapter 3.

- The complexity of the judgment has been made intelligible.
- Creativity has been substantiated, as human action motivated by meaning, above a certain level of routinicity, but not over-populated.
- The tension with previous understandings of copyright has been resolved, by revealing the continuity of the author's intellectual labor in conferring property.
- The incentive role of copyright has been restored, for intellectual labor.
- The appeal to nineteenth-century precedents by the Supreme Court can be understood as consistent with earlier forms of information technology.
- Consonance with natural justice has been revealed.
- The judgment has been precisely situated in relation to the digital age.
- The approach taken within the United States with its concern with creativity has been correlated with that of other jurisdictions which continue directly to emphasize labor.

The issues raised by the critiques can then be regarded as fully resolved.

The self-consistency of the decision, which was earlier assumed, has also been made specific and revealed, through careful analysis. The conceptual framework revealed has been rigorously followed. Its deepest component, creativity utterly lacking or the antithesis to creativity, has been grounded in a concept and practice of compelling contemporary significance, of computability.

Other qualities of the reading

The reading has further generally desirable qualities of comprehensiveness (it can be shown to pass a commutation test, by which all aspects of the judgment can be assigned to particular parts of the reading), final simplicity, and economy, amounting to parsimony. It also has high utility through its potential for practical application.

Overall summaries of the argument are given here, both in discursive and logical form and solely as a sequence of logical statements. They confirm the economy, progressive development, and self-consistency of the argument and assist its recollection as a whole.

Summary of argument

Originality was required for copyright

⊦ copyright ↔ originality

A work is original, if and only if, it has at least some minimal degree of creativity and is independently created.

Original ↔ ((at least some minimal degree of creativity) ∧ (independently created))

A minimal degree of creativity includes creativity.

A minimal degree of creativity → creativity

A minimal degree of creativity is differentiated from 'the creative spark … utterly lacking or so trivial as to be virtually nonexistent' (p. 358).

A minimal degree of creativity ↔ ~ (creative spark utterly lacking … so trivial as to be virtually nonexistent)

The 'creative spark … trivial as to be virtually nonexistent' (p. 358) also includes creativity.

creative spark so trivial as to be virtually nonexistent creativity → creativity

A minimal degree of creativity can be understood as contiguous with the creative spark so trivial as to be virtually nonexistent.

The 'creative spark … utterly lacking' (p. 358), by contrast, excludes creativity and can be understood as uniquely corresponding to the negative of or antithesis to creativity.

(creative spark utterly lacking) ↔ ~ creativity

As the antithesis to creativity, the not creative, can be understood to imply creativity as its own unique antithesis, or, creativity if, and only if, not creativity.

creativity ↔ ~ (~ creativity)

We could then proceed to elucidate creativity from this basis.

Creativity must apply to all works, extend from the lowest to the highest possible level, give rise to level and amount in combination, be knowable, and be consistent with ordinary discourse.

The creative spark utterly lacking for compilations was understood as

> A compilation has not the slightest trace of creativity if, and only if, it is constructed by a so mechanical or so … routine process and is an entirely typical or garden-variety end product.

Or

> **~ (A compilation has the slightest trace of creativity) ↔ ((so mechanical ∨ so … routine) ∧ (entirely typical ∨ garden-variety))**

The creative spark utterly lacking is analogous, or broadly equivalent, to the concept of computability.

> (so mechanical ∨ routine) ≈ computability

Mechanical in 'so mechanical' (p.362) was specifically equivalent to mechanical in a mechanical procedure

> mechanical (so mechanical) ≡ mechanical (automatic mechanical procedure)

'*[S]o* mechanical' [emphasis added] corresponds to the most intense form of mechanical procedure, to an *automatic* mechanical procedure.

> so mechanical ≡ automatic mechanical procedure

Automatic mechanical procedure was then substituted for *so mechanical* in the creative spark utterly lacking, to yield

> **A compilation has not the slightest trace of creativity if, and only if, it is constructed by an automatic mechanical procedure or so … routine process and is an entirely typical or garden-variety end product.**

Or

> **~ (A compilation has the slightest trace of creativity) ↔ ((automatic mechanical procedure ∨ so … routine) ∧ (entirely typical ∨ garden-variety))**

The statement was negated to yield a positive conception of creativity.

> **A compilation has the slightest trace of creativity if, and only if, it is not constructed by a so mechanical or so ... routine process and is not an entirely typical or garden-variety end product.**

Or

> **(A compilation has the slightest trace of creativity) ↔ ~ ((automatic mechanical procedure ∨ so ... routine) ∧ (entirely typical ∨ garden-variety))**

A not automatic mechanical procedure, above a certain level of routinicity, meets all the conditions for creativity.

> **A work is creative if, and only if, it is not an entirely typical or garden-variety end product constructed by an automatic mechanical procedure or a so ... routine process.**

Or

> **Creativity ↔ ~ ((automatic mechanical procedure ∨ so ... routine) ∧ (entirely typical ∨ garden-variety))**

The inclusion of creativity in a minimal degree of creativity and in the creative spark so trivial as to be virtually nonexistent meant that creativity alone will not necessarily give rise to copyright.

> (A minimal degree of creativity ∨ creative spark so trivial as to be virtually nonexistent) → creativity

> **A minimal degree of creativity consisted of creativity at an extremely low level, or more than a *de minimis* level, corresponding to an intellectual level, and a slight amount of creativity at that level.**

The existence of a minimal degree of creativity could be progressively determined.

- First, the required level can be read from the product, or, if necessary, by an enquiry into the circumstances of production.
- Second, the sufficient amount at that level can then be determined from the exchange values connected with the product.

The understanding of a minimal degree of creativity meets the conditions established for it, that it should consist of level and an amount at that level and that it should be knowable.

The creative spark so trivial as to be virtually nonexistent can be understood to include levels of creativity below the required level and also creativity at or above the required but of insufficient amount. Creativity as direct human engagement with meaning, above a certain level of routinicity, could be integrated with both a minimal degree of creativity and the creative spark so trivial as to be virtually nonexistent.

(A minimal degree of creativity ∨ creative spark so trivial as to be virtually nonexistent creativity) → creativity

The independent creation also required for originality was understood as related to, but less extensive than, a minimal degree of creativity. We could then return to our initial logical representation of the meaning of originality.

Original ↔ ((at least some minimal degree of creativity) ∧ (independently created))

and rewrite it as

((at least some minimal degree of creativity) ∧ (independently created)) ↔ Original

Finally, we returned to our initial proposition, that copyright requires originality or

⊦ copyright ↔ originality

but with a fuller understanding of the requirement as constitutional and embodied in statute and with a full and sufficient understanding of originality and its constituents.

⊦ **copyright ↔ originality.**

Summary of argument as logical statements

⊦ copyright ↔ originality

Original ↔ ((at least some minimal degree of creativity) ^ (independently created))

A minimal degree of creativity → creativity

A minimal degree of creativity ↔ ~ (creative spark … utterly lacking or so trivial as to be virtually nonexistent)

creative spark so trivial as to be virtually nonexistent creativity → creativity

(creative spark utterly lacking) ↔ ~ creativity

~ (A compilation has the slightest trace of creativity) ↔ ((so mechanical ∨ so … routine) ∧ (entirely typical ∨ garden-variety))

(so mechanical ∨ routine) ≈ computability

mechanical (so mechanical) ≡ mechanical (automatic mechanical procedure) so mechanical ≡ automatic mechanical procedure

~ (A compilation has the slightest trace of creativity) ↔ ((automatic mechanical procedure ∨ so … routine) ∧ (entirely typical ∨ garden-variety))

(A compilation has the slightest trace of creativity) ↔ ~ ((automatic mechanical procedure ∨ so … routine) ∧ (entirely typical ∨ garden-variety))

Creativity ↔ ~ ((automatic mechanical procedure ∨ so … routine) ∧ (entirely typical ∨ garden-variety))

(A minimal degree of creativity ∨ creative spark so trivial as to be virtually nonexistent creativity) → creativity

A minimal degree of creativity ↔ ~ (creative spark … utterly lacking or so trivial as to be virtually nonexistent)

((at least some minimal degree of creativity) ∧ (independently created)) ↔ Original

⊦ **copyright ↔ originality.**

Conclusion

The resolution of the issues raised by critiques, the revelation of the particular form of self-consistency of the judgment, and the further desirable qualities of the reading render it strongly proven and a basis for future judicial practice

The judgment, then, rather than being a radical misconstrual of copyright, emerges as extraordinarily far-sighted in its intentions and effects. The social benefits which can flow from the diffusion of technologies are also implicitly recognized, by removing a restriction on the development of particular technologies.

The need for the Supreme Court to revisit the judgment or for Congress to pass correcting legislation is greatly diminished. Judicial and legislative deliberation has opportunity costs, in diminishing the attention available for other purposes, and may only occur when anomalies between the operations and intended purpose of copyright are recognized, considered to be harmful, and perceived to be acute. Constitutionally, Congress, as the legislature, cannot override the Supreme Court and would have to pass *sui generis* type legislation, which would itself be questionable. The value of the interpretation here lies in the economy of its effects, reducing the need for further judicial or legislative deliberation, avoiding special provisions, resolving contradictions within the judgment, and integrating it with the historical development and synchronic scope for copyright, including establishing common criteria for property in databases and other writings.

In terms of a narrative motif, critiques of the judgment can be understood as the suitors, or false critics, whom Odysseus defeats on his return to Ithaca. We can dismiss the suitors, or false critics, and restore copyright to the deeply founded bed on which it rests and on which it can be renewed.

Resolving the issues raised by critiques, revealing the particular form of self-consistency of the judgment, substantiating creativity, and other desirable qualities, render the reading strongly proven and a strong basis for future judicial practice.

References

Feist (1991). Feist Publications, Inc. v. Rural Tel. Service Co., Inc. 499 U.S. 340 (1991).

Holmes, O.W. (1881/1991). *The common law*. With a new introduction by Sheldon M. Novick. New York: Dover.

10 Conclusion

The interaction of the twain

Introduction

We begin with the decision, move to the reading developed, and consider the approach and structure of the work, including its use of narrative motifs. Finally, we conclude on the narrative for the conclusion and the renewal of the case for copyright. The conclusion parallels the introduction and creates a symmetrical envelope for the work as whole.

The decision

The significance of the decision (Feist Publications, Inc. v. Rural Tel. Service Co., Inc., 1991) has been confirmed. It has also been substantiated and refined, through the incorporation of computability into the absence of creativity. The extensive diffusion of the decision, particularly of its standard for the lack of copyrightability, has been accompanied by the global diffusion of automatic computational processes in real world practice. The decision's status as law was accepted and formed the justification for elucidation rather than criticism. The decision's historical moment, in 1991, is confirmed as shortly after transition to computational technologies. A specific relation of the judgment to the determining forces of the digital age was revealed, by incorporating computational processes as the antithesis to creativity. We exposed the potential and scope for deliberate human action within an irreversible dynamic, in the contrast between the economy of action of the United States and the *sui generis* nature of some other jurisdictions' provisions.

An elucidation of the decision was entitled to assume its self-consistency and a deep connection to the digital age. It had then to reveal the particular form of self-consistency and connection.

Reading of the decision

The crux, or crucial turning point, for the reading of the decision developed was the correlation recognized between the opposite to creativity and computability. Creativity could then be conversely understood as residing in the non-computable, in human action motivated by meaning, above a certain level of routinicity. The particular form of the self-consistency of the judgment was revealed and used consistently and progressively through the argument. The correlation with computability established a deep, and specific, relation to the digital age. Economy and conviction followed from the use of single factor, the correlation with computability, to ground both the reading and the connection to the digital age.

The current – 2020 – understanding of the decision has been established after further, although still not full, growth in consciousness since the decision's historical moment in 1991, at an earlier stage of the diffusion of digital technologies.

The reading of the decision developed is full, persuasive, comprehensive, and practically implementable.

Approach

In accord, with Holmes' (1881/1991, p. 219) approach, logic was used to give organization, coherence, and clarity to experience. Logic resided in the method of development used, particularly incorporating negation, and experience lay in the connection to computability. Referral of the opposite to creativity to computability had not been anticipated. The analogy had not been previously noticed, plausibly because of the divide between the humanistic modes of thought embodied in legal scholarship and theoretical computer science. We have then brought logic and current, everyday experience together.

Structure

The parallels between the structure of the individual chapters, and the fitting of the chapters into an overall, broadly symmetrical structure, are indicative of strength, depth, and economy of the argument. The narrative motifs, and the overall conception as a journey, reveal its cohesion and development.

Conclusion

We began with the Twain – the judgment and the digital age – disassociate. The computational process has been incorporated as to the antithesis to creativity. The judgment and the digital age have been productively converged and can journey together harmoniously, rather than as potentially destructive opposites.

Crucially, what has been classically characterized as the uneasy case for copyright (Breyer, 1970), has been renewed. In a seminal article, of continuing relevance (Breyer, 2011), Breyer concluded:

> In sum, it is difficult to do other than take an ambivalent position of the question of whether current copyright protection – considered as a whole – is justified. One might compare this position with that of Professor Machlup, who, after studying the patent system, concluded, 'None of the empirical

> evidence at our disposal and none of the theoretical arguments presented either confirms or confutes the belief that the patent system has promoted the progress of the technical arts and the production of the economy.' The position suggests that the case for copyright in books rest not upon proven need, but rather upon uncertainty as to what would happen if protection were removed.
>
> (Breyer, 1970, p. 322)

The degree of certainty obtained may be characteristic of the outcome of studies in human and social domains. By correlating the judgment with computability, we have renewed the uneasy case for copyright for the digital age. Copyright and the digital age can move forward together.

In terms of our narrative motifs, we have reached home, as in James Joyce's *Ulysses*.

> He rests. He has travelled.
>
> With?
>
> Sinbad the Sailor and Tinbad the Tailor and Jinbad the Jailer and Whinbad the Whaler and Ninbad the Nailer and Finbad the Failer and Binbad the Bailer and Pinbad the Pailer and Minbad the Mailer and Hinbad the Hailer and Rinbad the Railer and Dinbad the Kailer and Vinbad the Quailer and Linbad the Yailer and Xinbad the Phthailer.
>
> (Joyce, 1922/1973, p. 658)

Leopold Bloom, the analogue to Odysseus in *Ulysses*, is accompanied by Stephen Daedalus, who partially corresponds to Telemachus in the *Odyssey*.

> What two temperaments did they individually represent?
>
> The scientific. The artistic.
>
> (Joyce, 1922/1973, p. 603)

For this work, scientific, or more strictly logical, and artistic perspectives are not just held by separate individuals but have been integrated with each other.

In 'The Uneasy Case for Copyright', Breyer continues on the degree of certainty for the value of copyright obtained.

> One may suspect that the risk of harm is small, but the world without copyright is nonetheless an 'undiscover'd country' which 'puzzles the will, / And makes us rather bear those ills we have / Than fly to others that we know not of …'
>
> (Breyer, 1970, p. 322)

We have chosen creativity and life, with all its uncertainty and complexity, over the Manichean certainties of computability.

References

Breyer, S. (1970). The uneasy case for copyright: A study of copyright in books, photocopies, and computer programs. *Harvard Law Review*. 84(2), 281–351.

Breyer, S. (2011). The uneasy case for copyright: A look back across four decades. *George Washington Law Review*. 79(6), 1635–1643.

Feist Publications, Inc. v. Rural Tel. Service Co., Inc. (1991). Feist Publications, Inc. v. Rural Tel. Service Co., Inc. 499 U.S. 340 (1991).

Holmes, O.W. (1881/1991). *The common law*. With a new introduction by Sheldon M. Novick. New York: Dover.

Joyce, J. (1922/1973). *Ulysses*. Harmondsworth: Penguin Books in association with Bodley Head.

Index

For Product Safety Concerns and Information please contact our EU representative GPSR@taylorandfrancis.com
Taylor & Francis Verlag GmbH, Kaufingerstraße 24, 80331 München, Germany

www.ingramcontent.com/pod-product-compliance
Ingram Content Group UK Ltd.
Pitfield, Milton Keynes, MK11 3LW, UK
UKHW022124190926
475702UK00013B/1629
9780367537142